Subject Headings
for
African American Materials

Other Titles of Interest from Libraries Unlimited

Subject Headings for African American Materials, CD Edition. By Lorene Byron Brown. 1995.

Electronic version with linked cross-references (BTs, NTs, etc.), providing unparalleled access to headings and subdivisions. Part of the *Libraries Unlimited Professional Collection CD*.

Headings for Children's Materials: An LCSH/Sears Companion. By Joanna Fountain. 1993.

An easy-to-use authority file for cataloging or conversion.

Conversion Tables: LC-Dewey, Dewey-LC. By Mona L. Scott. 1993.

Cataloging tool providing LC and Dewey equivalents. Available in Windows and DOS electronic versions. Part of the *Libraries Unlimited Professional Collection CD*.

Library of Congress Subject Headings: Principles and Application, 3d Edition. By Lois Mai Chan. 1995.

Definitive analysis of LCSH principles and description of applications.

Subject Headings
for
African American Materials

Lorene Byron Brown

1995
LIBRARIES UNLIMITED, INC.
Englewood, Colorado

To my husband, Paul,
and to the memory of my mother, Sallie

LIBRARIES UNLIMITED, INC.
P.O. Box 6633
Englewood, CO 80155-6633
1-800-237-6124

Production Editor: Stephen Haenel
Copy Editor: Christine J. Smith
Typesetter: Michael Florman
Editorial Assistant: Susan Sigman

Library of Congress Cataloging-in-Publication Data

Brown, Lorene Byron.
  Subject headings for African American materials / Lorene Byron
Brown.
    xvii, 118 p. 22x28 cm.
    Includes bibliographical references.
    ISBN 1-56308-252-7
    1. Subject headings--Afro-Americans. I. Title.
Z695.1.B57B76 1995
025.4'93058'96073--dc20   95-10847
                                                              CIP

Contents

Preface

The *Library of Congress Subject Headings* (Washington, D.C.: Library of Congress, annual.; *LCSH)* serves as the principal means of subject access for materials located in libraries and information centers in the United States. Notwithstanding its widespread use, this list is perceived as problematic and difficult to use by many librarians, subject specialists, and library patrons. As a result, the effective indexing, storage, and retrieval of information using this mode of subject access is limited.

As a corollary, subject headings listed in the *LCSH* that describe the African American experience continue to draw widespread discussion from librarians, documentalists, and users. These concerns are exacerbated by the variability and the multiformity of the language used in African American resources. Coupled with the above concerns is the fluctuation of language in materials written and developed from different philosophical, historical, and political perspectives.

This work represents a growth of an interest in the subject control of African American materials cultivated during my doctoral study at the University of Wisconsin-Madison. My thesis, *A Comparative Evaluation of Two Indexing Languages*, centered around Cutter's rule of the specific entry and later identified as specificity. The thesis study sought to ascertain which of two indexing languages contained African American history terms with the higher levels of specificity. The two languages were the list of *LCSH* and "A Thesaurus of African-American History Terms," a list I derived for my dissertation from 14 African American history sourcebooks.[1] By using the analysis of variance technique, I demonstrated that the African American history terms in the specially designed thesaurus were more specific, at a statistically significant level, than the African American history terms in *LCSH*. However, one of the most important implications of this study suggested that the combining of subject vocabularies through a systematic approach would provide the most economical and intellectual service to both information describers and information users.

This volume on the African American experience responds to the need of providing subject access for materials on all aspects of African American life and culture using *LCSH*. This publication lists approximately 5,000 subject headings that are interfaced and interlinked with *LCSH*. This list of subject headings contains some of the inherent problems that accompany the list of *LCSH* because it is based, for the most part, on the practices of subject cataloging at the Library of Congress. However, the interlinking and interjoining of the subject headings in this volume with the widely used list of *LCSH* should provide a logical continuum for the subject access of materials on the African American experience in the United States. This list should be used as an accompaniment to and not as a replacement for *LCSH*.

Users of These Subject Headings

The users of this list of subject headings may fall into three broad categories:

1. Patrons in school, academic, public, and special library/information centers requiring subject access to print and nonprint materials on the African American experience.

2. Librarians and information professionals responsible for the acquisition, collection, organization, and dissemination of print and nonprint resources on the African American experience.

3. Students and faculty members in secondary schools, colleges, and universities may use these concepts represented by the subject headings as a framework for understanding the complexity and multifariousness of the African American experience.

Notes

1. Lorene Sandra Byron, "A Comparative Evaluation of Two Indexing Languages." Ph.D. diss., University of Wisconsin-Madison, 1974.

Acknowledgments

For their assistance in the production of this manuscript, I am deeply grateful to:

David V. Loertscher, Vice President Editorial/Production, Libraries Unlimited, for suggesting that I compile this list of subject headings for African American materials.

Stephen Haenel, Production Editor, Libraries Unlimited, for his experienced technical and editorial assistance in the final production of this work.

Barbara Shlevin, Graduate Assistant, School of Library and Information Studies, Clark Atlanta University, and her husband, Harold H. Shlevin, for the final inputting, editing, and computer formatting of this manuscript.

Luci Barnes Leach, Valerie Lowery, and Karen Vernell, Graduate Assistants, School of Library and Information Studies, Clark Atlanta University, for their invaluable assistance in the inputting and proofreading of this manuscript.

Librarians at the Atlanta University Center Library, Atlanta-Fulton County Public Library, and the Georgia Institute of Technology for making their reference and cataloging sources readily available for use.

Introduction

This introduction serves as a guide for the use of *Subject Headings for African American Materials*. It presents a discussion of the elements of the entries including the types of headings, class numbers, scope notes, and term relationships. It also gives a commentary on the uses of subdivisions and an example of the filing arrangement of entries located in the *Library of Congress Subject Headings* (*LCSH*) and in this list of subject headings. This introduction should be of benefit, in particular, to high school and college students for an understanding of the seemingly complex but widely used *LCSH*.

The Construction of the Subject Headings

Terms were examined and extracted from the 16th edition of the *LCSH*, the *Cataloging Services Bulletin*, nos. 59-64 (Winter 1993-Spring 1994), and the *Library of Congress Subject Headings Weekly Lists* (January 1993-December 1993). This activity allowed for the inclusion of subject headings listed in the 17th edition of the *LCSH*. Also, subject headings are listed in this volume that will appear in the 18th edition of the *LCSH*, based on the *LCSH Weekly Lists* (January 1994-June 1994).

The *Subject Cataloging Manual: Subject Headings* (Washington, D.C.: Library of Congress, annual) was used extensively to provide directions for the uses of subdivisions and to serve as an authority for conforming to practices at the Library of Congress. The *Anglo-American Cataloging Rules, 2nd Ed. Rev.* (Chicago: American Library Association, 1988) was used to establish the entry headings for personal names, corporate bodies, and geographic entities.

Because the list of *LCSH* represents the chief subject access points for African American materials, it was decided at the onset to make only changes that were considered requirements for the construction of this volume. This decision was based on the rationale that restructuring a larger number of terms would decrease the interfacing and interlinking capabilities of this list of subject headings with the list of *LCSH*. However, two pronounced changes are noted, based on the principles of current usage and literary warrant (the use of concepts represented by subject headings based on the document). These two basic changes are the use of the subject heading *African American* for *Afro-American* and the use of the subject heading *Historically Black Colleges and Universities* for *African American Universities and Colleges*.

Afro-American
  USE African American
	African American
	  UF Afro-American

African American Universities and
  Colleges
  USE Historically Black Colleges
    and Universities
	**Historically Black Colleges and
	  Universities**
	  UF African American
	    Universities and Colleges

Elements of the Entries

The elements of the entries (see Fig. 1) in this list of subject headings follow closely the components of the entries outlined in *LCSH* to ensure interfacing and interlinking. A sample entry is listed below and a discussion of these elements follows. Each entry in this volume does not contain every element from *LCSH* (for example, the Narrower Term [NT] relationship is not located in the entry *Magnet schools*).

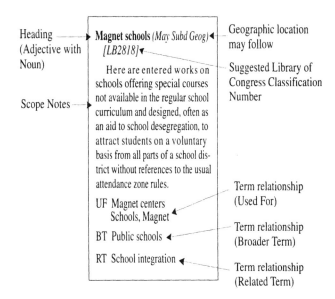

Fig. 1. Key to the Entries.

Headings

Table 1 (page xii) lists the types and examples of the grammatical structure of the *Subject Headings for African American Materials*.

Table 1. Grammatical structure of the subject headings.

Type	Example
Noun	Legend
Adjective with noun	Interethnic dating
Inverted adjective with noun	Migration, Internal
Noun with a preposition	Abolition of slavery
Prepositional phrase heading	Reverse discrimination in employment
Inverted prepositional phrase heading	Cities and towns, Movement to
Noun with a conjunction	Racism and language
Conjunctive phrase heading	Church and race problems
Parenthetical heading	Saxophone and piano music (Jazz)
Heading with a subdivision	Minorities—Employment

Class Numbers

This list of subject headings follows the practice of *LCSH* by including the suggested Library of Congress Classification Numbers in the entries. Caution must be taken in the use of the numbers as revisions are an ongoing process at the Library of Congress. For example,

Magnet Schools *[LB 2818]*
De facto school segregation *[LC212.6-LC212.63]*

In addition, if several facets of a topic are assigned different classification numbers, the number is given for each facet. For example,

Marginality, Social *[GN367 (Ethnology)] [HM136 (Sociology)] [HN50-HN942.5 (By country)]*
American literature—African American authors *[PS153.N5 (History)] [PS508.N3 (Collections)]*

Scope Notes

Scope notes are used in *LCSH* and in this list to ensure congruence and uniformity when using the subject heading in a particular entry. For example,

Demonstrations *(May Subd Geog)*
Here are entered works on large public gatherings, marches, etc., organized for non-violent protest or affirmation, even though incidental disturbances or incipient rioting may occur.
Inclusionary housing program *(May Subd Geog)*
Here are entered works on programs which oblige or encourage developers of upper income housing to include a number of low or moderate income units.

References: The Relationship Between Headings

Subject headings in this list are constructed to show equivalence (USE), hierarchical (Broader Term [BT], and Narrower Term [NT]), and associative (Related Term [RT]) relationships as displayed in the list of *LCSH*. Also, this list of subject headings employs general references (see also or SA). A discussion of each of these relationships follows.

The Equivalence Relationship: USE References

The USE reference is a technique of directing a term that is not preferred or not admissible to a term that is preferred or admissible. The admissible term is preceded by the code UF (Used For). The USE and UF symbols serve as reciprocals. The list below offers examples of the conditions of equivalence relationships.

1. *Synonyms or terms so nearly synonymous that they would cover the same kind of materials:*

Desegregation in education
  USE School Integration
School integration
  UF Desegregation in education

2. *The second part of a compound heading:*

Art and race
  UF Race and art
Race and art
  USE Art and race

3. *The second part of an inverted heading:*

Urban sociology
  USE Sociology, urban
Sociology, urban
  UF Urban sociology

4. *An inverted form to the normal order:*

Clergy, African American
  USE African American clergy
African American clergy
  UF Clergy, African American

5. *Varied spellings (including initialisms):*

NAACP
  USE National Association for
    the Advancement of Colored
    People

National Association for the Advancement of Colored People
  UF NAACP

6. *Subject headings located in a previous edition of the list of LCSH:*

Hairdressing of African Americans
  UF Hairdressing of Negroes
    [Former Heading]

Hairdressing of Negroes
  USE Hairdressing of African Americans

The Hierarchical Relationships: Broader Terms and Narrower Terms

The hierarchical relationships of terms located in the *LCSH* and in this volume are expressed by the symbols BT (Broader Term) and NT (Narrower Term). The BT reference indicates the class of which a given subject heading is a member. The NT reference is the reciprocal term of the BT reference. The Narrower Term (NT) indicates that the subject heading or subject headings are specific members of the class of concepts indicated by the BT. For example,

Federal aid to minority business enterprises
  BT Minority business enterprises—Finance

Minority business enterprises—Finance
  NT Federal aid to minority business enterprises

Hierarchical references serve to list subject headings that are broader or narrower than the headings consulted, thus providing the opportunity to create or use subject headings as broad or narrow as desired. Also, this class-structural display allows the user to conceptualize the headings in a hierarchical mode, for example:

Historically Black Colleges and Universities
  BT African Americans—Education
  NT United Negro College Fund Institutions

In this volume, a number of subject headings have been included that represent concepts broader than the African American experience. The use of these broad or generic terms provided the only technique for introducing the most precise or accurate term in a hierarchical or logical sequence. In the example that follows, it would be difficult to access the concepts *African American theater* or *Black theater* without using the broader term *Theater*. This hospitality of accessing narrower terms through the use of broader terms is located throughout this volume.

Theater *(May Subd Geog) [PN 2000-PN3299]*
  NT African American theater
    Black theater

The Associative Relationship: Related Topics

The Related Term (RT) reference indicates that under a given subject heading or subject headings, another heading or headings may be found that bears a nonstructural or a nonhierarchical relationship. For the most part, these associative terms are cross-referenced to provide the facility when examining one term for use, there occurs the existence of an associative or linking term, for example,

Affirmative action programs
  RT Minorities—Employment
Minorities—Employment
  RT Affirmative action programs

General References

Following the practice of the *LCSH*, this list employs the use of general references to refer from one subject heading to a group of subject headings. These groups of subject headings may represent, for example,

Specific headings
African Methodist Episcopal Church *(May Subd Geog)*
  SA *names of individual churches,* e.g. St. Paul A.M.E. Church (Tampa, Fla.)

Generic headings
Public schools
  SA *headings beginning with the word* School

General headings using subdivision
Armed Forces—Minorities
  SA *subdivision* Minorities *under military services,* e.g. United States. Navy—Minority

General headings containing USE references
Jazz ensembles
  USE *headings which include the words* jazz ensemble *as a medium qualifier, e.g.* Concertos (Flute with jazz ensemble); Flute with jazz ensemble; Jazz ensemble with orchestra; Suites (Jazz ensemble)

Subdivisions

As located in the *LCSH*, the four classes of subdivisions used in this volume are topical subdivisions, form subdivisions, chronological subdivisions, and geographical subdivisions. The *Subject Cataloging Manual: Subject Headings* gives specific instructions for assigning these subdivisions.

Topical Subdivisions

Topical subdivisions indicate the specific aspect of the subtopic to the main subject heading, for example,

School libraries—Services to Minorities

Form Subdivisions

Form subdivisions are used to express the form of the material on the subject. They may be used under any subject, for example,

African Americans—Directories
Horne, Lena, 1917—Bibliography

Chronological Subdivisions

These subdivisions indicate a particular period of time expressed by the dates given, for example,

Jazz—To 1921
Jazz—1921-1930

Geographical Subdivisions

The posting of *(May Subd Geog)* after a subject heading or subject signifies that a geographic entity may follow the subject heading or subdivision. The *Subject Cataloging Manual: Subject Headings* and the *Anglo-American Cataloging Rules, 2nd Ed. Rev.* may be used for establishing the appropriate forms for geographic entries. For example, materials on civil rights demonstrations in the following three geographic locations would appear:

Civil rights demonstrations—Alabama
**Civil rights demonstrations—Alabama—
  Montgomery**
Civil rights demonstrations—Alabama—Selma

Further geographic entities may be established using the *Anglo-American Cataloging Rules*, for example,

Lincoln University (Lincoln University, Pa.)
Lincoln University (Jefferson City, Mo.)

Free-Floating Subdivisions and Pattern Headings

As stated in the *Subject Cataloging Manual: Subject Headings*, the term free-floating refers to a form or topical subdivision that may be assigned by the subject cataloger under designated subjects without the usage being established editorially, and as a consequence, without the usage appearing in the SUBJECTS file under each individual subject heading.[1] The subject headings in this volume follow the practice of the *LCSH* in assigning free-floating subdivisions.

Five types of free-floating subdivisions are listed in the *Subject Cataloging Manual:*[2]

1. Form and topical subdivisions of general application. The Subject Cataloging Manual should be consulted for use with this list of subdivisions.

2. Subdivisions used under classes of persons and other groups. The Subject Cataloging Manual should be consulted for use with the subdivisions indicated for classes of persons. However, the subdivisions designated for ethnic groups have been integrated and established under the subject heading African Americans, for example,

African Americans—Directories
African Americans—Research

3. Subdivisions used under names of individual corporate bodies, persons, and families.

   a. *Corporate Bodies (individual)*
     The subdivision designating corporate bodies for this list have been integrated and established under the corporate body *National Association for the Advancement of Colored People* as:

**National Association for the Advancement of
  Colored People** *(May Subd Geog)*
  UF   NAACP
  BT   Civil rights organizations
Here are listed subdivisions that have been established by the LCSH for use under the names of individual corporate name headings. For example, a bibliography of the National Urban League would be constructed: National Urban League—Bibliography.

   b. *Persons*
     It would be impossible to list the names of all African Americans in this volume who may be noteworthy of subject access. However, the name of *King, Martin Luther, Jr., 1929-1968* has been selected as the pattern heading for persons.

King, Martin Luther, Jr., 1929-1968
  UF   King, Martin Luther *[Former Heading]*
The subdivisions provided under this heading represent, for the greater part, standard subdivisions established by *LCSH* useable under any person and do not necessarily pertain to Martin Luther King, Jr., e.g. Du Bois, William Edward Burghardt, 1868-1963—Archives.

c. *Families*

For the establishment of subdivisions for African American families, the *Subject Cataloging Manual* under Genealogy (H 1631) should be consulted. For example, subject headings for the *Dobbs Family of Atlanta* should be constructed:

Dobbs family

Atlanta (Ga.)—Genealogy

African Americans—Georgia—Atlanta—Genealogy

4. Subdivisions used under place names. The *Manual* should be consulted for subdivisions used under place names, including names of regions, countries, cities, etc., and names of bodies of water.

5. There are a number of subdivisions controlled by pattern headings listed in the *Manual* and designated for use with the *LCSH*. In this volume, three subdivisions controlled by pattern headings are included. They are educational institutions (individual), Christian denominations, and individual literary authors.

a. *Educational Institutions (individual)*

The subdivisions used to control each individual historically Black college and university is listed under Lincoln University. It is as follows:

Lincoln University (Lincoln University, Pa.)

BT   Historically Black Colleges and Universities—
      Pennsylvania
      Public Universities and Colleges

Here are listed subdivisions that have been established by LCSH for individual universities and colleges. For example, an alumni directory of Knoxville College would be constructed: Knoxville College (Knoxville, Tenn.)—Alumni and alumnae—Directories.

b. *Christian Denominations*

The subdivisions used to control the African American Christian denominations are located under African Methodist Episcopal Church, as follows:

African Methodist Episcopal Church *(May Subd Geog)*

UF   A.M.E. Church

BT   Religious institutions

SA   *names of churches e.g.* St. Paul A.M.E. Church
      (Tampa, Fla.)

Here are listed subdivisions that have been established by LCSH for Christian denominations. For example, a directory of African Methodist Episcopal Zion Churches would be constructed: African Methodist Episcopal Zion Churches—Directories.

c. *Individual literary authors*

The subdivisions used to control individual the African American literary authors are listed under Morrison, Toni, as follows:

Morrison, Toni, 1931-

The subdivisions provided under this heading represent, for the greater part, standard subdivisions usable under any literary author heading, and do not necessarily pertain to Toni Morrison, e.g. Hansberry, Lorraine, 1930-1965—Characters—African Americans; Haskins, James, 1941—Bibliography.

The Filing Arrangement of Entries

Entries in this volume are arranged following *LCSH*, which uses the *Library of Congress Filing Rules*. Headings are filed alphabetically, word by word. Headings with subdivisions (e.g., African American—Charities) precede headings with conjunctions and prepositional phrases (e.g., African Americans in the professions). Subdivisions are filed in the following order: period subdivision, arranged chronologically; form and topical subdivisions, arranged alphabetically; geographic subdivisions, arranged alphabetically. The following list illustrates these rules:

African American actors

African American bankers

African American Brethren (Church of the Brethren)

African American Jews

African American women chemists

African American wood carving

African Americans

African Americans—Charities

African Americans—Health and Hygiene

African Americans—Religion

African Americans—Social conditions

African Americans—Social conditions—To 1964

African Americans—Social conditions—1964-1974

African Americans—Social conditions—1975-

African Americans—Youth

African Americans—Appalachian Region

African Americans—New York (State)

African Americans—Puerto Rico

African Americans and libraries

African Americans and mass media

African Americans in the performing arts

African Americans on postage stamps

Notes

1. Library of Congress, *Subject Cataloging Manual: Subject Headings,* 4th ed. Washington, D.C.: Library of Congress Cataloging Distribution Service, 1991, H1095, p. 1.

2. Ibid.

Table of Pattern Headings

Category	Pattern Heading
Ethnic Groups	African Americans
Corporate Bodies	National Association for the Advancement of Colored People
Individuals	King, Martin Luther, Jr. 1929-1968
Educational Institutions	Lincoln University (Lincoln University, Pa.)
Christian Denominations	African Methodist Episcopal Church
Indiviual Literary Authors	Morrison, Toni, 1931-

Symbols

UF   Used for
BT   Broader Term
RT   Related Term
SA   See Also
NT   Narrower Term

(The following may be used as a guide for those libraries maintaining card catalogs.)

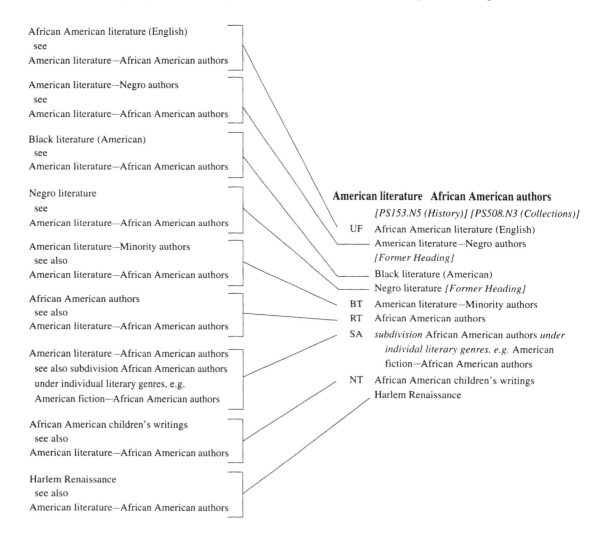

African American literature (English)
  see
American literature—African American authors

American literature—Negro authors
  see
American literature—African American authors

Black literature (American)
  see
American literature—African American authors

Negro literature
  see
American literature—African American authors

American literature—Minority authors
  see also
American literature—African American authors

African American authors
  see also
American literature—African American authors

American literature—African American authors
  see also subdivision African American authors
  under individual literary genres, e.g.
  American fiction—African American authors

African American children's writings
  see also
American literature—African American authors

Harlem Renaissance
  see also
American literature—African American authors

American literature   African American authors
[PS153.N5 (History)] [PS508.N3 (Collections)]
UF   African American literature (English)
     American literature—Negro authors
     [Former Heading]
     Black literature (American)
     Negro literature *[Former Heading]*
BT   American literature—Minority authors
RT   African American authors
SA   *subdivision* African American authors *under*
     individal literary genres, e.g. American
     fiction—African American authors
NT   African American children's writings
     Harlem Renaissance

Sources

Byron, Lorene Sandra. "A Comparative Evaluation of Two Indexing Languages." Ph.D. diss., University of Wisconsin-Madison, 1974.

Cutter, Charles A. *Rules for a Dictionary Catalog.* Washington, D.C.: Government Printing Office, U.S. Bureau of Education. Special Report of Libraries, 1876, pt. II.

Directory of the American Baptist Church in the USA. Valley Forge, PA: Distributed by the American Baptist Churches in the USA, 1982.

Encyclopedia of Associations. 28th ed. Detroit: Gale Research, 1994.

Library of Congress. *Cataloging Service Bulletin,* no. 59-64 (Winter 1993-Spring 1994). Washington, D.C.: Library of Congress, 1993-1994.

———. *Library of Congress Filing Rules.* Washington, D.C.: Library of Congress, 1980.

———. *Library of Congress Subject Headings,* 16th ed., 4 vols. Washington, D.C.: Library of Congress Cataloging Distribution Service, 1993.

———. *Library of Congress Subject Headings,* 17th ed., 4 vols. Washington, D.C.: Library of Congress Cataloging Distribution Service, 1994.

———. *Name Authorities Cumulative Microform Edition.* Washington, D.C.: Library of Congress, 1977- . Also available on CD-ROM as *CD MARC Names.*

———. *Subject Cataloging Manual: Subject Headings.* 4th ed., 2 vols. Washington, D.C.: Library of Congress Cataloging Distribution Service, 1991. Updated sheets were consulted for input.

———. Office for Subject Cataloging Policy. *Free-Floating Subdivisions: An Alphabetic Index.* 2nd ed. Washington, D.C.: Library of Congress Cataloging Distribution Service, 1990.

———. *LC Subject Headings Weekly Lists,* no. 01-51 (Jan. 1993-Dec. 1993) and no. 1-24 (Jan. 1994-June 1994). Washington, D.C.: Library of Congress Cataloging Distribution Service, 1993-1994.

Minority Organizations: A National Directory. 3rd ed. Garnett Park, Md.: Garnett Park Press, 1987.

"100 Most Influential Black Americans and Organization Leaders," *Ebony* 49, No. 7 (May 1994): 36-50.

Ploski, Harry and Ernest Kaiser. *The Negro Almanac.* New rev. ed. New York: Bellwether, 1971.

Roebuck, Julian B. and Komanduri S. Murty. *Historically Black Colleges and Universities: Their Place in American Higher Education.* Westport, Conn.: Praeger, 1993.

Thum, Marcella. *Exploring Black America: A History and Guide.* New York: Atheneum, 1975.

Who's Who Among Black Americans. 8th ed. Detroit: Gale Research, 1994-1995.

Wynar, Bohdan S. *Introduction to Cataloging and Classification.* 8th ed. by Arlene G. Taylor. Englewood, Colo.: Libraries Unlimited, 1992.

Subject Headings

100 Black Men of America, Inc. *(May Subd Geog)*
  RT   African American civic leaders
1890 Land-grant and Tuskegee University
  USE   State universities and colleges
A.M.E. Church
  USE   African Methodist Episcopal Church
A.M.E. Zion Church
  USE   African Methodist Episcopal Zion Church

A

Abolition of capital punishment
  USE   Capital punishment
Abolition of slavery
  USE   Slavery
Abolitionists *(May Subd Geog)*
  RT   Slavery—Anti-slavery movements
Abolitionists in literature *(Not Subd Geog)*
Academic libraries—Services to minorities *(May Subd Geog)*
  BT   Libraries and minorities
        Minorities—Services for
  RT   African American academic libraries
Academics (Learned societies)
  USE   Societies
Accordion and piano music (Jazz)
  USE   Jazz
Acculturation *(May Subd Geog)*
  SA   *subdivision* Cultural assimilation *under ethnic groups, e.g.* African Americans—Cultural assimilation
  NT   Ethnic relations
        Socialization
Acculturation in literature *(Not Subd Geog)*
Action, State (Civil rights)
  USE   State action (Civil rights)
Activity programs in education *(May Subd Geog)* [LB1027.25]
  UF   Activity schools
  NT   African Americans—Study and teaching—Activity programs
        Multicultural education—Activity programs
Activity programs in multicultural education
  USE   Multicultural education—Activity programs
Activity schools
  USE   Activity programs in education
Actors, African American
  USE   African American actors

Actors, Black
  UF   Black actors
        Negro actors *[Former Heading]*
  BT   Black theater
  NT   African American actors
Actresses, African American
  USE   African American actresses
Addiction to drugs
  USE   Drug abuse
Admirals, African American
  USE   African American admirals
Adoption *(May Subd Geog) [HV874.8-H875.7]*
  UF   Child placing
  NT   Interracial adoption
Advertising *(May Subd Geog) [HF5801-HF6182]*
  NT   African Americans in advertising
        Minorities in advertising
Aeronautics—United States
  NT   African Americans in aeronautics
Aesthetics, African American
  USE   African American aesthetics
Aesthetics, Black *(May Subd Geog)*
  UF   Black aesthetics
Affirmative action programs *(May Subd Geog)*
  UF   Equal employment opportunity
        Equal opportunity in employment
  BT   Discrimination in employment
        Personnel management
  RT   Minorities—Employment
  NT   Reverse discrimination in employment
Affirmative action programs—Law and legislation *(May Subd Geog)*
Africa—Civilization
  NT   African American art—African influences
        Afrocentrism
        United States—Civilization—African influences
Africa, West—Civilization
  NT   African American quilts—West African influences
African-African American relations
  USE   African Americans—Relations with Africans
African American
  UF   Afro-American
African American academic libraries *(May Subd Geog) [Z675.U5]*
  UF   Afro-American university and college libraries *[Former Heading]*
        Libraries, African American academic

BT   African Americans and libraries
RT   Academic libraries—Services to minorities

African American actors *(May Subd Geog)* *[PN2286]*
UF   Actors, African American
        Negro actors *[Former Heading]*
BT   Actors, Black
        African American entertainers
        African Americans in the performing arts
NT   African American gay actors
        African American motion picture actors and actresses

African American actresses *(May Subd Geog)*
UF   Actresses, African American
NT   African American motion picture actors and actresses

African American admirals *(May Subd Geog)*
UF   Admirals, African American

African American adolescent mothers
    USE   African American teenage mothers

African American aesthetics *(May Subd Geog)*
UF   Aesthetics, African American

African American-African relations
    USE   African Americans—Relations with Africans

African American aged *(May Subd Geog)*
UF   Aged, African American

African American agricultural economists *(May Subd Geog)*
UF   Agricultural economists, African American

African American agricultural laborers *(May Subd Geog)*
UF   African American farm workers
        Agricultural laborers, African American
        Negro agricultural laborers *[Former Heading]*

African American agriculturists *(May Subd Geog)*
UF   Agriculturists, African American

African American Air Force personnel
    USE   United States. Air Force—African Americans

African American air pilots *(May Subd Geog)*
UF   African American pilots
        Air pilots, African American
BT   African Americans in aeronautics
        United States. Air Force—African Americans

African American anthropologists *(May Subd Geog)*
UF   Anthropologists, African American

African American architects *(May Subd Geog)*
UF   Architects, African American

African American architecture *(May Subd Geog)*
UF   Architecture, African American
BT   Ethnic architecture—United States

African American art *(May Subd Geog)*
UF   Art, African American
        Negro art *[Former Heading]*
BT   Ethnic art—United States

African American art—African influences
BT   Africa—Civilization

African American art—European influences
BT   Europe—Civilization

African American art industries and trade
    USE   African American decorative arts

African American artisans *(May Subd Geog)*
UF   Artisans, African American

African American artists *(May Subd Geog)* *[N6538.N5]*
UF   Artists, African American
        Negro artists *[Former Heading]*
NT   African American photographers
        African American women artists

African American arts *(May Subd Geog)* *[NX512.3A35]*
UF   Arts, African American
        Negro arts *[Former Heading]*
NT   African Americans in the performing arts
        Harlem Renaissance

African American astronauts *(May Subd Geog)*
UF   Astronauts, African American

African American athletes *(May Subd Geog)*
UF   Athletes, African American
        Negro athletes *[Former Heading]*
NT   African American baseball players
        African American basketball players
        African American boxers
        African American football players
        African American women athletes

African American authors *(May Subd Geog)* *[PS153.N5]*
UF   Authors, African American
        Negro authors *[Former Heading]*
RT   American literature—African American authors
        African American historians
        African American women authors

African American automobile industry workers *(May Subd Geog)*
UF   Automobile industry workers, African American

African American automobile industry workers— Effect of technological innovations on *(May Subd Geog)*

African American bankers *(May Subd Geog)*
UF   Bankers, African American
BT   African American executives

African American banks *(May Subd Geog)*

African American Baptists *(May Subd Geog)*
UF   Baptists, African American
        Baptists, Negro *[Former Heading]*

African American baseball players *(May Subd Geog)*
UF   Baseball players, African American
BT   African American athletes

African American basketball players *(May Subd Geog)* *[GV884]*
UF   Basketball players, African American
BT   African American athletes

African American beauty operators *(May Subd Geog)*
UF   Beauty operators, African American

African American boxers *(May Subd Geog)*
UF   Boxers, African American
BT   African American athletes

African American boys *(May Subd Geog)*
BT   African American children

African American Brethren (Church of the Brethren) *(May Subd Geog)*
UF   Brethren, African American (Church of the Brethren)
BT   African Americans—Religion

African American business enterprises *(May Subd Geog)*
UF   Business enterprises, African American

African American business people
USE   African Americans in business

African American cabinetmakers *(May Subd Geog)*
UF   Cabinetmakers, African American

African American Catholics *(May Subd Geog)* *[BX1407.N4]*
UF   Catholics, African American
Catholics, Negro *[Former Heading]*
BT   African Americans—Religion

African American chemists *(May Subd Geog)*
UF   Chemists, African American
BT   African American scientists
NT   African American women chemists

African American children *(May Subd Geog)* *[E185.86]*
UF   African Americans—Children
Children, African American
Negro children *[Former Heading]*
NT   African American boys
Social work with African American children

African American children—Anthropometry

African American children—Games
USE   African American children's games

African American children—Language
RT   Black English

African American children—Nutrition

African American children's games *(May Subd Geog)* *[GR103 (Folklore)] [GV1204.12 (Recreation)]*
UF   African American children—Games
Children's games, African American

African American children's writings
UF   Children's writing, African American
Negro children's writings *[Former Heading]*
BT   American literature—African American authors

African American Christians (Disciples of Christ)
UF   African American Disciples of Christ (Christians)
Christians (Disciples of Christ), African American
Disciples of Christ, African American
Disciples of Christ, Negro *[Former Heading]*
BT   African Americans—Religion

African American Christians (General Convention of the Christian Church) *(May Subd Geog)*
UF   Christians (General Convention of the Christian Church), African American
BT   African Americans—Religion

African American churches *(May Subd Geog)*
UF   Churches, African American
Negro churches *[Former Heading]*
BT   African Americans—Religion
NT   African American Spiritual churches

African American civic leaders *(May Subd Geog)*
UF   Civic leaders, African American
RT   100 Black Men of America, Inc.
National Coalition of 100 Black Women, Inc.

African American civil rights workers *(May Subd Geog)*
UF   Civil rights workers, African American
NT   African American women civil rights workers

African American clergy *(May Subd Geog)*
UF   Clergy, African American
Negro clergy *[Former Heading]*
NT   African American women clergy

African American clergy in literature *(Not Subd Geog)*

African American coal miners *(May Subd Geog)*
UF   Coal miners, African American

African American college administrators *(May Subd Geog)*
UF   African American university administrators
College administrators, African American

African American college graduates *(May Subd Geog)*
UF   African American university graduates
College graduates, African American
Negro college graduates *[Former Heading]*

African American college students *(May Subd Geog)*
UF   African American university students
College students, African American
College students, Negro *[Former Heading]*
BT   African American students
African Americans—Education (Higher)

African American college students—Books and reading

African American college students—Fellowships
USE   African American college students—Scholarship, fellowships, etc.

African American college students—Political activity

African American college students—Religious life

African American college students—Scholarships, fellowships, etc. *(May Subd Geog)*
- UF African American college students—Fellowships
- BT African Americans—Scholarships, fellowships, etc.

African American college teachers *(May Subd Geog)*
- UF African American university teachers
  College teachers, African American
  Negro college teachers *[Former Heading]*
- BT African American teachers

African American college teachers—Appointment
- USE African American college teachers—Selection and appointment

African American college teachers—Selection and appointment *(May Subd Geog)*
- UF African American college teachers—Appointment

African American colleges
- USE Historically Black Colleges and Universities

African American colonization
- USE African Americans—Colonization

African American communication
- USE African Americans—Communication

African American communists *(May Subd Geog)*
- UF Communists, African American
  Communists, Negro *[Former Heading]*

African American composers *(May Subd Geog)*
- UF Composers, African American
- NT African American women composers

African American Congregationalists *(May Subd Geog)*
- UF Congregationalists, African American
- BT African Americans—Religion

African American construction workers *(May Subd Geog)*
- UF Construction workers, African American

African American consumers
- USE African Americans as consumers

African American cookery
- UF Cookery, Afro-American *[Former Heading]*
  Cookery, Negro *[Former Heading]*
  Soul food cookery

African American cooks *(May Subd Geog)*
- UF Cooks, African American
- NT African American women cooks

African American costume designers
- USE African American fashion designers

African American county agricultural agents *(May Subd Geog)*
- UF County agricultural agents, African American

African American cowboys *(May Subd Geog)*
- UF Cowboys, African American
  Negroes as cowboys *[Former Heading]*

African American criminals *(May Subd Geog)*
- UF Criminals, African American
  Negro criminals *[Former Heading]*
- NT African American outlaws

African American decorative arts *(May Subd Geog)*
[NK839.3.A35]
- UF Afro-American art, industries and trade *[Former Heading]*
  Decorative arts, African American

African American dentists *(May Subd Geog)*
[RK60.45]
- UF Dentists, African American
  Negro dentists *[Former Heading]*
- RT National Dental Association

African American dialect
- USE Black English

African American diplomats *(May Subd Geog)*
- UF Diplomats, African American
- NT African American women diplomats

African American Disciples of Christ (Christians)
- USE African American Christians (Disciples of Christ)

African American drama (English)
- USE American drama—African American authors

African American dramatists *(May Subd Geog)*
- UF Dramatists, African American

African American dropouts *(May Subd Geog)*
- UF Dropouts, African American
  Negro dropouts *[Former Heading]*

African American education
- USE African Americans—Education

African American elementary schools *(May Subd Geog)*
- UF Elementary schools, African American
  Negro elementary schools *[Former Heading]*
- BT African Americans—Education (Elementary)

African American engineers *(May Subd Geog)*
[TA157]
- UF Engineers, African American
  Negro engineers *[Former Heading]*

African American English
- USE Black English

African American entertainers *(May Subd Geog)*
- UF Entertainers, African American
  Negro entertainers *[Former Heading]*
- BT African Americans in the performing arts
- NT African American actors
  African American musicians

African American Episcopalians *(May Subd Geog)*
[BX5979-BX5980]
- UF Episcopalians, African American
  Episcopalians, Negro *[Former Heading]*
- BT African Americans—Religion

African American evangelists *(May Subd Geog)*
  UF   Evangelists, African American

African American executives *(May Subd Geog)*
  UF   Executives, African American
        Negro executives *[Former Heading]*
  BT   African Americans in business
        Minority executives
  NT   African American bankers
        African American women executives

African American explorers *(May Subd Geog)*
  UF   Explorers, African American

African American families *(May Subd Geog)*
  [E186.86]
  UF   African Americans—Families
          [Former Heading]
        Families, African American
        Negro families *[Former Heading]*
  NT   Church work with African American families

African American families—Religious life *(May Subd Geog)*

African American farm workers
  USE   African American agricultural laborers

African American farmers *(May Subd Geog)*
  UF   Farmers, African American
        Negroes as farmers *[Former Heading]*

African American fashion designers *(May Subd Geog)*
  UF   Afro-American costume designers *[Former Heading]*
        Fashion designers, African American

African American fiction (English)
  USE   American fiction—African American authors

African American fire fighters *(May Subd Geog)*
  UF   Afro-American firemen *[Former Heading]*
        Fire fighters, African American
        Negro firemen *[Former Heading]*

African American firemen
  USE   African American fire fighters

African American folk art *(May Subd Geog)*
  UF   Folk art, African American

African American football players *(May Subd Geog)*
  UF   Football players, African American
  BT   African American athletes

African American freemasonry *(May Subd Geog)*
  UF   Freemasonry, African American
        Freemasons. United States. Scottish Rite.
          National Supreme Council (Negro)
          [Former Heading]
        Freemasons, Afro-American *[Former Heading]*

African American freemasons *(May Subd Geog)*
  UF   Freemasons, Afro-American *[Former Heading]*
        Freemasons, Negro *[Former Heading]*

African American gardens *(May Subd Geog)*
  [SB457.527]
  UF   Gardens, African American

African American gay actors *(May Subd Geog)*
  UF   Gay Afro-American actors *[Former Heading]*
  BT   African American actors

African American gays *(May Subd Geog)*
  UF   Afro-American homosexuals *[Former Heading]*
        Gays, African American

African American generals *(May Subd Geog)*
  UF   Generals, African American

African American-German American relations
  USE   African Americans—Relations with German Americans

African American government executives *(May Subd Geog)*
  UF   Government executives, African American

African American hairdressing
  USE   Hairdressing of African Americans

African American handicapped *(May Subd Geog)*
  UF   Handicapped African Americans

African American healers *(May Subd Geog)*
  UF   Healers, African American

African American Heroines of Jericho
  USE   Heroines of Jericho, African American

African American historians *(May Subd Geog)*
  UF   Historians, African American
        Historians, Negro *[Former Heading]*
  BT   African American authors

African American Holiness church members *(May Subd Geog)*
  UF   Holiness church members, African American
  BT   African Americans—Religion

African American home economics extension workers *(May Subd Geog)*
  UF   Home economics extension workers, African American

African American homosexuals
  USE   African American gays

African American horsemen and horsewomen *(May Subd Geog)*
  UF   Horsemen and horsewomen, African American

African American-Indian relations
  USE   African Americans—Relations with Indians

African American infants *(May Subd Geog)*
  UF   Infants, African American

African American intellectuals *(May Subd Geog)*
  UF   Intellectuals, African American
  RT   African Americans—Intellectual life

African American inventors *(May Subd Geog)*
  UF   Inventors, African American
        Negro inventors *[Former Heading]*

African American iron and steel workers *(May Subd Geog)*
  UF   Iron and steel workers, African American

African American-Japanese relations
USE African Americans—Relations with Japanese
African American-Jewish relations
USE African Americans—Relations with Jews
African American Jews *(May Subd Geog)*
UF Black Jews (United States)
Jews, African American
Negro Jews *[Former Heading]*
African American journalism
USE African American press
African American journalists *(May Subd Geog)*
UF Journalists, African American
Negro journalists *[Former Heading]*
BT African American press
RT African Americans in the newspaper industry
National Association of Black Journalists
African American judges *(May Subd Geog)*
UF Judges, African American
Negro judges *[Former Heading]*
African American labor leaders *(May Subd Geog)*
UF Labor leaders, African American
African American law students *(May Subd Geog)*
UF Law students, African American
African American lawyers *(May Subd Geog)*
[KF299.A35]
UF Lawyers, African American
Negro lawyers *[Former Heading]*
BT Minority lawyers
RT National Bar Association
African American leadership *(May Subd Geog)*
UF Leadership, African American
Negro leadership *[Former Heading]*
African American legislators *(May Subd Geog)*
UF Legislators, African American
BT African American politicians
African American lesbians *(May Subd Geog)*
UF Lesbians, African American
African American librarians *(May Subd Geog)*
UF Librarians, African American
Negro librarians *[Former Heading]*
BT Minority librarians—United States
RT American Library Association—Black Caucus
African American libraries
USE African Americans and libraries
African American literature (English)
USE American literature—African American
authors
African American Lutherans *(May Subd Geog)*
UF Lutherans, African American
Lutherans, Negro *[Former Heading]*
BT African Americans—Religion
African American mass media *(May Subd Geog)*
[P94.5.A37]
UF Mass media, African American

BT Ethnic mass media—United States
NT African American press
African American radio stations
African American mathematicians *(May Subd Geog)*
UF Mathematicians, African American
NT African American women mathematicians
African American mayors *(May Subd Geog)*
UF Mayors, African American
Negro mayors *[Former Heading]*
BT African American politicians
RT National Conference of Black Mayors
African American mediums *(May Subd Geog)*
UF Mediums, African American
African American membership in associations,
institutions, etc.
USE Associations, institutions, etc.—Membership,
African American
African American membership in school boards
USE School boards—United States—Membership,
African American
African American men *(May Subd Geog)* *[E185.86]*
UF Men, African American
African American men in literature *(Not Subd Geog)*
African American Mennonites *(May Subd Geog)*
[BX8116.3.A37]
UF Mennonites, African American
BT African Americans—Religion
African American merchant seamen *(May Subd Geog)*
UF Merchant seamen, African American
BT African American seamen
African American messianism
USE Messianism, African American
African American Methodists *(May Subd Geog)*
UF Methodists, African American
Methodists, Negro *[Former Heading]*
BT African Americans—Religion
African American midwives *(May Subd Geog)*
UF Midwives, African American
African American militant organizations
USE Black militant organizations—United States
African American military personnel
USE African American soldiers
United States—Armed Forces—African Americans
African American militia movement
USE Reconstruction—African American troops
African American minstrel shows
USE Minstrel shows
African American missionaries *(May Subd Geog)*
UF Missionaries, African American
Missionaries, Negro *[Former Heading]*

African American Mormons *(May Subd Geog)*
    UF   Mormons, African American
           Mormons and Mormonism, Negro
              [Former Heading]
    BT   African Americans—Religion
African American mortality
    USE African Americans—Mortality
African American motion picture actors and actresses *(May Subd Geog)*
    UF   Motion picture actors and actresses, African American
           Negro moving-picture actors and actresses
              [Former Heading]
    BT   African American actors
           African American actresses
African American motion picture producers and directors *(May Subd Geog)*
    UF   Motion picture producers and directors, African American
African American music
    USE African Americans—Music
African American musicians *(May Subd Geog)*
    UF   Musicians, African American
           Negro musicians *[Former Heading]*
    BT   African American entertainers
           African Americans in the performing arts
    NT   African American orchestral musicians
           African American singers
           African American women musicians
African American musicians in literature *(Not Subd Geog)*
African American Muslims *(May Subd Geog)*
    UF   Muslims, African American
    BT   Muslims—United States
African American nationalism
    USE Black nationalism—United States
African American neighborhoods *(May Subd Geog)*
    UF   Neighborhoods, African American
    BT   Ethnic neighborhoods—United States
African American newspapers *(May Subd Geog)*
[PN4882.5]
    UF   Negro newspapers (American)
              [Former Heading]
African American novelists *(May Subd Geog)*
    UF   Novelists, African American
    BT   American fiction—African American authors
African American nurses *(May Subd Geog)* *[RT83.5]*
    UF   Negro nurses *[Former Heading]*
           Nurses, African American
African American optometrists *(May Subd Geog)*
    UF   Optometrists, African American
African American orators *(May Subd Geog)*
    UF   Negro orators *[Former Heading]*
           Orators, African American

African American orchestral musicians *(May Subd Geog)*
    UF   Orchestral musicians, African American
    BT   African American musicians
African American outlaws *(May Subd Geog)*
    UF   Outlaws, African American
    BT   African American criminals
African American painters *(May Subd Geog)*
    UF   Painters, African American
African American painting *(May Subd Geog)*
[ND238.N5]
    UF   Painting, African American
African American parents *(May Subd Geog)*
    UF   Parents, African American
African American Pentecostals *(May Subd Geog)*
[BR1644.3]
    UF   Pentecostals, African American
    BT   African Americans—Religion
African American periodicals *(May Subd Geog)*
    UF   Negro periodicals (American)
              [Former Heading]
           Periodicals, African American
    BT   African American Press
African American pharmacists *(May Subd Geog)*
[RS122.5]
    UF   Pharmacists, African American
    BT   African Americans in medicine
African American philosophy
    UF   Philosophy, African American
African American photographers *(May Subd Geog)*
    UF   Negro photographers *[Former Heading]*
           Photographers, African American
    BT   African American artists
African American physicians *(May Subd Geog)*
[R695]
    UF   Negro physicians *[Former Heading]*
           Physicians, African American
    RT   National Medical Association
African American pilots
    USE African American air pilots
African American pioneers
    UF   Pioneers, African American
African American poetry (English)
    USE American poetry—African American authors
African American poets *(May Subd Geog)*
    UF   Poets, African American
    NT   African American women poets
African American police *(May Subd Geog)*
    UF   Negro policemen *[Former Heading]*
           Police, African American
African American-Polish American relations
    USE African Americans—Relations with Polish Americans

African American political consultants *(May Subd Geog)*
    UF   Political consultants, African American
African American political scientists *(May Subd Geog)*
    UF   Negro political scientists *[Former Heading]*
          Political scientists, African American
African American politicians *(May Subd Geog)*
    UF   Politicians, African American
    NT   African American legislators
          African American mayors
African American preaching
    UF   Preaching, African American
    BT   African Americans—Religion
African American Presbyterians *(May Subd Geog)*
    UF   Presbyterians, African American
          Presbyterians, Negro
    BT   African Americans—Religion
African American press *(May Subd Geog) [PN4882.5]*
    UF   African American journalism
          Journalism, African American
          Negro press *[Former Heading]*
          Press, African American
    BT   African American mass media
          Ethnic press—United States
    NT   African American journalists
          African American periodicals
African American printmakers *(May Subd Geog)*
    UF   Printmakers, African American
African American prints *(May Subd Geog)*
    [NE539.3.A35]
    UF   Prints, African American
African American prisoners *(May Subd Geog)*
    UF   Prisoners, African American
African American prisoners—Mental health services
    (May Subd Geog) [RC451.5.N4)
African American prose literature (English)
    USE   American prose literature—African American
           authors
African American proverbs *(May Subd Geog)*
    UF   Proverbs, African American
          Proverbs, Negro *[Former Heading]*
African American psychics *(May Subd Geog)*
    UF   Psychics, African American
African American psychologists *(May Subd Geog)*
    [BF109]
    UF   Psychologists, African American
African American public worship *(May Subd Geog)*
    BT   African Americans—Religion
African American quiltmakers *(May Subd Geog)*
    UF   Quiltmakers, African American
African American quilts *(May Subd Geog)*
    UF   Quilts, African American

African American quilts—West African influences
    BT   Africa, West—Civilization
African American quotations
    USE   African Americans—Quotations
African American radio stations *(May Subd Geog)*
    UF   Radio stations, African American
    BT   African American mass media
          African Americans in radio broadcasting
          Ethnic radio broadcasting—United States
African American sailors
    USE   African American seamen
African American scholars *(May Subd Geog)*
    UF   Scholars, African American
African American scholarships
    USE   African Americans—Scholarships,
           fellowships, etc.
African American school board members
    USE   School boards—United States—Membership,
           African American
African American school principals *(May Subd Geog)*
    UF   Afro-American school superintendents and
           principals *[Former Heading]*
          School principals, African American
African American school superintendents *(May Subd Geog)*
    UF   Afro-American school superintendents and
           principals *[Former Heading]*
          School superintendents, African American
African American school superintendents and principals
    USE   African American school principals
           African American school superintendents
African American scientists *(May Subd Geog)*
    UF   Negro scientists *[Former Heading]*
          Scientists, African American
    NT   African American chemists
African American sculpture *(May Subd Geog)*
    UF   Sculpture, African American
African American seamen *(May Subd Geog)*
    Here are entered works on African American naval personnel or
    African American naval personnel and merchant seamen collectively.
    Works on the organization, administration, and history of African
    American units within the United States Navy are entered under
    United States. Navy—African Americans.
    UF   African American sailors
          Negroes as seamen *[Former Heading]*
          Seamen, African American
    BT   United States—Armed Forces—
           African Americans
    NT   African American merchant seamen
          United States. Navy—African Americans
African American Seminoles
    USE   Black Seminoles
African American sermons (English)
    USE   Sermons, American—African American
           authors

African American Seventh-Day Adventists *(May Subd Geog)*
UF   Seventh-Day Adventists, African American
       Seventh-Day Adventists, Negro
       [Former Heading]
BT   African Americans—Religion

African American ship captains *(May Subd Geog)*
UF   Ship captains, African American

African American short stories (English)
USE   Short stories, American—African American authors

African American singers *(May Subd Geog)*
UF   Singers, African American
BT   African American musicians

African American single people *(May Subd Geog)*
UF   Single people, African American

African American slave holders
USE   African American slaveholders

African American slave masters
USE   African American slaveholders

African American slave owners
USE   African American slaveholders

African American slaveholders *(May Subd Geog)*
UF   African American slave holders
       African American slave masters
       African American slave owners
       African American slavemasters
       African American slaveowners
       Slaveholders, African American
BT   Slaveholders—United States

African American slavemasters
USE   African American slaveholders

African American slaveowners
USE   African American slaveholders

African American slaves
NT   Freedmen

African American social workers *(May Subd Geog)*
UF   Negroes as social workers *[Former Heading]*
       Social workers, African American

African American sociologists *(May Subd Geog)*
[HM19-HM22]
UF   Negro sociologists *[Former Heading]*
       Sociologists, African American

African American soldiers *(May Subd Geog)*
Here are entered works on African American military personnel in the United States Army. Works on the organization, administration, and history of African American units within the United States Army are entered under United States. Army—African American troops.
UF   African American military personnel
       Negro soldiers *[Former Heading]*
       Negroes as soldiers *[Former Heading]*
       Soldiers, African American
BT   Soldiers, Black
       United States—Armed Forces—African Americans

SA   *subdivision* Participation, African American *under individual wars*
NT   Reconstruction—African American troops
       United States. Army—African American troops
       United States. Marine Corps—African American troops
       United States. Marine Corps—African Americans

African American songs
USE   African Americans—Music

African American Spiritual churches *(May Subd Geog) [BX6194.A46]*
UF   African American Spiritual movement
       Black Spiritual churches
       Black Spiritual movement
       Spiritual churches, African American
       Spiritual churches, Black
       Spiritualist churches, African American
       Spiritualist churches, Black
       Spiritualist movement, African American
       Spiritualist movement, Black
BT   African American churches

African American Spiritual movement
USE   African American Spiritual churches

African American spirituals
USE   Spirituals (Songs)

African American student movements *(May Subd Geog)*
UF   Student movements, African American

African American students *(May Subd Geog)*
UF   Negro students *[Former Heading]*
BT   African Americans—Education
       Students
NT   African American college students
       English language—Study and teaching—African American students

African American studies
USE   African Americans—Study and teaching

African American suffrage
USE   African Americans—Suffrage

African American Sunday schools *(May Subd Geog) [BV1523.A37]*
UF   Sunday schools, African American

African American surgeons *(May Subd Geog)*
UF   Surgeons, African American

African American teacher participation in the community
USE   African American teachers and the community

African American teachers *(May Subd Geog)*
UF   Negro teachers *[Former Heading]*
       Teachers, African American
BT   African Americans—Education
       Faculty integration—United States
NT   African American college teachers

African American teachers—In-service training *(May Subd Geog)*

African American teachers—Pensions *(May Subd Geog)*
- UF   Afro-American teachers—Salaries, pensions, etc. *[Former Heading]*

African American teachers—Salaries, etc. *(May Subd Geog)*
- UF   Afro-American teachers—Salaries, pensions, etc. *[Former Heading]*

African American teachers—Salaries, pensions, etc.
- USE   African American teachers—Pensions
-        African American teachers—Salaries, etc.

African American teachers—Training of *(May Subd Geog)*
- UF   Afro-American teachers, Training of *[Former Heading]*
-        Negro teachers, Training of *[Former Heading]*

African American teachers, Training of
- USE   African American teachers—Training of

African American teachers and the community *(May Subd Geog)*
- UF   African American teacher participation in the community
-        Community and African American teachers
-        Negro teachers and the community *[Former Heading]*
- BT   Community and school—United States

African American teenage boys *(May Subd Geog)*
- UF   Teenage boys, African American
- BT   African American teenagers

African American teenage girls *(May Subd Geog)*
- UF   Teenage girls, African American
- BT   African American teenagers

African American teenage mothers *(May Subd Geog)*
- UF   Afro-American adolescent mothers *[Former Heading]*
-        Teenage mothers, African American

African American teenagers *(May Subd Geog)*
- UF   Teenagers, African American
- NT   African American teenage boys
-        African American teenage girls

African American television producers and directors *(May Subd Geog)*
- UF   Television producers and directors, African American

African American theater *(May Subd Geog)* *[PN2270.A35]*
- BT   American drama—African American authors
-        Theater

African American theologians *(May Subd Geog)* *[BR563.N4]*
- UF   Theologians, African American
- BT   Black theology

African American theological seminaries *(May Subd Geog)*
- UF   Negro theological seminaries *[Former Heading]*
-        Theological seminaries, African American
- BT   Historically Black Colleges and Universities
- NT   Interdenominational Theological Center (Atlanta, Ga.)
-        Simmons University Bible School (Louisville, Ky.)
-        Virginia Seminary College (Lynchburg, Va.)

African American theology
- USE   Black theology

African American trade unionists
- USE   Trade-unions—African American membership

African American trappers *(May Subd Geog)*
- UF   Trappers, African American

African American union members
- USE   Trade-unions—African American membership

African American Unitarian Universalists *(May Subd Geog)*
- UF   Unitarian Universalists, African American
- BT   African Americans—Religion

African American universities and colleges
- USE   Historically Black Colleges and Universities

African American university administrators
- USE   African American college administrators

African American university and college libraries
- USE   African American academic libraries

African American university graduates
- USE   African American college graduates

African American university students
- USE   African American college students

African American university teachers
- USE   African American college teachers

African American veterans *(May Subd Geog)*
- UF   Negro veterans *[Former Heading]*
-        Veterans, African American
- BT   United States—Armed Forces—African Americans

African American veterinarians
- USE   African Americans in veterinary medicine

African American victims of crimes
- USE   African Americans—Crimes against

African American whalers *(May Subd Geog)*
- UF   Whalers, African American

African American wit and humor *[PN6231.N5]*
- UF   Black humor (African American)
-        Negro wit and humor *[Former Heading]*
-        Wit and humor, African American

African American women *(May Subd Geog)*
- UF   Women, African American
-        Women, Negro *[Former Heading]*

African American women—Alcohol use *(May Subd Geog)*

African American women—Education *(May Subd Geog)*
  BT   African Americans—Education

African American women artists *(May Subd Geog)*
  UF   Women artists, African American
  BT   African American artists

African American women athletes *(May Subd Geog)*
  UF   Women athletes, African American
  BT   African American athletes

African American women authors *(May Subd Geog)*
  UF   Women authors, African American
  BT   African American authors

African American women chemists *(May Subd Geog)*
  UF   Women chemists, African American
  BT   African American chemists

African American women civil rights workers *(May Subd Geog)*
  UF   Women civil rights workers, African American
  BT   African American civil rights workers
        Women civil rights workers—United States

African American women clergy *(May Subd Geog)*
  UF   Women clergy, African American
  BT   African American clergy

African American women composers *(May Subd Geog)*
  UF   Women composers, African American
  BT   African American composers

African American women cooks *(May Subd Geog)*
  UF   Women cooks, African American
  BT   African American cooks

African American women diplomats *(May Subd Geog)*
  UF   Women diplomats, African American
  BT   African American diplomats

African American women executives *(May Subd Geog)*
  UF   Women executives, African American
  BT   African American executives

African American women in literature *(Not Subd Geog)*

African American women in the professions *(May Subd Geog)*
  BT   African Americans in the professions

African American women mathematicians *(May Subd Geog)*
  UF   Women mathematicians, African American
  BT   African American mathematicians

African American women musicians *(May Subd Geog)*
  UF   Women musicians, African American
  BT   African American musicians

African American women poets *(May Subd Geog)*
  UF   Women poets, African American
  BT   African American poets

African American wood-carving *(May Subd Geog)*
  UF   Wood-carving, African American

African American youth *(May Subd Geog)*
  UF   African Americans—Youth
        Negro youth *[Former Heading]*
        Youth, African American
  NT   Church work with African American youth

African Americana
  USE   African Americans—Collectibles

African Americans *(May Subd Geog)* [E185]
  Here are entered works on citizens of the United States of black African descent. Works on blacks who temporarily reside in the United States, such as aliens, students from abroad, etc., are entered under Blacks—United States. Works on blacks outside the United States are entered under Blacks—[place].
  UF   African Americans—United States
        Afro-Americans
        Black Americans
        Colored people (United States)
        Negroes *[Former Heading]*
  BT   Africans—United States
        Blacks—United States
        Ethnology—United States
  SA   *subdivision* African Americans *under names of wars, e.g.* World War, 1939-1945—African Americans; *and headings beginning with* African American
  NT   Associations, institutions, etc.—Membership, African American
        Freedmen
        Mulattoes
        School boards—United States—Membership, African American
        Social work with African Americans
        United States—Civilization—African American influences

African Americans—Alcohol use

African Americans—Anniversaries, etc.
  UF   African Americans—Biography—Anniversaries, etc.
        African Americans—History—Anniversaries, etc.

African Americans—Archives

African Americans—Assaults against *(May Subd Geog)*

African Americans—Assimilation, Cultural
  USE   African Americans—Cultural assimilation

African Americans—Athletics
  USE   African Americans—Sports

African Americans—Attitudes
  Use for works on attitudes or opinions held by members of the group. For works on public opinion about the group, see African Americans—Public opinion

African Americans—Audiotape catalogs

African Americans—Autographs

African Americans—Bibliography

African Americans—Bibliography—Catalogs

African Americans—Bibliography— Microform catalogs

African Americans—Bibliography—Union lists

African Americans—Bio-bibliography

African Americans—Biography

African Americans—Biography—Anniversaries, etc.
 USE African Americans—Anniversaries, etc.

African Americans—Biography—Dictionaries

African Americans—Biography— History and criticism

African Americans—Book reviews

African Americans—Books and reading *[Z1039.B56]*
 UF African Americans—Reading habits or interests

African Americans—Caricatures and cartoons

African Americans—Case studies

African Americans—Census

African Americans—Ceremonies
 USE African Americans—Rites and ceremonies

African Americans—Charitable contributions *(May Subd Geog)*
 UF African Americans—Contributions, Charitable

African Americans—Charities

African Americans—Children
 USE African American children

African Americans—Civil rights *(May Subd Geog)* *[E185.61]*
 UF Discrimination against African Americans
 BT Civil rights—United States
   Race discrimination—United States
 NT African Americans—Suffrage
   Black power—United States
   Civil rights workers—United States
   Poor People's Campaign
   Selma-Montgomery Rights March, 1965

African Americans—Clothing *(May Subd Geog)*
 UF African Americans—Costume

African Americans—Collectibles *(May Subd Geog)*
 UF African Americana
   Black Americana
   Negrobilia

African Americans—Colonization *(May Subd Geog)* *[E448]*
 This heading may be subdivided by place colonized, e.g. African Americans—Colonization—Africa; African Americans—Colonization—Texas.
 UF African American colonization
   Colonization by African Americans
   Slavery—United States—Colonization

African Americans—Colonization—Africa
 UF Back to Africa movement

African Americans—Colonization—Texas

African Americans—Color
 UF Color of African Americans
 BT Color of man

African Americans—Comic books, strips, etc.

African Americans—Communication *[P94.5.A37]*
 UF African American communication

African Americans—Congresses

African Americans—Congresses—Attendance

African Americans—Contributions, Charitable
 USE African Americans—Charitable contributions

African Americans—Correspondence

African Americans—Costume
 USE African Americans—Clothing

African Americans—Counseling of *(May Subd Geog)*

African Americans—Craniology *[GN130.N5]*

African Americans—Crimes against *(May Subd Geog)*
 UF African American victims of crimes
   Crimes against African Americans

African Americans—Cultural assimilation *(May Subd Geog)*
 UF African Americans—Assimilation, Cultural

African Americans—Cultural life
 USE African Americans—Intellectual life

African Americans—Customs
 USE African Americans—Social life and customs

African Americans—Dancing
 BT African Americans—Social life and customs

African Americans—Death

African Americans—Demography
 USE African Americans—Population

African Americans—Dental care *(May Subd Geog)*

African Americans—Devotions
 USE African Americans—Prayer-books and devotions

African Americans—Diaries

African Americans—Dictionaries

African Americans—Directories

African Americans—Discography

African Americans—Diseases *(May Subd Geog)*

African Americans—Drama

African Americans—Drug Use *(May Subd Geog)*
 BT Drug abuse
   Drug utilization

African Americans—Dwellings
 Use for works discussing residential buildings for African Americans from the standpoint of architecture, construction, ethnology, etc. For works on social or economic aspects of the provision of housing for the group, see African Americans—Housing. For works discussing the actual homes of African Americans from an architectural or historical point of view, see African Americans—Homes and haunts.

BT Dwellings
African Americans—Early works to 1800
African Americans—Economic conditions *[E185.8]*
UF African-Americans—Socioeconomic status
NT African Americans—Employment
    African Americans in business
    Black power—United States
African Americans—Education *(May Subd Geog)*
[LC2701-LC2858]
UF African American education
RT School integration—United States
NT African American students
    African American teachers
    African American women—Education
    African Americans—Professional education
    African Americans—Scholarships, fellowships, etc.
    African Americans—Vocational education
    English language—Study and teaching—African
      American students
    Historically Black Colleges and Universities
    Segregation in education—United States
    Segregation in higher education—United States
**African Americans—Education—Agriculture,
[Reading, etc.]**
African Americans—Education—Law and legislation
(May Subd Geog)
**African Americans—Education
(Continuing education)** *(May Subd Geog)*
African Americans—Education (Early childhood)
(May Subd Geog)
African Americans—Education (Elementary) *(May
Subd Geog) [LC2771]*
NT African American elementary schools
African Americans—Education (Graduate) *(May
Subd Geog)*
African Americans—Education (Higher) *(May Subd
Geog) [LC2781]*
NT African American college students
African Americans—Education (Preschool) *(May
Subd Geog)*
African Americans—Education (Primary) *(May
Subd Geog)*
African Americans—Education (Secondary) *(May
Subd Geog) [LC2779]*
African Americans—Employment *(May Subd Geog)*
UF African Americans—Occupations
    African Americans—Working conditions
BT African Americans—Economic conditions
NT African Americans in business
African Americans—Employment—Foreign countries
African Americans—Employment—Law and legislation
(May Subd Geog)
African Americans—Encyclopedias

African Americans—Ethnic identity
UF African Americans—Identity, Ethnic
African Americans—Ethnobiology *(May Subd Geog)*
African Americans—Ethnobotany *(May Subd Geog)*
African Americans—Ethnozoology *(May Subd Geog)*
African Americans—Examinations, questions, etc.
African Americans—Exhibitions
African Americans—Families
    USE African American families
African Americans—Family relationships
    USE African Americans—Kinship
African Americans—Fellowships
    USE African Americans—Scholarships,
      fellowships, etc.
African Americans—Fiction
African Americans—Film catalogs
African Americans—Finance
African Americans—Finance—Law and legislation
(May Subd Geog)
African Americans—Finance, Personal
UF African Americans—Personal finance
African Americans—Folklore
NT John Henry (Legendary character)
African Americans—Food
African Americans—Foreign countries
African Americans—Foreign influences
UF African Americans—Influences, Foreign
African Americans—Funeral customs and rites
(May Subd Geog)
UF African Americans—Mortuary customs
African Americans—Gambling
African Americans—Games
African Americans—Genealogy
African Americans—Government
    USE African Americans—Politics and government
African Americans—Government policy *(May Subd
Geog)*
African Americans—Government relations
Use for relations between the group as a whole and the government
of the place in which they reside.
African Americans—Hairdressing
    USE Hairdressing of African Americans
African Americans—Haunts
    USE African Americans—Homes and haunts
African Americans—Health and hygiene *(May Subd
Geog) [RA448.5.N4]*
UF African Americans—Hygiene
NT African Americans—Medical care
African Americans—Historiography

African Americans—History
　　UF　Black history
African Americans—History—To 1863
African Americans—History—1863-1877 *[E185.2]*
African Americans—History—1877-1964 *[E185.6]*
African Americans—History—1964- *[E185.615]*
African Americans—History—Anniversaries, etc.
　　USE　African Americans—Anniversaries, etc.
African Americans—History—Sources
African Americans—Home care *(May Subd Geog)*
African Americans—Homes and haunts *(May Subd Geog)*
　　Use for works discussing the actual homes of individual African Americans from an architectural or historical point of view. Also use for works about the favorite places of African Americans or places they habitually frequent or with which they are associated. For works discussing residential buildings for African Americans from the standpoint of architecture, construction, ethnology, etc. see African Americans—Dwellings. For works on social or economic aspects of the provision of housing for African Americans, see African Americans—Housing.
　　UF　African Americans—Haunts
　　　　African Americans—Places frequented
African Americans—Hospital care *(May Subd Geog)*
African Americans—Hospitals *(May Subd Geog)*
African Americans—Housing *(May Subd Geog)*
　　[HD7288.72U]
　　Use for works on social or economic aspects of the provision of housing for African Americans. For works discussing residential buildings for African Americans from the standpoint of architecture, construction, ethnology, etc., see African Americans—Dwellings. For works discussing the actual homes of African Americans from an architectural or historical point of view, see African Americans—Homes and haunts.
　　UF　Housing, African American
　　BT　Discrimination in housing
　　RT　Housing
African Americans—Humor
African Americans—Hunting
African Americans—Hygiene
　　USE　African Americans—Health and hygiene
African Americans—Iconography
　　USE　African Americans—Pictorial works
African Americans—Identity, Ethnic
　　USE　African Americans—Ethnic identity
African Americans—Identity, Race
　　USE　African Americans—Race identity
African Americans—Indexes
African Americans—Influences, Foreign
　　USE　African Americans—Foreign influences
African Americans—Information services
African Americans—Injuries
　　USE　African Americans—Wounds and injuries
African Americans—Institutional care *(May Subd Geog)*

African Americans—Intellectual life
　　UF　African Americans—Cultural life
　　RT　African American intellectuals
African Americans—Intelligence levels
African Americans—Intelligence testing
African Americans—Interviews
African Americans—Jewelry
African Americans—Job stress *(May Subd Geog)*
African Americans—Juvenile drama
African Americans—Juvenile fiction
African Americans—Juvenile films
African Americans—Juvenile humor
African Americans—Juvenile literature
African Americans—Juvenile poetry
African Americans—Juvenile sound recordings
African Americans—Kinship *(May Subd Geog)*
　　UF　African Americans—Family relationships
African Americans—Land tenure
African Americans—Languages
　　NT　Black English
African Americans—Languages—Texts
African Americans—Law and legislation
　　USE　African Americans—Legal status, laws, etc.
African Americans—Legal status, laws, etc. *(May Subd Geog)*
　　UF　African Americans—Law and legislation
　　　　Discrimination against African Americans
African Americans—Library resources *[Z1361.N39]*
　　UF　Library resources on Negroes *[Former Heading]*
　　BT　African Americans—Study and teaching
African Americans—Life skills guides
African Americans—Literary collections
African Americans—Longitudinal studies
African Americans—Manuscripts
African Americans—Marriage customs and rites
African Americans—Material culture
African Americans—Mathematics
African Americans—Medical care *(May Subd Geog)*
　　[RA448.5.N4]
　　BT　African Americans—Health and hygiene
African Americans—Medical examinations *(May Subd Geog)*
African Americans—Medicine
African Americans—Mental health *(May Subd Geog)*
　　[RC451.5.N4]
　　UF　African Americans—Mental illness
　　　　[Former Heading]
African Americans—Mental health services

African Americans—Mental illness
  USE African Americans—Mental health
African Americans—Migrations
African Americans—Missions *(May Subd Geog)*
  [BV2783]
  UF Missions to African Americans
       [Former Heading]
       Missions to Negroes *[Former Heading]*
African Americans—Money
African Americans—Monuments
African Americans—Mortality *[HB1323.B5]*
  UF African American mortality
  BT African Americans—Statistics, Vital
African Americans—Mortuary customs
  USE African Americans—Funeral customs and rites
African Americans—Museums *(May Subd Geog)*
  RT Museums
African Americans—Music *[M1670-M1671 (Music)]*
  [ML3556 (History)]
  UF Afro-American music *[Former Heading]*
       Afro-American songs *[Former Heading]*
       Negro music *[Former Heading]*
       Negro sounds *[Former Heading]*
  NT Blues (Music)
       Gospel music
       Jazz
       Rhythm and blues music
       Soul music
       Spirituals (Songs)
African Americans—Music—Bibliography
African Americans—Music—Discography
African Americans—Music—History and criticism
African Americans—Newspapers
  Use only as a form subdivision under African Americans in the United States. For works about African American newspapers, use the heading African American newspapers.
African Americans—Nutrition
African Americans—Obituaries
African Americans—Occupations
  USE African Americans—Employment
African Americans—Outlines, syllabi, etc.
African Americans—Outside employment
  USE African Americans—Supplementary employment
African Americans—Pastoral counseling of *(May Subd Geog)*
African Americans—Pensions *(May Subd Geog)*
African Americans—Periodicals
  UF African Americans—Yearbooks
African Americans—Periodicals—Bibliography
African Americans—Periodicals—Bibliography—Catalogs
African Americans—Periodicals—Bibliography—Union lists
African Americans—Periodicals—Indexes
African Americans—Personal finance
  USE African Americans—Finance, Personal
African Americans—Photographs
  Use only for works consisting of actual photographs, i.e. photographic prints. Do not use for works consisting of reproductions of photographs.
African Americans—Physiology
African Americans—Pictorial works
  UF African Americans—Iconography
African Americans—Places frequented
  USE African Americans—Homes and haunts
African Americans—Poetry
African Americans—Political activity
  USE African Americans—Politics and government
African Americans—Politics and government
  Use for the internal or self-government of African Americans and/or the political activity of African Americans.
  UF African Americans—Government
       African Americans—Political activity
African Americans—Politics and suffrage
  USE African Americans—Suffrage
African Americans—Population
  UF African Americans—Demography
African Americans—Portraits
African Americans—Posters
African Americans—Prayer-books and devotions
  UF African Americans—Devotions
African Americans—Professional education *(May Subd Geog) [LC2785]*
  BT African Americans—Education
African Americans—Promotions *(May Subd Geog)*
African Americans—Prophesies
African Americans—Psychological testing *(May Subd Geog)*
African Americans—Psychology *[E185.625]*
African Americans—Public opinion
  Use for works on public opinion about African Americans. For works on the attitudes or opinions held by members of the group, use African Americans—Attitudes.
African Americans—Public welfare *(May Subd Geog)*
African Americans—Quotations
  Use for collections or discussions of quotations by or about African Americans.
  UF Afro-American quotations *[Former Heading]*
       African Americans—Quotations, maxims, etc.
       Negro quotations *[Former Heading]*
African Americans—Quotations, maxims, etc.
  USE African Americans—Quotations

African Americans—Race identity
 UF African Americans—Identity, Race
   Negritude
   Racial identity of African Americans
 BT Race awareness
 NT Black nationalism—United States
African Americans—Reading habits or interests
 USE African Americans—Books and reading

African Americans—Recreation

African Americans—Registers

African Americans—Rehabilitation

African Americans—Relations with Africans
 UF African-African American relations
   Africans—Relations with African Americans
   African American-African relations
   Blacks—Africa—Relations with African Americans

African Americans—Relations with German Americans
 UF African American-German American relations
   German American-African American relations
   German Americans—Relations with African
    Americans
 BT United States—Ethnic relations
   United States—Race relations

African Americans—Relations with Indians
 UF African American-Indian relations
   Indian-African American relations
   Indians of North America—Relations with African
    Americans
   Negro-Indian relations *[Former Heading]*
 BT United States—Race relations

African Americans—Relations with Japanese
 UF African American-Japanese relations
   Japanese—Relations with African Americans
   Japanese-African Americans relations
 BT Japan—Race relations
   United States—Race relations

African Americans—Relations with Jews
 UF African American-Jewish relations
   Jewish-African American relations
   Jews—Relations with African Americans
   Negro-Jewish relations *[Former Heading]*

African Americans—Relations with Polish Americans
 UF African American-Polish American relations
   Polish American-African American relations
   Polish Americans—Relations with African
    Americans
 BT United States—Ethnic relations
   United States—Race relations

African Americans—Relations with West Indians
 UF Blacks—West Indies—Relations with African
    Americans
   West Indians—Relations with African Americans
African Americans—Relations with whites
 USE United States—Race relations

African Americans—Radio stations
 BT Ethnic radio broadcasting—United States
African Americans—Religion
 RT Religious institutions
 NT African American Brethren (Church of the
   Brethren)
   African American Catholics
   African American Christians (Disciples of Christ)
   African American Christians (General Convention
    of the Christian Church)
   African American churches
   African American Congregationalists
   African American Episcopalians
   African American Holiness Church Members
   African American Lutherans
   African American Mennonites
   African American Methodists
   African American Mormons
   African American Pentecostals
   African American preaching
   African American Presbyterians
   African American public worship
   African American Seventh-Day Adventists
   African American Unitarian Universalists
   Black Muslims
   Black theology
   Jehovah's Witnesses
   Jesus Christ—African American interpretations

African Americans—Relocation *(May Subd Geog)*

African Americans—Research *(May Subd Geog)*

African Americans—Respite care *(May Subd Geog)*

African Americans—Retirement

African Americans—Rites and ceremonies
 UF African Americans—Ceremonies

African Americans—Scholarships, fellowships, etc.
 (May Subd Geog) [LC2707]
 UF African Americans—Fellowships
   African American scholarships
 BT African Americans—Education
 NT African American college students—Scholar-
   ships, fellowships, etc.

African Americans—Segregation *[E185.6]*
 BT African Americans—Social conditions
 NT Segregation in education—United States
   Segregation in higher education—United States
   Segregation in transportation—United States

African Americans—Services for *(May Subd Geog)*

African Americans—Social conditions *[E185.86]*
 UF African Americans—Socioeconomic status
 NT African Americans—Segregation

African Americans—Social conditions—To 1964

African Americans—Social conditions—1964-1975

African Americans—Social conditions—1975-

African Americans—Social life and customs
[E185.86]
  UF African Americans—Customs
  NT African Americans—Dancing

African Americans—Social networks

African Americans—Social work with
  USE Social work with African Americans

African Americans—Socialization

African Americans—Societies, etc.
  NT Black militant organizations—United States

African Americans—Socioeconomic status
  USE African Americans—Economic conditions
       African Americans—Social conditions

African Americans—Songs and music
  Use for music about African Americans. For music of African Americans, use African Americans—Music.
  UF Negro music *[Former Heading]*
       Negro songs *[Former Heading]*
       Topical songs (Negro) *[Former Heading]*
       Topical songs (Negroes) *[Former Heading]*

African Americans—Sports
  UF African Americans—Athletics

African Americans—Statistical services

African Americans—Statistics

African Americans—Statistics, Vital
  UF African Americans—Vital statistics
  BT Vital statistics
  NT African Americans—Mortality

African Americans—Study and teaching *(May Subd Geog) [E184.7]*
  UF Afro-American studies *[Former Heading]*
  NT African Americans—Library resources

African Americans—Study and teaching— Activity programs *(May Subd Geog)*
  BT Activity programs in education

African Americans—Study and teaching—Audio-visual aids

African Americans—Study and teaching (Continuing education) *(May Subd Geog)*

African Americans—Study and teaching (Early childhood) *(May Subd Geog)*

African Americans—Study and teaching (Elementary) *(May Subd Geog)*

African Americans—Study and teaching (Graduate) *(May Subd Geog)*

African Americans—Study and teaching (Higher) *(May Subd Geog)*

African Americans—Study and teaching (Internship) *(May Subd Geog)*

African Americans—Study and teaching (Preschool) *(May Subd Geog)*

African Americans—Study and teaching (Primary) *(May Subd Geog)*

African Americans—Study and teaching (Secondary) *(May Subd Geog)*

African Americans—Substance use *(May Subd Geog)*

African Americans—Suffrage *(May Subd Geog)*
[JK1923-JK1929]
  UF African American suffrage
       African Americans—Politics and suffrage
       [Former Heading]
  BT African Americans—Civil rights
       Suffrage—United States

African Americans—Suicidal behavior *(May Subd Geog)*

African Americans—Supplementary employment *(May Subd Geog)*
  UF African Americans—Outside employment

African Americans—Surgery *(May Subd Geog)*

African Americans—Taxation *(May Subd Geog)*

African Americans—Time management

African Americans—Tobacco use *(May Subd Geog)*

African Americans—Transportation

African Americans—Travel *(May Subd Geog)*

African Americans—Travel restrictions *(May Subd Geog)*

African Americans—Trapping

African Americans—Video catalogs

African Americans—Vital statistics
  USE African Americans—Statistics, Vital

African Americans—Vocational education *(May Subd Geog) [LC2780]*
  BT African Americans—Education

African Americans—Warfare *(May Subd Geog)*

African Americans—Wars *(May Subd Geog)*
  Use for works discussing collectively the wars in which African Americans have participated.

African Americans—Working conditions
  USE African Americans—Employment

African Americans—Wounds and injuries *(May Subd Geog)*
  UF African Americans—Injuries

African Americans—Yearbooks
  USE African Americans—Periodicals

African Americans—Youth
  USE African American youth

African Americans—Appalachian Region
  NT Melungeons

African Americans—Florida
  NT Gullahs

African Americans—Georgia
  NT Gullahs

African Americans—Maryland
  NT Wesorts

African Americans—Massachusetts

African Americans—New Jersey
    NT   Ramapo Mountain people

African Americans—New York (State)
    NT   Ramapo Mountain people

African Americans—Puerto Rico
    UF   Blacks—Puerto Rico

African Americans—South Carolina
    NT   Gullahs

African Americans—United States
    USE   African Americans

African Americans and libraries *(May Subd Geog)*
    UF   African American libraries
           Libraries, African Americans
           Libraries and African Americans
           Libraries and Negroes *[Former Heading]*
           Library services to African Americans
    BT   Libraries and minorities
    NT   African American academic libraries

African Americans and mass media *(May Subd Geog) [P94.5.A37]*
    UF   Mass media and African Americans

African Americans as consumers *(May Subd Geog)*
    UF   African American consumers
           Negroes as consumers *[Former Heading]*

African Americans in advertising *(May Subd Geog)*
    Here are entered works on the portrayal of African Americans in advertising.
    BT   Advertising

African Americans in aeronautics *(May Subd Geog)*
    UF   Negroes in aeronautics *[Former Heading]*
    BT   Aeronautics—United States
    NT   African American air pilots

African Americans in art
    UF   Negroes in art *[Former Heading]*

African Americans in astronautics *(May Subd Geog)*

African Americans in business *(May Subd Geog) [E185.8]*
    UF   African American business people
           Businessmen, African American
           Negro businessmen *[Former Heading]*
           Negroes as businessmen
    BT   African Americans—Economic conditions
           African Americans—Employment
           Minority business enterprises—United States
    NT   African American executives

African Americans in dentistry *(May Subd Geog) [RK60.45]*
    UF   Negroes in dentistry *[Former Heading]*

African Americans in drama
    USE   African Americans in literature

African Americans in fiction
    USE   African Americans in literature

African Americans in literature
    UF   African Americans in drama
           African Americans in fiction
           African Americans in poetry
           Negroes in literature *[Former Heading]*
    SA   *subdivision* Characters—African Americans *under names of individual literary authors, e.g.* Johnson, James Weldon, 1871-1938—Characters—African Americans

African Americans in mass media *(May Subd Geog) [P94.5.A37]*

African Americans in medicine *(May Subd Geog) [R695]*
    UF   Negroes in medicine *[Former Heading]*
    NT   African American pharmacists

African Americans in military service
    USE   United States—Armed Forces—African Americans

African Americans in motion pictures
    Here are entered works discussing the portrayal of African Americans in motion pictures. Works discussing all aspects of involvement of African Americans in motion pictures are entered under African Americans in the motion picture industry. Works discussing specific aspects of African American involvement are entered under the particular subject, e.g. African American motion picture actors and actresses.
    UF   Negroes in moving-pictures *[Former Heading]*

African Americans in poetry
    USE   African Americans in literature

African Americans in radio broadcasting
    UF   African Americans in the radio industry *[Former Heading]*
           Negroes in radio *[Former Heading]*
    NT   African American radio stations
    BT   Radio broadcasting—United States

African Americans in television *(May Subd Geog)*
    Here are entered works on the portrayal of African Americans on television. Works on the employment of African Americans in television are entered under African Americans in television broadcasting.
    UF   African Americans on television

African Americans in television broadcasting *(May Subd Geog) [PN1992.8.A34]*
    Here are entered works on the employment of African Americans in television. Works on the portrayal of African Americans on television are entered under African Americans in television.
    UF   African Americans in the television industry *[Former Heading]*

African Americans in the Armed Forces
    USE   United States—Armed Forces—African Americans

African Americans in the civil service *(May Subd Geog)*
    UF   African Americans in the civil service—United States
           Civil service—African American employment

African Americans in the civil service—United States
    USE   African Americans in the civil service

African Americans in the motion picture industry
(May Subd Geog) [PN1995.9.N4]
 Here are entered works discussing all aspects of African American involvement in motion pictures. Works discussing the portrayal of African Americans in motion pictures are entered under African Americans in motion pictures. Works discussing specific aspects of African American involvement are entered under the particular subject, e.g. African American motion picture actors and actresses.
  UF   Negroes in the moving-picture industry
         [Former Heading]

African Americans in the newspaper industry *(May Subd Geog)*
  BT   Mass media and minorities
  RT   African American journalists

African Americans in the performing arts *(May Subd Geog)*
  UF   Negroes in the performing arts
         [Former Heading]
  BT   African American arts
  NT   African American actors
        African American entertainers
        African American musicians
        Minstrel shows

African Americans in the press *(May Subd Geog)*
 Here are entered works discussing the portrayal of African Americans by the press.
  BT   Press

African Americans in the professions *(May Subd Geog)*
  NT   African American women in the professions
African Americans in the radio industry
  USE   African Americans in radio broadcasting
African Americans in the television industry
  USE   African Americans in television broadcasting

African Americans in veterinary medicine *(May Subd Geog)*
  UF   African American veterinarians
        Negroes in veterinary medicine *[Former Heading]*

African Americans on postage stamps *[HE6185.A35]*
  BT   Postage stamps
African Americans on television
  USE   African Americans in television

African cooperation
  RT   Pan-Africanism

African diaspora *(Not Subd Geog)*
 Here are entered works dealing with the dispersion of black Africans to countries outside of the African Continent, together with a description of life, attitude and outlook in their new surroundings.
  UF   Black diaspora
  RT   Africans—Migrations

African Methodist Episcopal Church *(May Subd Geog)*
  UF   A.M.E. Church
  BT   Religious institutions
  SA   *names of individual churches, e.g.* St. Paul A.M.E. Church (Tampa, Fla.)
 Here are listed subdivisions that have been established by LCSH for Christian denominations. For example, a directory of African

Methodist Episcopal Zion Churches would be constructed: African Methodist Episcopal Zion Churches—Directories.

—**Adult education**

—**Anecdotes**

—**Anniversaries, etc.**

—**Apologetic works**

—**Apologetic works—History and criticism**

—**Benefices** *(May Subd Geog)*

—**Bibliography**

—**Bio-bibliography**

—**Bishops**

—**Bishops—Appointment, call and election**

—**Bishops—Biography**

—**Bishops—Correspondence**

—**Bishops—Directories**

—**Bishops—Interviews**

—**Caricatures and cartoons**

—**Catechisms**

—**Catechisms—History and criticism**

—**Charities**

—**Clergy**

—**Clergy—Appointment, call and election**

—**Clergy—Biography**

—**Clergy—Correspondence**

—**Clergy—Degradation**

—**Clergy—Deposition**

—**Clergy—Deprivation of the clerical garb**

—**Clergy—Health and hygiene** *(May Subd Geog)*

—**Clergy—Installation**

—**Clergy—Pensions** *(May Subd Geog)*

—**Clergy—Portraits**

—**Clergy—Psychology**

—**Clergy—Rating of**

—**Clergy—Religious life**

—**Clergy—Salaries, etc.** (*May Subd Geog*)

—**Clergy—Secular employment**

—**Clergy—Sexual behavior**

—**Clergy—Societies, etc.**

—**Clergy—Supply and demand** (*May Subd Geog*)

—**Clergy—Training of** (*May Subd Geog*)

—**Comparative studies**

—**Congresses**

—**Controversial literature**

—**Controversial literature—History and criticism**

—**Creeds**

—**Creeds—History and criticism**

—**Customs and practices**

—**Dictionaries**

—**Dictionaries, Juvenile**

—**Dioceses** (*May Subd Geog*)

—**Diplomatic service**

—**Directories**

—**Discipline**

—**Doctrines**

—**Education** (*May Subd Geog*)

—**Education—Societies, etc.**

—**Employees**

—**Exhibitions**

—**Finance**

—**Foreign relations** (*May Subd Geog*)

—**Government**

—**Handbooks, manuals, etc.**

—**Historiography**

—**History**

—**History—19th century**

—**History—20th century**

—**History—1965-**

—**History—Maps**

—**History—Societies, etc.**

—**History—Sources**

—**Humor**

—**Hymns**

—**Hymns—History and criticism**

—**Hymns—Texts**

—**In literature**

—**Infallibility**

—**Influence**

—**Liturgy**

—**Liturgy—Calendar**

—**Liturgy—History**

—**Liturgy—Study and teaching** (*May Subd Geog*)

—**Liturgy—Texts**

—**Liturgy—Texts—Concordances**

—**Liturgy—Texts—History and criticism**

—**Liturgy—Texts—Illustrations**

—**Liturgy—Texts—Manuscripts**

—**Liturgy—Theology**

—**Liturgy, Experimental**

—**Maps**

—**Membership**

—**Missions** (*May Subd Geog*)

—**Missions—Congresses**

—**Missions—Pictorial works**

—**Missions—Societies, etc.**

—**Museums** (*May Subd Geog*)

—**Name**

—**On postage stamps**

—**Pastoral letters and charges**

—**Periodicals**

—**Pictorial works**

—**Political activity**

—**Prayer-books and devotions**

—**Prayer-books and devotions—History and criticism**

—**Public opinion**

—**Publishing** *(May Subd Geog)*

—**Relations**

—**Sermons**

—**Sermons—History and criticism**

—**Societies, etc.**

—**Statistics**

—**Teaching office**

—**Terminology**

African Methodist Episcopal Zion Church *(May Subd Geog)*
  UF   A.M.E. Zion Church
  BT   Religious institutions
  SA   *names of individual churches, e.g.* Shaw Temple
         A.M.E. Zion Church (Atlanta, Ga.)

African relations
  USE Pan-Africanism

Africans *(May Subd Geog)*
  BT   Ethnology—Africa

Africans—Migrations
  RT   African diaspora

Africans—Relations with African Americans
  USE African Americans—Relations with Africans

Africans—United States
  NT   African Americans

Afro (Hair style)
  USE Hairdressing of African Americans
         Hairdressing of Blacks

Afro-American
  USE African American

Afro-Americans
  USE African Americans

Afrocentricity
  USE Afrocentrism

Afrocentrism *(May Subd Geog)*
  UF   Afrocentricity
  BT   Africa—Civilization
         Civilization, Western—African influences
         Ethnocentrism

Aged, African American
  USE African American aged

Agricultural economists, African American
  USE African American agricultural economists

Agricultural laborers, African American
  USE African American agricultural laborers

Agriculturists, African American
  USE African American agriculturists

Air Force personnel, African American
  USE United States. Air Force—African Americans

Air pilots, African American
  USE African American air pilots

Airlines—Minority employment
  BT   Minorities—Employment

Alabama Agricultural and Mechanical University (Normal, Ala.)
  BT   Historically Black Colleges and Universities—
         Alabama
         Public universities and colleges
         State universities and colleges

Alabama State University (Montgomery, Ala.)
  BT   Historically Black Colleges and Universities—
         Alabama
         Public universities and colleges

Albany State College (Albany, Ga.)
  BT   Historically Black Colleges and Universities—
         Georgia
         Public universities and colleges

Alcorn State University (Lorman, Miss.)
  BT   Historically Black Colleges and Universities
         Public universities and colleges
         State universities and colleges

Aldermen
  USE City Council members

Allen University (Columbia, S.C.)
  BT   Historically Black Colleges and Universities—
         South Carolina
         Private universities and colleges

Alonzo Franklin Herndon Home (Atlanta, Ga.)
  UF   Herndon Home
  BT   Dwellings—Georgia

Alpha Kappa Alpha Sorority
  BT   Greek letter societies

Alpha Phi Alpha Fraternity
  BT   Greek letter societies

Alumnae and alumni
  USE *subdivision* Alumni and alumnae *under types
         of educational institutions and under
         names of individual educational institu-
         tions, e.g.* Public universities and colleges—
         Alumni and alumnae; Talladega College
         (Talladega, Ala.)—Alumni and alumnae

American Black Achievement Awards
  BT   Awards

American black dialect
  USE Black English

American drama—African American authors
UF   African American drama (English)
       American drama—Negro authors
          [Former Heading]
       Black drama (American)
       Negro drama *[Former Heading]*
NT   African American theater

American drama—Negro authors
    USE American drama—African American authors

American fiction—African American authors
UF   African American fiction (English)
       American fiction—Negro authors
          [Former Heading]
       Black fiction (American)
       Negro fiction *[Former Heading]*
NT   African American novelists

American fiction—Negro authors
    USE American fiction—African American authors

American hymns
    USE Hymns, English—United States

American Library Association—Black Caucus
UF   Black Caucus of the American Library Association
RT   African American librarians

American literature—African American authors
[PS153.N5 (History)] [PS508.N3 (Collections)]
UF   African American literature (English)
       American literature—Negro authors
          [Former Heading]
       Black literature (American)
       Negro literature *[Former Heading]*
BT   American literature—Minority authors
RT   African American authors
SA   *subdivision* African American authors *under*
       individual literary genres, e.g. American
       fiction—African American authors
NT   African American children's writings
       Harlem Renaissance

American literature—Minority authors
UF   Ethnic literature (American)
       Minority literature (American)
NT   American literature—African American authors

American literature—Negro authors
    USE American literature—African American
          authors

American Muslim Mission
    USE Black Muslims

American poetry—African American authors
[PS591.N4]
UF   African American poetry (English)
       American poetry—Negro authors
          [Former Heading]
       Black poetry (American)
       Negro poetry *[Former Heading]*
BT   American poetry—Minority authors
NT   Toasts (African American folk poetry)

American poetry—Minority authors
UF   Ethnic poetry (American)
       Minority literature (American)
NT   American poetry—African American authors

American poetry—Negro authors
    USE American poetry—African American authors

American prose literature—African American
authors *(May Subd Geog)*
UF   African American prose literature (English)
       American prose literature—Negro authors
          [Former Heading]
       Black prose literature (American)

American prose literature—Negro authors
    USE American prose literature—African American
          authors

American slaves' writings
    USE Slaves' writings, American

Amistad Research Center (New Orleans, La.)
BT   Archives—African American

Ancestry
    USE Genealogy

Ancient Egyptian Arabic Order Nobles Mystic
Shrine, Inc. *(May Subd Geog)*
UF   Shriners
BT   Secret societies

Anniversaries
UF   Celebrations, anniversaries, etc.
       Commemorations
RT   Holidays
SA   *subdivision* Anniversaries, etc. *under names*
       of countries, cities, etc., names of individ-
       ual persons and corporate bodies, and un-
       der historic and social movements,
       historic events, classes of persons and eth-
       nic groups; and subdivision Centennial
       celebrations, etc. *under names of cities,*
       countries, etc., and individual corporate
       bodies, and under historic events.
NT   Black Family Celebration
       Emancipation Day

Anthropologists, African American
    USE African American anthropologists

Anti-apartheid movements *(May Subd Geog)*
UF   Movements against apartheid
BT   Civil rights movements
RT   Apartheid

Anti-discrimination laws
    USE Discrimination—Law and legislation

Antipathies
    USE Prejudices

Antisemitism *(May Subd Geog) [DS145]*
BT   Prejudices
       Race relations
       Racism

Antislavery
USE Slavery

Antislavery movements
USE Slavery—Antislavery movements

Apartheid *(May Subd Geog)*
Here are entered works on the political, economic, and social policies of the government of South Africa designed to keep racial groups in South Africa and Namibia separated.
RT Anti-apartheid movements

Apollo Theater (New York, N.Y.)
USE Apollo Theatre (New York, N.Y.)

Apollo Theatre (New York, N.Y.)
UF Apollo Theater (New York, N.Y.)
[Former Heading]
Bryant Theatre (New York, N.Y.)
BT Theaters—New York (State)

Architects, African American
USE African American architects

Architecture, African American
USE African American architecture

Archives—African American *(May Subd Geog)*
[CD931-CD4279]
SA *subdivision* Archival resources *under topical headings and under names of countries, cities, etc., e.g.* Slavery—Archival resources; *subdivision* Archives *under types of corporate bodies, classes of persons, and ethnic groups, and under names of individual persons, families, and corporate bodies for collections of documents of historical records, including notes, correspondence, minutes, photographs, legal papers etc., e.g.* Mays, Benjamin Elijah, 1895-1984—Archives; African Methodist Episcopal Church—Archives
NT Amistad Research Center (New Orleans, La.)
Atlanta University Center Special Collections and Archives (Atlanta, Ga.)
Moorland-Spingarn Research Center (Washington, D.C.)
Schomberg Center for Research in Black Culture (New York, N.Y.)

Archives, Family
USE Family archives

Arkansas Baptist College (Little Rock, Ark.)
BT Historically Black Colleges and Universities
Private universities and colleges

Arkansas at Pine Bluff, University of (Pine Bluff, Ark.)
UF University of Arkansas at Pine Bluff (Pine Bluff, Ark.)
BT Historically Black Colleges and Universities
Public universities and colleges
State universities and colleges

Armed Forces—Minorities
UF Minorities in Armed Forces

BT Minorities
SA *subdivision* Minorities *under military services, e.g.* United States. Navy—Minorities

Art, African American
USE African American art

Art, Black *(May Subd Geog)*
UF Black art
Negro art *[Former Heading]*

Art, Ethnic
USE Ethnic art

Art and nationalism
USE Nationalism and art

Art and race
UF Race and art
BT Ethnopsychology

Art centers *(May Subd Geog)*
Here are entered works on community art centers in general. Works on an individual art center are entered under its name.
UF Community art centers
NT Centers for the performing arts

Art festivals *(May Subd Geog)*
UF Arts festivals
BT Festivals

Art in African American universities and colleges *(May Subd Geog)*
UF Art in Negro universities and colleges *[Former Heading]*
BT Historically Black Colleges and Universities

Art in Negro universities and colleges
USE Art in African American universities and colleges

Artisans, African American
USE African American artisans

Artists, African American
USE African American artists

Artists, Black *(May Subd Geog)*
UF Black artists
Negro artist *[Former Heading]*

Arts, African American
USE African American arts

Arts, Black
UF Black arts
Negro arts *[Former Heading]*

Arts festivals
USE Art festivals

Assimilation (Sociology)
UF Cultural assimilation
BT Socialization
RT Minorities
NT Discrimination
Ethnic relations
Multicultural education
Marginality, Social

Associations, institutions, etc. *(May Subd Geog)*
  UF   Institutions, associations, etc.
        Networks (Associations, institutions, etc.)
        Organizations
        Voluntary associations
        Voluntary organizations
  RT   Societies
        Voluntarism
  SA   *subdivision* Societies, etc. *under names of individual persons, families, and corporate bodies, and under classes of persons, ethnic groups, and topical headings; and names of individual associations, institutions, etc., e.g.* Southern Christian Leadership Conference; *and subdivisions under* National Association for the Advancement of Colored People.
  NT   Civil rights organizations
        Clubs
        Religious institutions
        Trade and professional associations
        Women—Societies and clubs

Associations, institutions, etc.—Membership, African American
  UF   African American membership in associations, institutions, etc.
        Associations, institutions, etc.—Membership, Negro *[Former Heading]*
  BT   African Americans

Associations, institutions, etc.—Membership, Negro
    USE Associations, institutions, etc.—Membership, African American

Astronauts, African American
    USE African American astronauts

Athletes, African American
    USE African American athletes

Athletes, Black
  UF   Black athletes
        Negro athletes *[Former Heading]*

Atlanta University
    USE Clark Atlanta University (Atlanta, Ga.)

Atlanta University Center Special Collections and Archives (Atlanta, Ga.)
  BT   Archives—African American

Attorneys, County
    USE County attorneys

Authors, African American
    USE African American authors

Authors, Black *(May Subd Geog)*
  UF   Black authors
        Negro authors *[Former Heading]*

Automobile industry workers, African American
    USE African American automobile industry workers

Awards *(May Subd Geog)*
  UF   Prizes (Rewards)
        Rewards (Prizes, etc.) *[Former Heading]*
  SA   *subdivision* Awards *under names of individual persons and corporate bodies, and under topical headings, e.g.* Lincoln University (Lincoln University, Pa.)—Awards
  NT   American Black Achievement Awards

B

Back to Africa movement
  BT   African Americans—Colonization—Africa

Bankers, African American
    USE African American bankers

Baptists, African American
    USE African American Baptists

Baptists, Black *(May Subd Geog)*
  UF   Baptists, Negro *[Former Heading]*
        Black Baptists

Baptists, Negro
    USE African American Baptists
         Baptists, Black

Barber-Scotia College (Concord, N.C.)
  BT   Historically Black Colleges and Universities—North Carolina
        Private universities and colleges
        United Negro College Fund Institutions

Base-ball
    USE Baseball

Baseball *(May Subd Geog) [GV862-GV880.6]*
  UF   Base-ball *[Former Heading]*
  NT   Negro leagues

Baseball—Biography *[GV865]*

Baseball players, African American
    USE African American baseball players

Basic rights
    USE Civil rights

Basketball—Biography

Basketball players, African American
    USE African American basketball players

Be-bop (Music)
    USE Bop (Music)

Beauty contestants *(May Subd Geog)*
  UF   Beauty queens
        Contestants, Beauty

Beauty contests *(May Subd Geog)*
  UF   Beauty pageants
        Pageants, Beauty

Beauty operators, African American
    USE African American beauty operators

Beauty pageants
    USE Beauty contests

Beauty queens
    USE Beauty contestants
Bebop (Music)
    USE Bop (Music)
Behavior, Child
    USE Child psychology
Behavior, Consumer
    USE Consumer behavior
Benedict College (Columbia, S.C.)
    BT   Historically Black Colleges and Universities—
         South Carolina
         Private universities and colleges
         United Negro College Fund Institutions
Benefit societies
    USE Friendly societies
Bennett College (Greensboro, N.C.)
    BT   Historically Black Colleges and Universities—
         North Carolina
         Private universities and colleges
         United Negro College Fund Institutions
         Women's colleges
Bethune-Cookman College (Daytona Beach, Fla.)
    BT   Historically Black Colleges and Universities—
         Florida
         Private universities and colleges
         United Negro College Fund Institutions
Bi-racial children
    USE Children of interracial marriage
Bi-racial dating
    USE Interracial dating
Bias, Job
    USE Discrimination in employment
Bias (Psychology)
    USE Prejudices
Bias crimes
    USE Hate crimes
Bias in tests
    USE Test bias
Bias in textbooks
    USE Textbook bias
Bias-related crimes
    USE Hate crimes
Bible—Black interpretations
    Here are entered works on Biblical interpretations from a black and/or African American perspective, emphasizing such motifs as skin color, slavery, freedom, and geography.
    RT   Black theology
Bible—Blacks
    USE Blacks in the Bible
Biculturalism *(May Subd Geog)*
    BT   Pluralism (Social sciences)
Big band music *(May Subd Geog)* *[M1366 (Music)]*
    [ML3518 (History and Criticism)]

    UF   Big band music—United States
         Dance band music
         Jazz band music
    BT   Jazz
    NT   Jazz vocals
Big band music—United States
    USE Big band music
Big bands *(May Subd Geog)*
    [ML3518 (History and Criticism)]
    UF   Dance bands
         Jazz bands
    BT   Dance orchestras
         Jazz
Bigotry
    USE Toleration
Bilalians
    USE Black Muslims
Bills of sale
    NT   Slave bills of sale
Biography *[CT]*
    UF   History—Biography
         Life histories
         Memoirs
    RT   Genealogy
    SA   *subdivision* Biography *under names of countries, cities, etc. names of individual literary authors and corporate bodies, uniform titles of sacred works, and under classes of persons e.g.* African American physicians—Georgia—Biography *and historic events e.g.* March on Washington for Jobs and Freedom, Washington, D.C., 1963—Biography
Biography—Anniversaries, etc.
    SA   *subdivision* Anniversaries, etc. *under names of individual persons and under classes of persons and ethnic groups. e.g.* King, Martin Luther, Jr., 1929-1968—Anniversaries
Biracial children
    USE Children of interracial marriage
Biracial dating
    USE Interracial dating
Biracial minorities
    USE Racially mixed people
Birth records
    USE Registers of births, etc.
Birthday of Martin Luther King, Jr.
    USE Martin Luther King, Jr., Day
Births, Registers
    USE Registers of births, etc.
Bishop (S.D.) State Junior College (Mobile, Ala.)
    BT   Historically Black Colleges and Universities—
         Alabama
         Junior Colleges
         Public universities and colleges

Black—Folklore
    UF   Black (in religion, folk-lore, etc.)
              [Former Heading]
Black—Religious aspects
    UF   Black (in religion, folk-lore, etc.)
              [Former Heading]
Black (in religion, folk-lore, etc.)
    USE   Black—Folklore
              Black—Religious aspects
Black actors
    USE   Actors, Black
Black aesthetics
    USE   Aesthetics, Black
Black American...
    USE   *subject headings beginning with the words*
              African American
Black Americana
    USE   African Americans—Collectibles
Black Americans
    USE   African Americans
Black art
    USE   Art, Black
Black artists
    USE   Artists, Black
Black arts
    USE   Arts, Black
Black athletes
    USE   Athletes, Black
Black authors
    USE   Authors, Black
Black Baptists
    USE   Baptists, Black
Black business enterprises *(May Subd Geog)*
    BT   Minority business enterprises
Black Caucus of the American Library Association
    USE   American Library Association—Black Caucus
Black children
    USE   Children, Black
Black Christians
    USE   Christians, Black
Black college graduates
    USE   College graduates, Black
Black college students
    USE   College students, Black
Black college teachers
    USE   College teachers, Black
Black colleges
    USE   Historically Black Colleges and Universities
Black communication
    USE   Blacks—Communication

Black composers
    USE   Composers, Black
Black Congressional Caucus
    USE   United States. Congress—Black Caucus
Black diaspora
    USE   African diaspora
Black dolls *(May Subd Geog) [NK4894.3B53]*
    UF   Dolls, Black
Black drama
    USE   Drama—Black authors
Black drama (American)
    USE   American drama—African American authors
Black English *(May Subd Geog)*
        [PE3102.N4-PE3102.N48]
    UF   African American dialect
              African American English
              American black dialect
              Negro-English dialects *[Former Heading]*
    BT   African Americans—Languages
    RT   African American children—Language
              English language—Study and teaching—
                  African American students
    NT   Sea Islands Creole dialect
Black English in mass media *(May Subd Geog)*
Black executives
    USE   Executives, Black
Black explorers
    USE   Explorers, Black
Black families
    USE   Families, Black
Black Family Celebration
    BT   Anniversaries
              Family festivals
Black fiction
    USE   Fiction—Black authors
Black fiction (American)
    USE   American fiction—African American authors
Black Film Collection, Tyler, Texas
    USE   Tyler, Texas, Black Film Collection
Black folk art
    USE   Folk art, Black
Black hairdressing
    USE   Hairdressing of Blacks
Black history
    USE   African Americans—History
              Blacks—History
Black History Month
    BT   Special months
Black humor (African American)
    USE   African American wit and humor

Black humor (Black authors)
 USE Wit and humor—Black authors
Black-Indian relations
 USE Blacks—Relations with Indians
Black-Jewish relations
 USE Blacks—Relations with Jews
Black Jews (United States)
 USE African American Jews
Black libraries
 USE Libraries and Blacks
Black literature
 USE Literature—Black authors
Black literature (American)
 USE American literature—African American
   authors
Black literature (English)
 USE English literature—Black authors

Black militant organizations *(May Subd Geog)*
 UF Militant organizations, Black
 BT Black power

Black militant organizations—United States
 UF African American militant organizations
 BT African Americans—Societies, etc.

Black musicians
 USE Musicians, Black

Black Muslims *(May Subd Geog)*
 [BP221-BP223 (Religion)] [E185.61 (Race question)]
 Here are entered works on the movement known as the Nation of
 Islam or Black Muslims. Works on persons of the Black race who are
 Muslims are entered under Muslims, Black.
 UF American Muslim Mission
   Bilalians
   Black Muslims—United States
   Nation of Islam
   World Community of al-Islam in the West
 BT African Americans—Religion
   Black nationalism
   Black nationalism—United States
   Muslims—United States
   Religious institutions

Black Muslims—Controversial literature
 UF Black Muslims—Doctrinal and controversial
   works

Black Muslims—Dietary laws
 UF Dietary laws, Black Muslims
 BT Food—Religious aspects—Black Muslims
   Nutrition—Religious aspects—Black Muslims

Black Muslims—Doctrinal and controversial works
 USE Black Muslims—Controversial literature
   Black Muslims—Doctrines

Black Muslims—Doctrines
 UF Black Muslims—Doctrinal and controversial
   works *[Former Heading]*

Black Muslims—United States
 USE Black Muslims

Black nationalism *(May Subd Geog)*
 UF Black separatism
   Nationalism—Blacks
   Nationalism, Black
   Separatism, Black
 BT Blacks—Politics and government
   Blacks—Race identity
 RT Black power
 NT Black Muslims
   Ras Tafari movement

Black nationalism—United States
 UF African American nationalism
 BT African Americans—Race identity
 NT Black Muslims

Black newspapers *(May Subd Geog)*
 UF Newspapers, Black

Black painters
 USE Painters, Black

Black painting
 USE Painting, Black

Black Panthers Trial, New York, 1970-1971
 USE Black Panthers Trial, New York, N.Y., 1970-1971

Black Panthers Trial, New York, N.Y., 1970-1971
 UF Black Panthers Trial, New York, 1970-1971
   [Former Heading]
   Bomb Conspiracy Trial, New York, N.Y.,
   1970-1971
   New York 21 Trial, New York, N.Y., 1970-1971
   New York City Bomb Conspiracy Trial, New
   York, N.Y., 1970-1971
   Panther 21 Trial, New York, N.Y., 1970-1971
 BT Trials (Conspiracy)—New York (State)

Black pioneers
 USE Pioneers, Black

Black poetry
 USE Poetry—Black authors

Black poetry (American)
 USE American poetry—African American authors

Black poetry (English)
 USE English poetry—Black authors

Black poets
 USE Poets, Black

Black police
 USE Police, Black

Black power *(May Subd Geog)*
 UF Power, Black
 RT Black nationalism
 NT Black militant organizations

Black power—United States
 BT African Americans—Civil rights
   African Americans—Economic conditions

Black prints
    USE Prints, Black
Black prose literature (American)
    USE American prose literature—African American
         authors
Black proverbs
    USE Proverbs, Black
Black race
    Here are entered theoretical works discussing the Black race from
    an anthropological point of view. Works on blacks as an element in
    the populations are entered under Blacks.
    UF   Negro race [Former Heading]
    BT   Race
Black race—Color
    UF   Blacks—Color
    BT   Color of man
Black Seminole Indians
    USE Black Seminoles
Black Seminoles
    UF   African American Seminoles
         Black Seminole Indians
         Seminole Indians, Black
    BT   Ethnology—United States
         Mulattoes—United States
         Seminole Indians—Mixed descent
Black separatism
    USE Black nationalism
Black short stories (American)
    USE Short stories, American—African American
         authors
Black soldiers
    USE Soldiers, Black
Black Spiritual churches
    USE African American Spiritual churches
Black Spiritual movement
    USE African American Spiritual churches
Black students
    USE Students, Black
Black studies
    USE Blacks—Study and teaching
Black teachers
    USE Teachers, Black
Black theater
    BT   Theater
    NT   Actors, Black
Black theology [BT82.7]
    UF   African American theology
         Theology, African American
         Theology, Black
    BT   African Americans—Religion
         Blacks—Religion
    RT   Bible—Black interpretations
    NT   African American theologians

Black trade-unions
    USE Trade-unions, Black
Black universities and colleges
    USE Historically Black Colleges and Universities
Black university students
    USE College students, Black
Black university teachers
    USE College teachers, Black
Black women
    USE Women, Black
Black women artists
    USE Women artists, Black
Black women authors
    USE Women authors, Black
Black women composers
    USE Women composers, Black
Black youth
    USE Youth, Black
Blacklisting, Labor (May Subd Geog)
    BT   Discrimination in employment
Blacks (May Subd Geog)
    Here are entered works on blacks as an element in the population.
    Theoretical works discussing the Black race from an anthropological
    point of view are entered under Black race.
    Works on black people in countries whose racial composition is
    predominately black are assigned headings appropriate for the coun-
    try as a whole without the use of the heading Blacks. The heading
    Blacks is assigned to works on such countries only if the work
    discusses blacks apart from other groups in the country.
    UF   Negroes [Former Heading]
    BT   Ethnology
    SA   subdivision Blacks under individual wars, e.g.
         World War, 1939-1945—Blacks; headings
         beginning with the word Black; and subdi-
         visions under African Americans
    NT   Libraries and Blacks
         Mulattoes
         Soldiers, Black
Blacks—Anthropometry
Blacks—Attitudes
Blacks—Children
    USE Children, Black
Blacks—Civil rights (May Subd Geog)
    NT   Blacks—Politics and government
Blacks—Color
    USE Black race—Color
Blacks—Communication [P94.5B55]
    UF   Black communication
Blacks—Cultural assimilation (May Subd Geog)
Blacks—Dancing
    UF   Dancing—Blacks
Blacks—Education (May Subd Geog)
    [LC2699-LC2913]

NT   Students, Black
        Historically Black Colleges and Universities

Blacks—Employment *(May Subd Geog)*

Blacks—Employment—Law and legislation *(May Subd Geog)*
    BT   Labor laws and legislation

Blacks—Families
    USE Families, Black

Blacks—Funeral customs and rites
    UF   Funeral rites and ceremonies *[Former Heading]*

Blacks—Hairdressing
    USE Hairdressing of Blacks

Blacks—History
    UF   Black history

Blacks—Jewelry
    UF   Jewelry, Black *[Former Heading]*

Blacks—Missions *(May Subd Geog)*
    UF   Missions to Blacks *[Former Heading]*
        Missions to Negroes *[Former Heading]*

Blacks—Politics and government
    BT   Blacks—Civil Rights
    NT   Black nationalism

Blacks—Puerto Rico
    USE African Americans—Puerto Rico

Blacks—Quotations
    UF   Negro quotations *[Former Heading]*
        Quotations, Black *[Former Heading]*

Blacks—Race identity
    UF   Negritude
        Racial identity of Blacks
    BT   Ethnicity
        Race awareness
    NT   Black nationalism

Blacks—Relations with Indians
    UF   Black-Indian relations
        Indian-Black relations
        Indians—Relations with Blacks

Blacks—Relations with Jews
    UF   Black-Jewish relations
        Jewish-Black relations
        Jews—Relations with Blacks
        Negro-Jewish relations *[Former Heading]*

Blacks—Religion
    NT   Black theology
        Muslims, Black
        Ras Tafari movement

Blacks—Relocation *(May Subd Geog)*
    UF   Blacks—Resettlement
        Relocation of Blacks
        Removal of Blacks
        Resettlement of Blacks
    BT   Race relations
        Segregation

Blacks—Relocation—Religious aspects

Blacks—Resettlement
    USE Blacks—Relocation

Blacks—Segregation
    BT   Blacks—Social conditions
        Segregation

Blacks—Social conditions
    NT   Blacks—Segregation

Blacks—Songs and music
    UF   Negro music *[Former Heading]*
        Negro songs *[Former Heading]*
        Topical songs (Negro) *[Former Heading]*
        Topical songs (Negroes) *[Former Heading]*

Blacks—Study and teaching *(May Subd Geog)*
    UF   Black studies

Blacks—Africa—Relations with African Americans
    USE African Americans—Relations with Africans

Blacks—United States
    Here are entered works on blacks who temporarily reside in the United States, such as aliens, students from abroad, etc. Works on citizens of the United States of black African descent are entered under African Americans.
    NT   African Americans

Blacks—West Indies
    NT   Maroons

Blacks—West Indies—Relations with African Americans
    USE African Americans—Relations with West Indians

Blacks and libraries
    USE Libraries and Blacks

Blacks as consumers *(May Subd Geog)*
    UF   Negroes as consumers *[Former Heading]*

Blacks in art
    UF   Negroes in art *[Former Heading]*

Blacks in literature
    UF   Negroes in literature *[Former Heading]*

Blacks in mass media *(May Subd Geog) [P94.5B55]*

Blacks in medicine *(May Subd Geog) [R695]*
    UF   Negroes in medicine *[Former Heading]*

Blacks in motion pictures *[PN1995.9.N4]*
    Here are entered works on the portrayal of Blacks in motion pictures. Works on all aspects of Black involvement in motion pictures are entered under Blacks in the motion picture industry. Works on specific aspects of Black involvement are entered under the particular subject, e.g. Actors, Black.
    UF   Negroes in moving-pictures *[Former Heading]*

Blacks in television broadcasting *(May Subd Geog)*
    UF   Blacks in the television industry
            [Former Heading]

Blacks in the Bible
    UF   Bible—Blacks
        Negro race in the Bible *[Former Heading]*

Blacks in the motion picture industry *(May Subd Geog) [PN 1995.9.N4]*
　Here are entered works on all aspects of Black involvement in motion pictures. Works on the portrayal of Blacks in motion pictures are entered under Blacks in motion pictures. Works on specific aspects of Black involvement are entered under the particular subject, e.g. Actors, Black.
　　UF　Negroes in the moving-picture industry
　　　　[Former Heading]
　　BT　Motion picture industry

Blacks in the performing arts *(May Subd Geog)*
　　UF　Negroes in the performing arts
　　　　[Former Heading]
　　NT　Musicians, Black

Blacks in the press *(May Subd Geog)*
　　BT　Press

Blacks in the television industry
　　USE　Blacks in television broadcasting

Bluefield State College (Bluefield, W.Va.)
　　BT　Historically Black Colleges and Universities
　　　　Public universities and colleges

Blues (Music) *(May Subd Geog)*
[ML3521 (History and criticism)]
　　UF　Blues (Music)—United States
　　　　Blues (Songs, etc.) *[Former Heading]*
　　BT　African Americans—Music
　　　　Folk music—United States
　　　　Popular music
　　SA　*subdivisions* Methods (Blues) *and* Studies and
　　　　　exercises (Blues) *under names of instruments*
　　NT　Boogie woogie (Music)
　　　　Guitar—Methods (Blues)
　　　　Guitar music (Blues)
　　　　Piano music (Blues)

Blues (Music)—to 1931

Blues (Music)—1931-1940

Blues (Music)—1941-1950

Blues (Music)—1951-1960

Blues (Music)—1961-1970

Blues (Music)—1971-1980

Blues (Music)—1981-1990

Blues (Music)—1991-2000

Blues (Music)—Religious aspects

Blues (Music)—United States
　　USE　Blues (Music)

Blues (Songs, etc.)
　　USE　Blues (Music)

Blues musicians *(May Subd Geog)*
　　BT　Musicians

Bomb Conspiracy Trial, New York, N.Y., 1970-1971
　　USE　Black Panthers Trial, New York, N.Y., 1970-1971

Boogie woogie (Music) *(May Subd Geog)*
　　UF　Boogie woogie (Music)—United States

　　BT　Blues (Music)
　　　　Jazz
　　NT　Piano music (Boogie woogie)

Boogie woogie (Music)—United States
　　USE　Boogie woogie (Music)

Book awards
　　USE　Literary prizes

Book prizes
　　USE　Literary prizes

Bop (Music) *(May Subd Geog)*
　　UF　Be-bop (Music)
　　　　Bebop (Music)
　　　　Bop (Music)—United States
　　　　Rebop (Music)
　　BT　Jazz

Bop (Music)—United States
　　USE　Bop (Music)

Bossa nova (Music) *(May Subd Geog)*
　　BT　Jazz—Brazil

Boston (Mass.)—Antislavery movement, 1830-1863
(Not Subd Geog)

**Boston African American National Historic Site
(Boston, Mass.)** *(Not Subd Geog)*
　　BT　Historic Sites—Massachusetts
　　　　National parks and reserves—Massachusetts

Bowie State College (Bowie, Md.)
　　BT　Historically Black Colleges and Universities—
　　　　Maryland
　　　　Public universities and colleges

Boxers, African American
　　USE　African American boxers

Boycott
　　USE　Boycotts

Boycotts *(May Subd Geog) [HD 5461 (Labor disputes)]*
　　UF　Boycott *[Former Heading]*
　　　　Consumer boycotts
　　　　Secondary boycotts
　　BT　Consumer behavior
　　　　Passive resistance

Brethren, African American (Church of the Brethren)
　　USE　African American Brethren (Church of the
　　　　Brethren)

Brotherhood Week *(May Subd Geog)*
　　BT　Special weeks

Brown Farm State Historic Site (North Elba, N.Y.)
　　USE　John Brown Farm State Historic Site
　　　　(North Elba, N.Y.)

**Brown v. Board of Education National Historic Site
(Topeka, Kan.)**
　　BT　Historic sites—Kansas
　　　　National parks and reserves—Kansas

Bryant Theatre (New York, N.Y.)
　　USE　Apollo Theatre (New York, N.Y.)

Burial clubs
  USE Insurance, Burial
Burial insurance
  USE Insurance, Burial
Burial statistics
  USE Registers of births, etc.
Burying-grounds
  USE Cemeteries
Business enterprises, African American
  USE African American business enterprises
Business enterprises, Minority
  USE Minority business enterprises
Businessmen, African American
  USE African Americans in business
Busing for school integration (*May Subd Geog*)
  [LC214.5-LC214.53]
  UF Busing of school children
     School busing for integration
     Student busing for school integration
  BT School integration
     Segregation in education
Busing for school integration—Law and legislation
(May Subd Geog)
Busing of school children
  USE Busing for school integration
Buyer behavior
  USE Consumer behavior

C

C.C.M.
  USE Contemporary Christian music
C.M.E. Church
  USE Christian Methodist Episcopal Church
CORE
  USE Congress of Racial Equality
Cabinetmakers, African American
  USE African American cabinetmakers
Caldecott Awards
  USE Caldecott Medal
Caldecott Medal
  UF Caldecott Awards
     Caldecott Medal books
  BT Illustration of books—Awards—United States
Caldecott Medal books
  USE Caldecott Medal
Camp-meeting hymns
  USE Revivals—Hymns
Capital punishment (*May Subd Geog*)
  [HV8694-HV8699]
  UF Abolition of capital punishment
     Death penalty

Carver State Technical College (Mobile, Ala.)
  BT Historically Black Colleges and Universities—Alabama
     Junior Colleges
     Public universities and colleges
Catholics, African American
  USE African American Catholics
Catholics, Negro
  USE African American Catholics
Caucus *[JF2085]*
  SA *subdivision* Caucuses *under names of individual legislative bodies, e.g.* United States. Congress—Black Caucus
Celebrations, anniversaries, etc.
  USE Anniversaries
Cemeteries (*May Subd Geog*)
  Here are entered general works on cemeteries and burying grounds.
  UF Burying-grounds
     Churchyards
     Graves
     Graveyards
Centers for the performing arts (*May Subd Geog*)
  [PN1585-PN1589]
  UF Performing art centers
  BT Art Centers
  SA *names of individual centers*
Central cities
  USE Inner cities
Central State University (Wilberforce, Ohio)
  BT Historically Black Colleges and Universities—Ohio
     Public universities and colleges
Charles H. Mason Theological Seminary (Church of God in Christ)
  BT Interdenominational Theological Center (Atlanta, Ga.)
Charles R. Drew University of Medicine and Science (Los Angeles, Calif.)
  UF Drew, Charles R., University of Medicine and Science
  BT Historically Black Colleges and Universities—California
     Medical colleges
     Private universities and colleges
Charleston (S.C.)—History—Slave Insurrection, 1822
(Not Subd Geog)
  UF Charleston (S.C.)—Slave insurrection, 1822
     [Former Heading]
Charleston (S.C.)—Slave insurrection, 1822
  USE Charleston (S.C.)—History—Slave Insurrection, 1822
Chemists, African American
  USE African American chemists

Cheyney State University (Cheyney, Pa.)
>BT Historically Black Colleges and Universities—
>>Pennsylvania
>>Public universities and colleges

Child behavior
>USE Child psychology

Child placing
>USE Adoption

Child psychology *(May Subd Geog)* *[BF721-BF723]*
>Here are entered works on the psychological growth and characteristics of children.
>UF Behavior, Child
>>Child behavior
>>Child study *[Former Heading]*
>>Children—Psychology
>>Psychology, Child
>NT Prejudices in children
>>Race awareness in children

Child psychology—Cross-cultural studies

Child study
>USE Child psychology

Children—Education
>USE Education

Children—Drug effects
>USE Pediatric pharmacology

Children—Psychology
>USE Child psychology

Children, African American
>USE African American children

Children, Black *(May Subd Geog)*
>UF Black children
>>Blacks—children
>>Negro children *[Former Heading]*

Children of interracial marriage *(May Subd Geog)*
[HQ777.9]
>UF Bi-racial children
>>Biracial children
>>Interracial marriage, Children of
>>Mixed race children
>BT Interracial marriage
>>Racially mixed people

Children of minorities *(May Subd Geog)*
>UF Minority children
>>Minority group children
>BT Minorities

Children of single parents
>BT Single parents

Children's games, African American
>USE African American children's games

Children's writing, African American
>USE African American children's writings

Christian colleges
>USE Church colleges

Christian contemporary music
>USE Contemporary Christian music

Christian Methodist Episcopal Church *(May Subd Geog)*
>UF C.M.E. Church
>BT Religious institutions
>SA *names of individual churches, e.g.* West Side Community C.M.E. Church (Atlanta, Ga.)

Christian music, Contemporary
>USE Contemporary Christian music

Christian popular music
>USE Contemporary Christian music

Christian schools
>USE Church schools

Christians, Black *(May Subd Geog)*
>UF Black Christians

Christians (Disciples of Christ), African American
>USE African American Christians (Disciples of Christ)

Christians (General Convention of the Christian Church), African American
>USE African American Christians (General Convention of the Christian church)

Chronicle history (Drama)
>USE Historical drama

Chronicle play
>USE Historical drama

Church and college *(May Subd Geog)* *[LC3832]*
>Here are entered works on the influence of religious denominations and sects on colleges. Works on colleges supported and/or administered by a religious denomination or sect are entered under Church colleges.
>UF College and church
>BT Historically Black Colleges and Universities

Church and minorities *(May Subd Geog)*
[BV639.M56]
>UF Minorities and the church
>BT Minorities

Church and race problems
>USE Race relations—Religious aspects—Christianity

Church and race relations
>USE Race relations—Religious aspects—Christianity

Church and slavery
>USE Slavery and the church

Church colleges *(May Subd Geog)* *[LC427-LC629]*
>Here are entered works on colleges supported and/or administered by a religious denomination or sect, e.g. Xavier University (New Orleans, La.). Works on the influence of religious denominations and sects on colleges are entered under Church and college.
>UF Christian colleges
>>Church-related colleges
>>Denominational colleges
>BT Historically Black Colleges and Universities

Church of God in Christ, Inc. *(May Subd Geog)*
>BT Religious institutions
>SA *names of individual churches, e.g.* Ingram Temple Church of God in Christ (Atlanta, Ga.)

Church-related colleges
    USE Church colleges

Church schools *(May Subd Geog) [LC427-LC629]*
    Here are entered works on elementary and secondary schools operated under church auspices, control, or support. Works on the schools of a particular denomination are entered under the name of the denomination with subdivision Education, e.g. Presbyterian Church in the U.S.A.—Education.
    UF   Christian schools
            Denominational schools
            Diocesan schools
            Parish schools
            Parochial schools
            Schools, Denominational
            Schools, Parochial
    BT   Private schools

Church societies
    BT   Societies

Church work with African American families *(May Subd Geog)*
    BT   African American families

Church work with African American youth *(May Subd Geog)*
    BT   African American youth

Church work with minorities *(May Subd Geog)*
    BT   Minorities

Churches, African American
    USE African American churches

Churchyards
    USE Cemeteries

Cimarrones
    USE Maroons

Cities and state
    USE Urban policy

Cities and towns *(May Subd Geog) [HT101-HT395] [HV6177 (Influence on crime)]*
    UF   Urban areas
            Urbanisms
    RT   Sociology, Urban
    NT   Education, Urban
            Inner cities
            Tenement-houses
            Urban dialects
            Urbanization

Cities and towns—Growth *[HB2161-HB2370 (Statistics)] [HT371 (City problem)]*
    UF   Cities and towns, Movement to
            Urban development
    BT   Migration, Internal

Cities and towns, Movement to
    USE Cities and towns—Growth
           Rural-urban migration
           Urbanization

Citizen participation
    USE Political participation

Citizenship *(May Subd Geog) [JF800-JF823] [JK1751-JK1788 (United States)] [LC1091 (Education for)]*
    UF   Nationality (Citizenship)
    RT   Political rights

City council members *(May Subd Geog)*
    UF   Aldermen
            City councilors
            City councilmen *[Former Heading]*
            Council members, City
            Councilors, City
            Councilmen, City
    NT   Women city council members

City councilors
    USE City council members

City councilmen
    USE City council members

City councilwomen
    USE Women city council members

City-country migration
    USE Urban-rural migration

City schools
    USE Urban schools

Civic leaders, African American
    USE African American civic leaders

Civic rights
    USE Political rights

Civil disorders
    USE Riots

Civil liberation movements
    USE Civil rights movements

Civil liberties
    USE Civil rights

Civil rights *(May Subd Geog) [JC571-JC628 (Political science)] [K3236-K3268 (Law)]*
    Here are entered works on citizens' rights as established by law and protected by the United States constitution.
    UF   Basic rights
            Civil liberties
            Constitutional rights
            Fundamental rights
            Rights, Civil
    NT   Discrimination—Law and legislation
            Equality before the law
            Political rights

Civil rights—United States
    NT   African Americans—Civil rights
            State action (Civil rights)

Civil rights and communism
    USE Civil rights and socialism

Civil rights and socialism *(May Subd Geog)*
    UF   Civil rights and communism
            Communism and civil rights

Civil rights demonstrations *(May Subd Geog)*
- UF   Freedom marches (Civil rights)
           Sit-ins (Civil rights)
- BT   Civil rights movements
           Demonstrations

Civil rights demonstrations—Washington (D.C.)
- NT   March on Washington for Jobs and Freedom, Washington, D.C., 1963

Civil rights movements *(May Subd Geog)*
- UF   Civil liberation movements
           Liberation movements (Civil rights)
           Protest movements (Civil rights)
- NT   Anti-apartheid movements
           Civil rights demonstrations

Civil rights organizations *(May Subd Geog)*
- BT   Associations, institutions, etc.
- SA   *names of other civil rights organizations under names of individual civil rights organizations*
- NT   Congress of Racial Equality
           Martin Luther King, Junior, Center for Nonviolent Social Change (Atlanta, Ga.)
           National Association for the Advancement of Colored People
           National Rainbow Coalition
           National Urban Coalition
           National Urban League
           Opportunities Industrial Centers of America
           Southern Christian Leadership Conference
           Student Nonviolent Coordinating Committee
           TransAfrica Forum

Civil rights workers *(May Subd Geog)*
- UF   Race relations reformers
- NT   Women civil rights workers

Civil rights workers—United States
- BT   African Americans—Civil rights
- NT   African American civil rights workers

Civil rights workers, African American
- USE   African American civil rights workers

Civil service—African American employment
- USE   African Americans in the civil service

Civil service—Minority employment
- UF   Minorities in the civil service *[Former Heading]*
- BT   Minorities—Employment

Civil service, Municipal
- USE   Municipal officials and employees

Civilization, Western—African influences
- NT   Afrocentrism

Claflin College (Orangeburg, S.C.)
- BT   Historically Black Colleges and Universities—South Carolina
           Private universities and colleges
           United Negro College Fund Institutions

Clarinet and piano music (Jazz)
- USE   Jazz

Clark Atlanta University (Atlanta, Ga.)
- UF   Atlanta University
           Clark College
- BT   Historically Black Colleges and Universities—Georgia
           Private universities and colleges
           United Negro College Fund Institutions

Clark College
- USE   Clark Atlanta University (Atlanta, Ga.)

Classical music
- USE   Music

Clergy—Education
- USE   Theological seminaries

Clergy, African American
- USE   African American clergy

Clerks, County
- USE   County clerks

Clinton Junior College (Rock Hill, S.C.)
- BT   Historically Black Colleges and Universities—South Carolina
           Junior Colleges
           Private universities and colleges

Closed schools
- USE   School closings

Closing of schools
- USE   School closings

Closings of schools
- USE   School closings

Clubs *(May Subd Geog)* *[HS2501-HS3200 (Social)]*
- BT   Associations, institutions, etc.
- RT   Societies
- SA   *subdivision* Societies and clubs *under ages or age groups; and names of individual clubs, e.g.* The October Club (Atlanta, Ga.)
- NT   Women—Societies and clubs

Clubs, Burial
- USE   Insurance, Burial

Coahoma Junior College (Clarksdale, Miss.)
- BT   Historically Black Colleges and Universities—Mississippi
           Junior Colleges
           Public universities and colleges

Coal miners, African American
- USE   African American coal miners

Coalition of Black Trade Unionists
- BT   Trade-unions
- RT   Trade-unions—African American membership

College administrators, African American
- USE   African American college administrators

College and church
- USE   Church and college

College athletes *(May Subd Geog)*

College athletes—Recruiting *(May Subd Geog)*
   [GV350.5]
   UF   Recruiting of college athletes
College desegregation
   USE   College integration
College fraternities
   USE   Greek letter societies
College graduates, African American
   USE   African American college graduates
College graduates, Black *(May Subd Geog)*
   UF   Black college graduates
          Negro college graduates *[Former Heading]*
College integration *(May Subd Geog)*
   UF   College desegregation
          Desegregation in higher education
          Integration in higher education
   BT   Education, Higher
          School integration
College integration—Law and legislation *(May Subd Geog)*
   BT   Educational law and legislation
College presidents *(May Subd Geog)*
   UF   Presidents, College
          University presidents
   SA   *subdivision* Presidents *under names of individual universities and colleges, e.g.* Lincoln University (Lincoln University, Pa.)—Presidents.
   NT   Community college presidents
          Women college presidents
College sororities
   USE   Greek letter societies
College sports *(May Subd Geog)*
   SA   *subdivision* Sports *under names of colleges, universities, etc,. e.g.* Lincoln University (Lincoln University, Pa.)—Sports
College students, African American
   USE   African American college students
College students, Black *(May Subd Geog)*
   UF   Black college students
          Black university students
   BT   Students, Black
College students, Minority
   USE   Minority college students
College students, Negro
   USE   African American college students
College teachers, African American
   USE   African American college teachers
College teachers, Black *(May Subd Geog)*
   UF   Black college teachers
          Black university teachers
          Negro college teachers *[Former Heading]*
          University teachers, Black
   BT   Teachers, Black

Colleges, African American
   USE   Historically Black Colleges and Universities
Colleges, Black
   USE   Historically Black Colleges and Universities
Colleges for women
   USE   Women's colleges
Colonization by African Americans
   UF   African Americans—Colonization
Color of African Americans
   USE   African Americans—Color
Color of man *[GN197]*
   UF   Pigmentation
          Skin, Color of
          Skin pigmentation
   BT   Physical anthropology
          Skin
   NT   African Americans—Color
          Black race—Color
          Melanism
Colored people (United States)
   USE   African Americans
Commemorations
   USE   Anniversaries
Communism and civil rights
   USE   Civil rights and socialism
Communists, African American
   USE   African American communists
Communists, Negro
   USE   African American communists
Community and African American teachers
   USE   African American teachers and the community
Community and school—United States
   NT   African American teachers and the community
Community art centers
   USE   Art centers
Community college presidents *(May Subd Geog)*
   BT   College presidents
Community colleges *(May Subd Geog) [LB2328]*
   UF   Community junior colleges
          Local junior colleges
          Municipal junior colleges *[Former Heading]*
          Public community colleges
          Public junior colleges
          Public two-year colleges
          Two-year colleges
Community health services *(May Subd Geog)*
   UF   Neighborhood health centers
Community junior colleges
   USE   Community colleges
Composers, African American
   USE   African American composers
Composers, Black *(May Subd Geog)*
   UF   Black composers

Comprehensive high schools *(May Subd Geog)*
   BT   High schools
Compromise of 1850 *[E423]*
   UF   Omnibus bill, 1850
   BT   Slavery—United States
   NT   Fugitive slave law of 1850
Concordia College (Selma, Ala.)
   BT   Historically Black Colleges and Universities—
         Alabama
         Junior Colleges
         Private universities and colleges
Conflict, Ethnic
   USE Ethnic relations
Conflict of cultures
   USE Culture conflict
Congregationalists, African American
   USE African American Congregationalists
Congress of Racial Equality
   UF   CORE
   BT   Civil rights organizations
Constitutional rights
   USE Civil rights
Construction workers, African American
   USE African American construction workers
Consumer behavior *(May Subd Geog)*
   [HF5415.32-HF 5415.33]
   Here are entered works on the decision-making processes, external factors, and individual characteristics of consumers that determine their purchasing behavior.
   UF   Behavior, Consumer
         Buyer behavior
         Decision-making, Consumer
   NT   Boycotts
Consumer boycotts
   USE Boycotts
Consumer credit *(May Subd Geog)*
   [HG3755-HG3756]
   UF   Credit, Consumer
   NT   Discrimination in consumer credit
Contemporary Christian music *(May Subd Geog)*
   [ML3187.5 (History and criticism)]
   UF   CCM
         Christian contemporary music
         Christian music, Contemporary
         Christian popular music
         Evangelical popular music
         Jesus music
         Popular music, Christian
   BT   Gospel music
         Popular music
Contestants, Beauty
   USE Beauty contestants
Cookbooks
   USE Cookery

Cookery
   UF   Cookbooks
Cookery, African American
   USE African American cookery
Cookery, Negro
   USE African American cookery
Cooks, African American
   USE African American cooks
Coppin State College (Baltimore, Md.)
   BT   Historically Black Colleges and Universities—
         Maryland
         Public universities and colleges
Core curriculum
   USE Education—Curricula
Coretta Scott King Book Award
   BT   Illustration of books—Awards—United States
         Literary prizes
Cornet and piano music (Jazz)
   USE Jazz
Corporations—Personnel management
   USE Personnel management
Council members, City
   USE City council members
Council members, County
   USE County council members
Councillors, City
   USE City council members
Councilmen, City
   USE City council members
Councilmen, County
   USE County council members
Councilwomen, City
   USE Women city council members
Councilwomen, County
   USE Women county council members
Country-city migration
   USE Rural-urban migration
Country musicians *(May Subd Geog)*
   UF   Hillbilly musicians
   NT   Gospel musicians
County agricultural agents, African American
   USE African American county agricultural agents
County attorneys *(May Subd Geog)*
   UF   Attorneys, County
         County counsels
         County law officers
         County solicitors
   BT   County officials and employees
County clerks *(May Subd Geog)*
   UF   Clerks, County
   BT   County officials and employees

County council members *(May Subd Geog)*
    UF   Council members, County
             Councilmen, County
             County councilmen
    BT   County officials and employees
             Legislators
    NT   Women county council members

County councilmen
    USE   County council members

County councilwomen
    USE   Women county council members

County counsels
    USE   County attorneys

County law officers
    USE   County attorneys

County officers
    USE   County officials and employees

County officials and employees *(May Subd Geog)*
    UF   County officers
             Town officers
    BT   Local officials and employees
    NT   County attorneys
             County clerks
             County council members
             Ordinaries

County solicitors
    USE   County attorneys

Courses of study
    USE   Education—Curricula

Covenants running with land
    USE   Real covenants

Cowboys, African American
    USE   African American cowboys

Craft fairs
    USE   Craft festivals

Craft festivals *(May Subd Geog)* *[TT6]*
    UF   Craft fairs
             Craft shows
             Crafts fairs
             Crafts festivals
             Crafts shows
             Fairs, Craft
             Handicraft festivals
             Shows, Craft
    BT   Festivals

Craft shows
    USE   Craft festivals

Crafts fairs
    USE   Craft festivals

Crafts festivals
    USE   Craft festivals

Crafts shows
    USE   Craft festivals

Credit, Consumer
    USE   Consumer credit

Credit card redlining
    USE   Discrimination in credit cards

Creole dialects, English *(May Subd Geog)*
[PM7871-PM7874]
    UF   English Creole languages
             Negro-English dialects *[Former Heading]*

Creole dialects, English—Florida
    NT   Sea Islands Creole dialect

Creole dialects, English—Georgia
    NT   Sea Islands Creole dialect

Creole dialects, English—South Carolina
    NT   Sea Islands Creole dialect

Creoles *(May Subd Geog)* *[F380.C87 (Louisiana)]*
    BT   Racially mixed people

Crimes against African Americans
    USE   African Americans—Crimes against

Crimes against humanity
    NT   Slavery

Crimes against minorities
    USE   Minorities—Crimes against

Criminal justice, Administration of
    NT   Discrimination in criminal justice administration
             Lynching

**Criminal justice, Administration of—Cross cultural
studies**

Criminals, African American
    USE   African American criminals

Cross-cultural dating
    USE   Interethnic dating

Cross-cultural psychology
    USE   Ethnopsychology

Cults *(May Subd Geog)*
    Here are entered works on groups or movements whose system of
    religious beliefs or practices differs significantly from the major world
    religions and which are often gathered around a specific deity or person.
    NT   Ras Tafari movement

Cultural anthropology
    USE   Ethnology

Cultural assimilation
    USE   Assimilation (Sociology)

Cultural diversity policy
    USE   Multiculturalism

Cultural pluralism policy
    USE   Multiculturalism

Culturally deprived
    USE   Socially handicapped

Culturally disadvantaged
    USE   Socially handicapped

Culturally handicapped
    USE   Socially handicapped

Culture conflict *(May Subd Geog) [BF740 (Psychology)]*
  UF   Conflict of cultures
  BT   Ethnic relations
        Ethnopsychology
        Race relations
  NT   Marginality, Social
Curricula (Courses of study)
  USE   Education—Curricula

D

Dance
  USE   Dancing
Dance band music
  USE   Big band music
Dance bands
  USE   Big bands
        Dance orchestras
Dance music—United States
  NT   Rap (Music)
Dance orchestra
  USE   Dance orchestras
Dance orchestras *(May Subd Geog)*
  UF   Dance bands
        Dance orchestra *[Former Heading]*
  NT   Big bands
        Instrumentation and orchestration (Dance orchestra)
Dancing *(May Subd Geog) [GV1580-GV1799]*
  UF   Dance
  NT   Jazz dance
Dancing—Blacks
  USE   Blacks—Dancing
Dating, Bi-racial
  USE   Interracial dating
Dating, Biracial
  USE   Interracial dating
Dating, Interethnic
  USE   Interracial dating
Dating, Interracial
  USE   Interracial dating
De facto school segregation *(May Subd Geog)*
  [LC212.6-LC212.63]
  UF   Token integration
  BT   Discrimination in education
        School integration
        Segregation in education
Death penalty
  USE   Capital punishment
Deaths, Registers of
  USE   Registers of births, etc.
Decision-making, Consumer
  USE   Consumer behavior
Decorative arts, African American
  USE   African American decorative arts

Defamation against groups
  USE   Hate speech
Delaware State College (Dover, Del.)
  BT   Historically Black Colleges and Universities—
          Delaware
        Public universities and colleges
        State universities and colleges
Delivery of health care
  USE   Medical care
Delivery of medical care
  USE   Medical care
Delta Sigma Theta Sorority
  BT   Greek letter societies
Demography *(May Subd Geog) [HB848-HB3697]*
  UF   Historical demography
  RT   Population
        Vital statistics
  SA   *subdivision* Population *under names of cities, etc.*
Demonstrations *(May Subd Geog)*
    Here are entered works on large public gatherings, marches, etc.,
    organized for non-violent protest or affirmation, even though inciden-
    tal disturbances or incipient rioting may occur.
  UF   Public Demonstrations
  RT   Riots
  NT   Civil rights demonstrations
Demonstrations—Law and legislation *(May Subd Geog)*
Denmark Technical College (Denmark, S.C.)
  BT   Historically Black Colleges and Universities—
          South Carolina
        Junior Colleges
        Public universities and colleges
Denominational colleges
  USE   Church colleges
Denominational schools
  USE   Church schools
Dentists, African American
  USE   African American dentists
Descent
  USE   Genealogy
Desegregation
  USE   Segregation
Desegregation, Faculty
  USE   Faculty integration
Desegregation in education
  USE   School integration
Desegregation in higher education
  USE   College integration
        Segregation in higher education
Destitution
  USE   Poverty
Dialects, Urban
  USE   Urban dialects

Dietary laws, Black Muslims
USE Black Muslims—Dietary laws

Dillard University (New Orleans, La.)
BT   Historically Black Colleges and Universities—
       Louisiana
     Private universities and colleges
     United Negro College Fund Institutions

Diocesan schools
USE Church schools

Diplomats, African American
USE African American diplomats

Direct action
NT   Passive resistance

Disadvantaged, Culturally
USE Socially handicapped

Disadvantaged, Socially
USE Socially handicapped

Disadvantaged children
USE Socially handicapped children

Disciples of Christ, African American
USE African American Christians (Disciples of Christ)

Disciples of Christ, Negro
USE African American Christians (Disciples of Christ)

Discrimination *(May Subd Geog)*
   Here are entered general works on social discrimination based on
   race, religion, sex, social minority status or other factors.
BT   Assimilation (Sociology)
     Ethnic relations
     Prejudices
RT   Minorities
     Toleration
NT   Race discrimination
     Reverse discrimination
     Segregation

Discrimination—Law and legislation *(May Subd
Geog)*
UF   Anti-discrimination laws
BT   Civil rights

Discrimination, Racial
USE Race discrimination

Discrimination against African Americans
USE African Americans—Civil rights
     African Americans—Legal status, laws, etc.

Discrimination in colleges and universities
USE Discrimination in higher education

Discrimination in consumer credit *(May Subd Geog)*
UF   Race discrimination in consumer credit
BT   Consumer credit

Discrimination in credit cards *(May Subd Geog)*
UF   Credit card redlining
     Race discrimination in credit cards
     Red lining
     Redlining

Discrimination in credit cards—Law and legislation
(May Subd Geog)

Discrimination in criminal justice administration
(May Subd Geog)
UF   Race discrimination in criminal justice
       administration
BT   Criminal justice, administration of

Discrimination in education *(May Subd Geog)*
[LC212-LC212.863]
UF   Educational discrimination
     Race discrimination in education
BT   Education
RT   Segregation in education
NT   De facto school segregation
     Racism in textbooks
     Test bias
     Textbook bias

Discrimination in education—Law and legislation
(May Subd Geog)
BT   Educational law and legislation

Discrimination in employment *(May Subd Geog)*
[HD4903-HD4903.5]
UF   Bias, Job
     Employment discrimination
     Equal employment opportunity
     Equal opportunity in employment
     Fair employment practice
     Job bias
     Job discrimination
     Race discrimination in employment
RT   Trade-unions—Minority membership
SA   *subdivision* Employment *under names of racial
       or social groups, e.g.* African Americans—
       Employment
NT   Affirmative action programs
     Blacklisting, Labor
     Equal pay for equal work
     Reverse discrimination in employment

Discrimination in employment—Law and legislation
(May Subd Geog)
BT   Labor laws and legislation

Discrimination in higher education *(May Subd Geog)*
[LC212.4-LC212.43]
UF   Discrimination in colleges and universities
     Race discrimination in higher education
BT   Education, Higher

Discrimination in housing *(May Subd Geog)*
UF   Fair housing
     Housing, Discrimination in
     Open housing
     Race discrimination in housing
     Segregation in housing
BT   Housing
NT   African Americans—Housing
     Minorities—Housing
     Zoning, Exclusionary

Discrimination in housing—Law and legislation
  (May Subd Geog)
  RT   Real covenants
Discrimination in insurance *(May Subd Geog)*
  UF   Race discrimination in insurance
  BT   Insurance
Discrimination in insurance—Law and legislation
  BT   Insurance law
Discrimination in law enforcement *(May Subd Geog)*
  UF   Race discrimination in law enforcement
  BT   Law enforcement
Discrimination in medical care *(May Subd Geog)*
  UF   Race discrimination in medical care
  BT   Medical care
Discrimination in medical care—Law and legislation
  (May Subd Geog)
Discrimination in medical education *(May Subd
Geog)*
  UF   Race discrimination in medical education
  BT   Medical education
**Discrimination in medical education—Law and
legislation**
  BT   Educational law and legislation
Discrimination in mental health services *(May Subd
Geog)*
  UF   Race discrimination in mental health services
  BT   Mental health services
Discrimination in mortgage loans *(May Subd Geog)*
  UF   Race discrimination in mortgage loans
          Red lining
          Redlining
  BT   Mortgage loans
Discrimination in mortgage loans—Law and legislation
  (May Subd Geog)
Discrimination in municipal services *(May Subd
Geog)*
  UF   Race discrimination in municipal services
  BT   Municipal services
**Discrimination in municipal services—Law and
legislation** *(May Subd Geog)*
Discrimination in public accommodations *(May Subd
Geog)*
  UF   Public accommodations, Discrimination in
          Race discrimination in public accommodations
          Segregation in public accommodations
  NT   Segregation in transportation
**Discrimination in public accommodations—Law
and Legislation** *(May Subd Geog)*
Discrimination in sports *(May Subd Geog)*
  UF   Integration in sports
          Race discrimination in sports
          Racial integration in sports
          Segregation in sports *[Former Heading]*
  BT   Sports

Discrimination in transportation
  USE Segregation in transportation
Diseases *(May Subd Geog)*
  UF   Illness
          Morbidity
          Sickness
  BT   Medicine
          Sick
  RT   Health
  SA   *specific diseases, e.g.* Cancer; *and* African
          Americans—Diseases
District of Columbia, University of the (Washington, D.C.)
  UF   University of the District of Columbia
          (Washington, D.C.)
  BT   Historically Black Colleges and Universities—
          District of Columbia
          Public universities and colleges
Divinity schools
  USE Theological seminaries
Dixieland music *(May Subd Geog) [M1366 (Music)]*
  [ML3505.8-ML3509 (History and criticism)]
  UF   Dixieland music—United States
          Music, Dixieland
Dixieland music—United States
  USE Dixieland music
Docudrama
  USE Historical drama
Documentary drama
  USE Historical drama
Dolls, Black
  USE Black dolls
Donations
  USE Endowments
Double-bass and piano music (Jazz)
  USE Jazz
Drake (J.F.) Technical College (Huntsville, Ala.)
  BT   Historically Black Colleges and Universities—
          Alabama
          Junior Colleges
          Public universities and colleges
Drama—Black authors
  UF   Black drama
          Negro drama *[Former Heading]*
Drama festivals
  UF   Theater festivals
  BT   Festivals
Drama, Historical
  USE Historical drama
Dramatists, African American
  USE African American dramatists
Drew, Charles R., University of Medicine and Science
  USE Charles R. Drew University of Medicine and
          Science (Los Angeles, Calif.)

Dropouts, African American
USE African American dropouts

Drug abuse *(May Subd Geog) [HV5800-HV5840]*
Here are entered works on the abuse or misuse of drugs in a broad sense such as aspirin, bromides, caffeine, sedatives, alcohol, LSD and narcotics.
UF Addiction to drugs
Drug addiction
Drug habit
Drug use
NT African Americans—Drug use

Drug addiction
USE Drug abuse

Drug habit
USE Drug abuse

Drug use
USE Drug abuse
Drug utilization

Drug utilization *(May Subd Geog)*
Here are entered works on the use of therapeutic drugs as reported by government agencies, hospitals, physicians and drug firms.
UF Drugs—Utilization
Utilization of drugs
NT African Americans—Drug use

Drugs—Utilization
USE Drug utilization

Due process of law
NT Fair trial

Duke Ellington Memorial (Portrait Sculpture)
USE Graham, Robert, 1938- Duke Ellington Memorial

Dwellings *(May Subd Geog)*
Here are entered works on the history and description of human shelter. Works on the social and economic aspects of housing are entered under Housing.
NT African Americans—Dwellings

Dwellings—Georgia
NT Alonzo Franklin Herndon House (Atlanta, Ga.)
Martin Luther King, Junior, Birthplace (Atlanta, Ga.)

Dwellings—New York (State)
NT Harriet Tubman Home (Auburn, N.Y.)

Dwellings—Washington (D.C.)
NT Frederick Douglass Home (Washington, D.C.)
Mary McLeod Bethune Council House (Washington, D.C.)

E

Early childhood education *(May Subd Geog)*
[LB1139.2-LB1139.4]
Here are entered works on the activities and schooling that are intended to effect developmental changes in children from birth through elementary grade 3. Works on the structured education of children before entering kindergarten or grade 1 in elementary school are entered under Education, Preschool.
BT Education

SA *subdivision* Education (Early Childhood) *under African Americans and subdivision* Study and teaching (Early Childhood) *under African Americans*

East Harlem (New York, N.Y.) *(Not Subd Geog)*
UF Harlem, East (New York, N.Y.)
New York (N.Y.) East Harlem

Ebony's Gertrude Johnson Williams Writing Contest
BT Literary prizes

Ecclesiastical institutions
USE Religious institutions

Education *(May Subd Geog) [L]*
UF Children—Education
Education of children *[Former Heading]*
Human resource development
Instruction
Pedagogy
Youth-Education
RT Schools
Students
NT Discrimination in education
Early childhood education
Education, Elementary
Islamic education

Education—Cross-cultural Studies

Education—Curricula *[LB1570-LB1571 (Elementary schools)]*
UF Core Curriculum
Courses of study
Curricula (Courses of study)
Schools—Curricula Study, Courses of
SA *subdivision* Curricula *under individual educational institutions, and under types of education and educational institutions, for listings of courses offered, or discussions about them, e.g.* Morehouse College (Atlanta, Ga.)—Curricula; Technical education—Curricula; Historically Black Colleges and Universities—Curricula.

Education—Integration
USE School integration

Education—Segregation
USE Segregation in education

Education, Elementary *(May Subd Geog)*
[LB1555-LB1601]
Here are entered works on education in grades one through six or eight. Works on education limited to grades one through three or four are entered under Education, Primary.
UF Elementary education
BT Education
SA *subdivision* Education (Elementary) *under African Americans and subdivision* Study and teaching *under African Americans*

Education, Higher
UF Higher education

SA   *subdivision* Education (Higher) *under* African
Americans *and* African American women
RT   Historically Black Colleges and Universities
NT   College integration
Discrimination in higher education

Education, Higher—Segregation
USE Segregation in higher education

Education, Islamic
USE Islamic education

Education, Medical
USE Medical education

Education, Muslim
USE Islamic education

Education, Preschool *(May Subd Geog)*
[LB1140-LB1140.5]
Here are entered works on the structured education of children
before entering kindergarten or grade one in elementary school.
Works on activities and schooling that are intended to effect devel-
opmental changes in children from birth through elementary grade
three are entered under Early childhood education.
UF   Infant education
Preschool education
SA   *subdivision* Education (Preschool) *under*
African Americans

Education, Primary *(May Subd Geog)*
[LB1501-LB1547]
Here are entered works on education limited to grades one through
three or four. Works on education in grades one through six or eight
are entered under Education, Elementary.
UF   Primary education
SA   *subdivision* Education (Primary) *under* African
Americans

Education, Secondary *(May Subd Geog)*
UF   High school education
Secondary education
Secondary schools
RT   High schools
SA   *subdivision* Education (Secondary) *under*
African Americans; Minorities

Education, Urban *(May Subd Geog)*
[LC5101-LC5143]
UF   Inner city education
Urban education
BT   Cities and towns
Urban policy

Education and employment
USE Labor supply—Effect of education on

Education of children
USE Education

Educational administration
USE School management and organization

Educational discrimination
USE Discrimination in education

Educational endowments
USE Endowments

Educational law and legislation *(May Subd Geog)*
NT   College integration—Law and legislation
Discrimination in education—Law and legislation
Discrimination in medical education—Law and
legislation
Faculty integration—Law and legislation
Minorities—Education—Law and Legislation
Public school closings—Law and legislation
School children—Transportation—Law and
legislation
Segregation in education—Law and legislation
Socially handicapped children—Education—
Law and legislation

Edward Waters College (Jacksonville, Fla.)
BT   Historically Black Colleges and Universities—
Florida
Private universities and colleges
United Negro College Fund Institutions

Elementary education
USE Education, Elementary

Elementary schools
BT   Schools

Elementary schools, African American
USE African American elementary schools

Elizabeth City State University (Elizabeth City, N.C.)
BT   Historically Black Colleges and Universities—
North Carolina
Public universities and colleges

Elks
USE Improved Benevolent Protective Order of Elks
of the World

Emancipation of slaves
USE Slaves—Emancipation

Emancipation Day
BT   Anniversaries

Employees—Legal status, laws, etc.
USE Labor laws and legislation

Employment and education
USE Labor supply—Effect of education on

Employment discrimination
USE Discrimination in employment

Employment management
USE Personnel management

Employment quotas
USE Reverse discrimination in employment

Enculturation
USE Socialization

Endowed charities
USE Endowments

Endowments *(May Subd Geog) [HV16-HV25 (Chari-*
ties)] [LB2336-LB2337 (Higher education)]
Here are entered general works on endowed institutions, endow-
ment funds and donations to such funds.

UF   Donations
     Educational endowments
     Endowed charities
     Foundations (Endowments)
     Philanthropy
SA   *subdivision* Endowments *under names of individual corporate bodies, e.g.* United Negro College Fund—Endowments *and under types of corporate bodies and disciplines, e.g.* Spelman College (Atlanta, Ga.)—Endowments

Enforcement of law
     USE   Law enforcement

Engineers, African American
     USE   African American engineers

English Creole languages
     USE   Creole dialects, English

English language—Study and teaching—African American students
     UF   English language—Study and teaching—Negro students *[Former Heading]*
     BT   African American students
          African Americans—Education
     RT   Black English

English language—Study and teaching—Negro students
     USE   English language—Study and teaching—African American students

English literature—Black authors
     UF   Black literature (English)

English literature—Minority authors
     BT   Minorities

English poetry—Black authors
     UF   Black poetry (English)
          English poetry—Negro authors *[Former Heading]*

English poetry—Negro authors
     USE   English poetry—Black authors

Entertainers, African American
     USE   African American entertainers

Episcopalians, African American
     USE   African American Episcopalians

Episcopalians, Negro
     USE   African American Episcopalians

Equal employment opportunity
     USE   Affirmative action programs
          Discrimination in employment

Equal opportunity in employment
     USE   Affirmative action programs
          Discrimination in employment

Equal pay for equal work *(May Subd Geog)*
     Here are entered works on equal pay for jobs that require identical skills, responsibilities and effort.
     BT   Discrimination in employment

Equality before the law *(May Subd Geog)*
     Here are entered discussions of the principle of just legislation and administration of justice.
     BT   Civil rights

Ethnic aged
     USE   Minority aged

Ethnic architecture—United States
     NT   African American architecture

Ethnic art *(May Subd Geog)*
     Here are entered works on art produced by members of a group who share a common heredity and cultural tradition.
     UF   Art, Ethnic
     BT   Ethnic groups
          Minorities

Ethnic art—United States
     NT   African American art

Ethnic attitudes *(May Subd Geog)*
     BT   Ethnic relations
          Minorities
     RT   Race awareness

Ethnic barriers *(May Subd Geog) [JX4115-JX4181]*
     BT   Ethnology

Ethnic conflict
     USE   Ethnic relations

Ethnic groups *(May Subd Geog) [GN495.4]*
     Here are entered theoretical works on the concept of groups of people who are bound together by common ties of ancestry and culture. Works on the subjective sense of belonging to an individual ethnic group are entered under Ethnicity. Works on the discipline of ethnology, and works on the origin, distribution, and characteristics of the elements of the population of a particular region or country are entered under Ethnology, with appropriate local subdivision. General works on racial, religious, ethnic, or other minority groups are entered under Minorities.
     UF   Groups, Ethnic
     BT   Ethnology
     NT   Ethnic art
          Ethnic relations
          Ethnicity
          Minorities
          Racially mixed people

Ethnic groups—Psychology
     USE   Ethnopsychology

Ethnic handicapped
     USE   Minority handicapped

Ethnic identity
     USE   Ethnicity

Ethnic journalism
     USE   Ethnic press

Ethnic literature (American)
     USE   American literature—Minority authors

Ethnic mass media *(May Subd Geog) [P94.5.M55]*
     UF   Minority mass media
          Multicultural mass media
     NT   Ethnic press
          Ethnic radio broadcasting
          Ethnic television broadcasting

Ethnic mass media—United States
  NT   African American mass media
Ethnic minorities
  USE Minorities
Ethnic neighborhoods—United States
  NT   African American neighborhoods
Ethnic performing arts
  UF   Minority performing arts
Ethnic poetry (American)
  USE American poetry—Minority authors
Ethnic politics
  USE Minorities—Political activity
Ethnic press
  UF   Ethnic journalism
       Journalism, Ethnic
       Minority press
  BT   Ethnic mass media
       Mass media and minorities
       Minorities
Ethnic press—United States
  NT   African American press
Ethnic psychology
  USE Ethnopsychology
Ethnic radio broadcasting *(May Subd Geog)*
  [PN1991.8.E84]
  UF   Minority radio broadcasting
  BT   Ethnic mass media
Ethnic radio broadcasting—United States
  NT   African American radio stations
Ethnic relations *[GN496-GN498 (Ethnology)]*
  UF   Conflict, Ethnic
       Ethnic conflict
       Interethnic relations
       Relations among ethnic groups
  BT   Acculturation
       Assimilation (Sociology)
       Ethnic groups
       Ethnology
       Social problems
  RT   Minorities
       Race relations
  SA   *subdivision* Ethnic relations *under names of*
       regions, countries, cities, etc.
  NT   Culture conflict
       Discrimination
       Ethnic attitudes
Ethnic studies
  USE Minorities—Study and teaching
Ethnic television broadcasting *(May Subd Geog)*
  [PN1992.8.E]
  UF   Minority television broadcasting
  BT   Ethnic mass media

Ethnic theater *(May Subd Geog)*
  UF   Minority theater
  BT   Minorities
Ethnic wit and humor *(May Subd Geog)*
  UF   Minorities—Humor
Ethnicity *(May Subd Geog) [GN495.6 (Ethnology)]*
  Here are entered works on the subjective sense of belonging to an
  individual ethnic group. Theoretical works on the concept of groups
  of people who are bound together by common ties of ancestry and
  culture are entered under Ethnic groups. Works on the discipline of
  ethnology, and works on the origin, distribution, and characteristics
  of the elements of the population of a particular region or country are
  entered under Ethnology with appropriate local subdivision. General
  works on racial, religious, ethnic, or other minority groups are en-
  tered under Minorities.
  UF   Ethnic identity
       Group identity, Ethnic
  RT   Multiculturalism
       Pluralism (Social sciences)
  SA   *subdivisions* Race identity *or* Ethnic identity
       under individual races or ethnic groups,
       e.g. African Americans—Race identity
  NT   Blacks—Race identity
       Ethnicity in children
Ethnicity in children *(May Subd Geog)*
  BT   Ethnicity
Ethnocentrism *(May Subd Geog)*
  BT   Ethnopsychology
       Prejudices
       Race
  NT   Afrocentrism
       Racism
Ethnography
  USE Ethnology
Ethnology *(May Subd Geog) [GN]*
  UF   Cultural anthropology
       Ethnography
       Races of man
       Social anthropology
  NT   Blacks
       Ethnic barriers
       Ethnic groups
       Ethnic relations
       Manners and customs
       Race relations
       Socialization
Ethnology—Africa
  NT   Africans
Ethnology—Maryland
  NT   Wesorts
Ethnology—New Jersey
  NT   Ramapo Mountain people
Ethnology—New York (State)
  NT   Ramapo Mountain people
Ethnology—United States
  NT   African Americans
       Black Seminoles

Ethnopsychology *(May Subd Geog) [GN270-GN279]*
UF   Cross-cultural psychology
        Ethnic groups—Psychology
        Ethnic psychology
        Folk-psychology
        Psychology—Cross cultural studies
        Psychology, Ethnic
        Psychology, Racial
        Race psychology
SA   *subdivision* Psychology *under names of racial*
        or ethnic groups, e.g. African Americans—
        Psychology
NT   Art and race
        Culture conflict
        Ethnocentrism
        Music and race
        Race awareness

Europe—Civilization
NT   African American art—European influences

Evangelical popular music
    USE   Contemporary Christian music

Evangelists, African American
    USE   African American evangelists

Even Start programs
BT   Socially handicapped children—Education
        (Preschool)—United States

Ex-slaves
    USE   Freedmen

Exclusionary zoning
    USE   Zoning, Exclusionary

Executives, African American
    USE   African American executives

Executives, Black *(May Subd Geog)*
UF   Black executives *[Former Heading]*
        Negro executives *[Former Heading]*

Executives, Minority
    USE   Minority executives

Explorers, African American
    USE   African American explorers

Explorers, Black *(May Subd Geog)*
UF   Black explorers

Extemporization (Music)
    USE   Improvisation (Music)

F

Faculty (Education)
    USE   *subdivision* Faculty *under names of specific*
        universities, etc. e.g. Lincoln University
        (Lincoln University, Pa.)—Faculty

Faculty integration *(May Subd Geog)*
UF   Desegregation, Faculty
        Integration, Faculty
        Teachers—Integration
BT   School integration

Faculty integration—Law and legislation *(May Subd*
Geog)
BT   Educational law and legislation

Faculty integration—United States
NT   African American teachers

Fair employment practice
    USE   Discrimination in employment

Fair housing
    USE   Discrimination in housing

Fair trial *(May Subd Geog)*
    Here are entered works on legal hearings before an impartial and
disinterested tribunal carried out in an atmosphere devoid of prejudice. Works on the regular administration of the law, according to
which no citizen may be denied his or her legal rights and all laws
must conform to fundamental, accepted legal principles are entered
under Due process of law.
UF   Right to a fair trial
        Trial, Fair
BT   Due process of law
NT   Free press and fair trial

Fair trial and free press
    USE   Free press and fair trial

Fairs, Craft
    USE   Craft festivals

Families, African American
    USE   African American families

Families, Black *(May Subd Geog)*
UF   Black families *[Former Heading]*
        Blacks—Families *[Former Heading]*
        Negro families *[Former Heading]*

Family archives *(May Subd Geog) [CO]*
UF   Archives, Family
SA   *subdivision* Archives *under names of individual*
        families

Family festivals *(May Subd Geog)*
BT   Festivals
NT   Black Family Celebration

Family history
    USE   Genealogy

Family reunions *(May Subd Geog)*
UF   Reunions, Family

Family trees
    USE   Genealogy

Farmers, African American
    USE   African American farmers

Fashion designers, African American
    USE   African American fashion designers

Fayetteville State University (Fayetteville, N.C.)
BT   Historically Black Colleges and Universities—
        North Carolina
        Public universities and colleges

Federal aid to minority business enterprises *(May*
Subd Geog)
UF   Minority business enterprises—Federal aid
BT   Minority business enterprises—Finance

Festivals *(May Subd Geog) [GT3930-GT4995 (Manners and customs)] [LB3560-LB3575 (Educational)]*
- RT   Pageants
- NT   Art festivals
  - Craft festivals
  - Drama festivals
  - Family festivals
  - Parades

Fiction—Black authors
- UF   Black fiction
  - Negro fiction *[Former Heading]*

Fiction, Historical
- USE Historical fiction

Film industry (Motion pictures)
- USE Motion picture industry

Fire fighters, African American
- USE African American fire fighters

Fisk University (Nashville, Tenn.)
- BT   Historically Black Colleges and Universities—Tennessee
  - Private universities and colleges
  - United Negro College Fund Institutions

Florida Agricultural and Mechanical University (Tallahassee, Fla.)
- BT   Historically Black Colleges and Universities—Florida
  - Public universities and colleges
  - State universities and colleges

Florida Memorial College (Miami, Fla.)
- BT   Historically Black Colleges and Universities—Florida
  - Private universities and colleges
  - United Negro College Fund Institutions

Folk art, African American
- USE African American folk art

Folk art, Black *(May Subd Geog)*
- UF   Black folk art

Folk beliefs
- USE Folklore

Folk-lore
- USE Folklore

Folk music—United States
- NT   Blues (Music)

Folk-psychology
- USE Ethnopsychology

Folk songs, English—United States
- NT   Spirituals (Songs)

Folk-tales
- USE Legends

Folk tales
- USE Tales

Folklore *(May Subd Geog) [GR]*
- UF   Folk beliefs
  - Folk-lore *[Former Heading]*
  - Traditions
- RT   Oral tradition
  - Storytelling
- SA   *subdivision* Folklore *under ethnic, national or occupational groups, e.g.* African Americans—Folklore; African American coal miners—Folklore
- BT   Manners and customs
- NT   Urban folklore

Folktales
- USE Tales

Folkways
- USE Manners and customs

Food—Religious aspects—Black Muslims
- NT   Black Muslims—Dietary laws

Football players, African American
- USE African American football players

Fort Valley State College (Fort Valley, Ga.)
- BT   Historically Black Colleges and Universities—Georgia
  - Public universities and colleges
  - State universities and colleges

Foundations (Endowments)
- USE Endowments

Franchise
- USE Suffrage

Fraternal benefit societies
- USE Friendly societies

Fraternal insurance
- USE Insurance, Fraternal

Fraternal organizations
- USE Friendly societies
  - Greek letter societies

Fraternities
- USE Greek letter societies
  - Initiations (into trades, societies, etc.)
  - Secret societies

Fraternity songs *[M1960]*
- UF   Greek letter societies—Songs and music
  - Sorority songs
- BT   Students' songs—United States
- SA   *subdivision* Songs and music *under names of individual fraternities, e.g.* Alpha Kappa Alpha Sorority—Songs and music

Frederick Douglass Home (Washington, D.C.)
- BT   Dwellings—Washington (D.C.)

Free press and fair trial *(May Subd Geog)*
- UF   Fair trial and free press
- BT   Fair trial

Freed slaves
- USE Freedmen

Freedmen *(May Subd Geog)* *[E185.2 (United States)]* *[HT731 (General)]*
- UF   Ex-slaves
  Freed slaves
  Refugees, African American
- BT   African Americans
  Slaves

Freedom marches (Civil rights)
- USE   Civil rights demonstrations

Freemasonry, African American
- USE   African American freemasonry

Freemasons. United States. Scottish Rite. National Supreme Council (Negro)
- USE   African American freemasonry

Freemasons, African American
- USE   African American freemasonry
  African American freemasons

Freemasons, Negro
- USE   African American freemasons

Friendly societies *(May Subd Geog)* *[HG9201-HG9245 (Fraternal insurance)]* *[HS1501-HS1510 (Societies)]*
- UF   Benefit societies
  Fraternal benefit societies
  Fraternal organizations
  Mutual aid societies
  Mutual benefit associations
  Societies, Benefit
- BT   Societies
- NT   Insurance, Fraternal

Fugitive slave law of 1793
- BT   Fugitive slaves—United States

Fugitive slave law of 1850
- BT   Compromise of 1850
  Fugitive slaves—United States

Fugitive slaves *(May Subd Geog)*
- UF   Runaway slaves
  Slavery—Fugitive slaves
- BT   Slaves

Fugitive slaves—Ohio—History
- NT   Oberlin-Wellington Rescue, 1858

Fugitive slaves—Pennsylvania

Fugitive slaves—United States
- UF   Refugees, African American
- RT   Underground railroad
- NT   Fugitive slave law of 1793
  Fugitive slave law of 1850

Fugitive slaves—West Indies
- NT   Maroons

Fundamental rights
- USE   Civil rights

Funeral rites and ceremonies, Black
- USE   Blacks—Funeral customs and rites

G

Games
- SA   *subdivision* Games *under* African Americans

Games, Olympic
- USE   Olympics

Gammon Theological Seminary (United Methodist)
- BT   Interdenominational Theological Center (Atlanta, Ga.)

Gardens, African American
- USE   African American gardens

Gay African American actors
- USE   African American gay actors

Gays, African American
- USE   African American gays

Geechee dialect
- USE   Sea Islands Creole dialect

Genealogical research
- USE   Genealogy

Genealogy *(Not Subd Geog)* *[CS]*
- UF   Ancestry
  Descent
  Family history
  Family trees
  Genealogical research
- RT   Biography
- SA   *subdivision* Family *under names of individual persons; also* Genealogy *under names of countries, cities, etc., names of individual corporate bodies and under classes of persons and ethnic groups; and names of individual families.*
- NT   Registers of births, etc.

Generals, African American
- USE   African American generals

George Washington Carver National Monument (Mo.) *(Not Subd Geog)*
- BT   National monuments—Missouri

German American-African American relations
- USE   African Americans—Relations with German Americans

German Americans—Relations with African Americans
- USE   African Americans—Relations with German Americans

Ghettos, Inner city
- USE   Inner cities

Gospel music *(May Subd Geog)* *[M2198-M2199 (Music)]* *[ML3186.8-ML3187 (History and criticism)]*
- UF   Gospel music—United States
  Music, Gospel
- BT   African Americans—Music
  Popular music
  Sacred songs
- NT   Contemporary Christian music
  Revivals—Hymns

Gospel music—United States
    USE Gospel music
Gospel musicians *(May Subd Geog) [ML385-ML403]*
    BT   Country musicians
              Musicians
Government executives, African American
    USE African American government executives
Government housing
    USE Public housing
Graham, Robert, 1938- Duke Ellington Memorial
    (Not Subd Geog)
    UF   Duke Ellington Memorial (Portrait Sculpture)
Grambling State University (Grambling, La.)
    BT   Historically Black Colleges and Universities—
              Louisiana
              Public universities and colleges
Grammar schools
    USE Public schools
Graves
    USE Cemeteries
Graveyards
    USE Cemeteries
Greek letter societies *(May Subd Geog) [LJ]*
    UF   College fraternities
              College sororities
              Fraternal organizations
              Fraternities
              Sororities, Greek letter
    BT   Societies
    SA   *names of individual Greek letter societies*
    NT   Alpha Kappa Alpha Sorority
              Alpha Phi Alpha Fraternity
              Delta Sigma Theta Sorority
              Iota Phi Lambda Sorority
              Kappa Alpha Psi Fraternity
              Omega Psi Phi Fraternity
              Phi Beta Sigma Fraternity
              Phi Delta Kappa Fraternity
              Sigma Gamma Rho Sorority
              Sigma Pi Phi Fraternity
              Zeta Phi Beta Sorority
Greek letter societies—Songs and music
    USE Fraternity songs
Group defamation
    USE Hate speech
Group identity, Ethnic
    USE Ethnicity
Group libel
    USE Hate speech
Groups, Ethnic
    USE Ethnic groups
Guineas (Mixed bloods, United States)
    USE Mulattoes—United States

Guitar—Methods (Blues) *[MT582]*
    BT   Blues (Music)
Guitar music (Blues) *[M125-M129]*
    BT   Blues (Music)
Gullah dialect
    USE Sea Islands Creole dialect
Gullahs *(May Subd Geog)*
    Here are entered works on a group of people of African ancestry inhabiting the Sea Islands and coastal areas of South Carolina, Georgia, and northern Florida.
    BT   African Americans—Florida
              African Americans—Georgia
              African Americans—South Carolina

H

Hairdressing of African Americans
    UF   Afro (Hair style)
              African American hairdressing
              African Americans—Hairdressing
              Hairdressing of Negroes *[Former Heading]*
Hairdressing of Blacks
    UF   Afro (Hair style)
              Black hairdressing
              Blacks—Hairdressing
              Hairdressing of Negroes *[Former Heading]*
Hairdressing of Negroes
    USE Hairdressing of African Americans
              Hairdressing of Blacks
Hampton University (Hampton, Va.)
    BT   Historically Black Colleges and Universities—
              Virginia
              Private universities and colleges
Handicapped African Americans
    USE African American handicapped
Handicraft festivals
    USE Craft festivals
Hard-core unemployed *(May Subd Geog) [HD5708.8-HD5708.85 (Labor market)] [HF5549.5.H3 (Personnel management)]*
    UF   Socially handicapped—Employment
    BT   Unemployed
Harlem, East (New York, N.Y.)
    USE East Harlem (New York, N.Y.)
Harlem Renaissance
    UF   New Negro Movement
              Renaissance, Harlem
    BT   African American arts
              American literature—African American authors
Harpers Ferry (W.Va.)—John Brown's Raid, 1859
    USE Harpers Ferry (W.Va.)—History—
              John Brown's Raid, 1859

Harpers Ferry (W.Va.)—History—John Brown's Raid, 1859 *[E45]*
  UF   Harpers Ferry (W.Va.)—John Brown's Raid, 1859 *[Former Heading]*
        Harpers Ferry Raid, Harpers Ferry, W.Va., 1859
        John Brown's Raid, Harpers Ferry, W.Va., 1859
Harpers Ferry Raid, Harpers Ferry, W.Va., 1859
  USE Harpers Ferry (W.Va.)—History—John Brown's Raid, 1859
Harriet Tubman Day *(May Subd Geog)*
  BT   Special days
Harriet Tubman Home (Auburn, N.Y.)
  BT   Dwellings—New York (State)
Harris-Stowe State College (St. Louis, Mo.)
  BT   Historically Black Colleges and Universities—Missouri
        Public universities and colleges
Harvest festivals—United States
  NT   Kwanzaa
Hate crimes *(May Subd Geog)*
  UF   Bias crimes
        Bias-related crimes
        Hate motivated crimes
        Hate offenses
Hate crimes in the press *(May Subd Geog)*
  BT   Press
Hate motivated crimes
  USE Hate crimes
Hate offenses
  USE Hate crimes
Hate speech *(May Subd Geog)*
  UF   Defamation against groups
        Group defamation
        Group libel
        Racist speech
        Speech, Hate
  BT   Libel and slander
HBCUS
  USE Historically Black Colleges and Universities
Head Start programs *(May Subd Geog)*
  BT   Socially handicapped children—Education (Preschool)—United States
Healers, African American
  USE African American healers
Health *[RA773-RA790]*
  Here are entered works on optimal physical, mental, and social well-being, as well as how to achieve and preserve it.
  UF   Personal health
        Wellness
  RT   Diseases
  SA   *subdivision* Health *under names of individual persons; also subdivision* Health and hygiene *under classes of persons and ethnic groups; and subdivision* Health aspects *under subjects, e.g.* African Americans—Health and hygiene
Health and race *(May Subd Geog)*
  BT   Race
Health care
  USE Medical care
Health care delivery
  USE Medical care
Health services
  USE Medical care
Herndon Home
  USE Alonzo Franklin Herndon Home (Atlanta, Ga.)
Heroines of Jericho, African American
  UF   African American Heroines of Jericho
        Heroines of Jericho, Negro *[Former Heading]*
Heroines of Jericho, Negro
  USE Heroines of Jericho, African American
High school education
  USE Education, Secondary
High schools *(May Subd Geog)* *[LB1603-LB1694]*
  UF   Secondary schools
  BT   Public schools
        Schools
  RT   Education, Secondary
  NT   Comprehensive high schools
Higher education
  USE Education, Higher
Hillbilly musicians
  USE Country musicians
Hinds Junior College (Utica, Miss.)
  BT   Historically Black Colleges and Universities—Mississippi
        Junior Colleges
        Public universities and colleges
Historians, African American
  USE African American historians
Historians, Negro
  USE African American historians
Historic sites *(May Subd Geog)*
  UF   Historical sites
Historic sites—Alabama
  NT   Tuskegee Institute National Historic Site (Tuskegee, Ala.)
Historic sites—Georgia
  NT   Martin Luther King, Junior, National Historic Site (Atlanta, Ga.)
        Savannah Historic District (Savannah, Ga.)
Historic sites—Kansas
  NT   Brown v. Board of Education National Historic Site (Topeka, Kan.)
Historic sites—Massachusetts
  NT   Boston African American National Historic Site (Boston, Mass.)

Historic sites—New York (State)
  NT   John Brown Farm State Historic Site
           (North Elba, N.Y.)

Historic sites—Washington (D.C.)
  NT   Mary McLeod Bethune Council House National
           Historic Site (Washington, D.C.)

Historical demography
  USE Demography

Historical drama *[PN1870-PN1879*
(History and criticism)]
  UF   Chronicle history (Drama)
           Chronicle play
           Docudrama
           Documentary drama
           Drama, Historical
           History—Drama
  SA   *subdivision* History—Drama *or subdivision*
           History—[period subdivisions]—Drama
           under names of countries, cities, etc.;
           and subdivision Drama *under names of*
           historical events and persons

Historical fiction *[PN3441]*
  UF   Fiction, Historical
           History—Fiction
  SA   *subdivision* History—Fiction *or subdivision*
           History—[period subdivision]—Fiction
           under names of countries, cities, etc.;
           and subdivision Fiction *under names of*
           historical events and persons

Historical sites
  USE Historic sites

Historically Black Colleges and Universities *(May*
Subd Geog) [LC2781]
  UF   African American colleges
           African American universities and colleges
           Black colleges
           Black universities and colleges
           Colleges, African American
           Colleges, Black
           HBCUS
           Negro universities and colleges *[Former Heading]*
           Universities and colleges, African American
           Universities and colleges, Black
  BT   African Americans—Education
           Blacks—Education
           Schools
  RT   Education, Higher
  SA   *subdivisions under* Lincoln University (Lincoln
           University, Pa.)
  NT   African American theological seminaries
           Art in African American universities and colleges
           Church and college
           Church colleges
           Junior Colleges
           State universities and colleges
           Medical colleges
           Private universities and colleges

           Public universities and colleges
           United Negro College Fund Institutions
           Women's colleges

Historically Black Colleges and Universities—
Alabama
  NT   Alabama Agricultural and Mechanical Univer-
           sity (Normal, Ala.)
           Alabama State University (Montgomery, Ala.)
           Bishop (S.D.) State Junior College (Mobile, Ala.)
           Carver State Technical College (Mobile, Ala.)
           Concordia College (Selma, Ala.)
           Drake (J.F.) Technical College (Huntsville, Ala.)
           Lawson State Community College
              (Birmingham, Ala.)
           Miles College (Birmingham, Ala.)
           Oakwood College (Huntsville, Ala.)
           Selma University (Selma, Ala.)
           Stillman College (Tuscaloosa, Ala.)
           Talladega College (Talladega, Ala.)
           Trenholm State Technical College
              (Montgomery, Ala.)
           Tuskegee University (Tuskegee, Ala.)

Historically Black Colleges and Universities—
Arkansas
  NT   Arkansas Baptist College (Little Rock, Ark.)
           Arkansas at Pine Bluff, University of
              (Pine Bluff, Ark.)
           Philander Smith College (Little Rock, Ark.)
           Shorter College (North Little Rock, Ark.)

Historically Black Colleges and Universities—
California
  NT   Charles R. Drew University of Medicine and
           Science (Los Angeles, Calif.)

Historically Black Colleges and Universities—
Delaware
  NT   Delaware State College (Dover, Del.)

Historically Black Colleges and Universities—
District of Columbia
  NT   District of Columbia, University of the
              (Washington, D.C.)
           Howard University (Washington, D.C.)

Historically Black Colleges and Universities—
Florida
  NT   Bethune-Cookman College
              (Daytona Beach, Fla.)
           Edward Waters College (Jacksonville, Fla.)
           Florida Agricultural and Mechanical University
              (Tallahassee, Fla.)
           Florida Memorial College (Miami, Fla.)

Historically Black Colleges and Universities—
Georgia
  NT   Albany State College (Albany, Ga.)
           Clark Atlanta University (Atlanta, Ga.)
           Fort Valley State College (Fort Valley, Ga.)
           Interdenominational Theological Center
              (Atlanta, Ga.)
           Morehouse College (Atlanta, Ga.)

Morehouse School of Medicine (Atlanta, Ga.)
Morris Brown College (Atlanta, Ga.)
Paine College (Augusta, Ga.)
Savannah State College (Savannah, Ga.)
Spelman College (Atlanta, Ga.)

Historically Black Colleges and Universities—Kentucky
NT Kentucky State University (Frankfort, Ky.)
Simmons University Bible School (Louisville, Ky.)

Historically Black Colleges and Universities—Louisiana
NT Dillard University (New Orleans, La.)
Grambling State University (Grambling, La.)
Southern University (Baton Rouge, La.)
Southern University (New Orleans, La.)
Southern University (Shreveport, La.)
Xavier University (New Orleans, La.)

Historically Black Colleges and Universities—Maryland
NT Bowie State College (Bowie, Md.)
Coppin State College (Baltimore, Md.)
Maryland Eastern Shore, University of (Princess Anne, Md.)
Morgan State University (Baltimore, Md.)

Historically Black Colleges and Universities—Michigan
NT Lewis College of Business (Detroit, Mich.)

Historically Black Colleges and Universities—Mississippi
NT Alcorn State University (Lorman, Miss.)
Coahoma Junior College (Clarksdale, Miss.)
Hinds Junior College (Utica, Miss.)
Jackson State University (Jackson, Miss.)
Mary Holmes College (West Point, Miss.)
Mississippi Valley State University (Itta Bena, Miss.)
Natchez Junior College (Natchez, Miss.)
Prentiss Institute Junior College (Prentiss, Miss.)
Rust College (Holly Springs, Miss.)
Tougaloo College (Tougaloo, Miss.)

Historically Black Colleges and Universities—Missouri
NT Harris-Stowe State College (St. Louis, Mo.)
Lincoln University (Jefferson City, Mo.)

Historically Black Colleges and Universities—North Carolina
NT Barber-Scotia College (Concord, N.C.)
Bennett College (Greensboro, N.C.)
Elizabeth City State University (Elizabeth City, N.C.)
Fayetteville State University (Fayetteville, N.C.)
Johnson C. Smith University (Charlotte, N.C.)
Livingstone College (Salisbury, N.C.)
North Carolina Agricultural and Technical State University (Greensboro, N.C.)
North Carolina Central University (Durham, N.C.)
Saint Augustine's College (Raleigh, N.C.)

Shaw University (Raleigh, N.C.)
Winston-Salem State University (Winston-Salem, N.C.)

Historically Black Colleges and Universities—Ohio
NT Central State University (Wilberforce, Ohio)
Wilberforce University (Wilberforce, Ohio)

Historically Black Colleges and Universities—Oklahoma
NT Langston University (Langston, Okla.)

Historically Black Colleges and Universities—Pennsylvania
NT Cheyney State University (Cheyney, Pa.)
Lincoln University (Lincoln University, Pa.)

Historically Black Colleges and Universities—South Carolina
NT Allen University (Columbia, S.C.)
Benedict College (Columbia, S.C.)
Claflin College (Orangeburg, S.C.)
Clinton Junior College (Rock Hill, S.C.)
Denmark Technical College (Denmark, S.C.)
Morris College (Sumter, S.C.)
South Carolina State College (Orangeburg, S.C.)
Voorhees College (Denmark, S.C.)

Historically Black Colleges and Universities—Tennessee
NT Fisk University (Nashville, Tenn.)
Knoxville College (Knoxville, Tenn.)
Knoxville College-Morristown Campus (Morristown, Tenn.)
Lane College (Jackson, Tenn.)
LeMoyne-Owen College (Memphis, Tenn.)
Meharry Medical College (Nashville, Tenn.)
Tennessee State University (Nashville, Tenn.)

Historically Black Colleges and Universities—Texas
NT Huston-Tillotson College (Austin, Tex.)
Jarvis Christian College (Hawkins, Tex.)
Paul Quinn College (Dallas, Tex.)
Prairie View Agricultural and Mechanical University (Prairie View, Tex.)
Saint Philip's College (San Antonio, Tex.)
Southwestern Christian College (Terrell, Tex.)
Texas College (Tyler, Tex.)
Texas Southern University (Houston, Tex.)
Wiley College (Marshall, Tex.)

Historically Black Colleges and Universities—Virgin Islands
NT Virgin Islands, University of the (St. Thomas, V.I.)

Historically Black Colleges and Universities—Virginia
NT Hampton University (Hampton, Va.)
Norfolk State University (Norfolk, Va.)
Saint Paul's College (Lawrenceville, Va.)
Virginia Seminary College (Lynchburg, Va.)
Virginia State University (Petersburg, Va.)
Virginia Union University (Richmond, Va.)

**Historically Black Colleges and Universities—
West Virginia**
- NT   Bluefield State College (Bluefield, W.Va.)
  West Virginia State College (Institute, W.Va.)

History—Biography
- USE Biography

History—Drama
- USE Historical drama

History—Fiction
- USE Historical fiction

Holidays
- RT   Anniversaries

Holidays—United States
- NT   Martin Luther King, Jr., Day

Holiness church members, African American
- USE African American Holiness church members

Home economics extension workers, African American
- USE African American home economics extension workers

Homelessness *(May Subd Geog)*
- BT   Housing
  Poverty

Horsemen and horsewomen, African American
- USE African American horsemen and horsewomen

House-raising parties *(May Subd Geog)*
- UF   Houseraising parties
  Parties, House-raising

Houseraising parties
- USE House-raising parties

Housing *(May Subd Geog) [HD7285-HD7391]*
> Here are entered works on the social and economic aspects of housing. Works on the history and the description of human shelters are entered under Dwellings.
- UF   Housing—Social aspects
  Slum clearance
  Urban housing
- SA   *subdivision* Housing *under classes of persons and ethnic groups*
- RT   African Americans—Housing
- NT   Discrimination in housing
  Homelessness
  Minorities—Housing
  Public housing
  Slums
  Tenement-houses
  Welfare recipients—Housing

Housing—Social aspects
- USE Housing

Housing, African American
- USE African Americans—Housing

Housing, Discrimination in
- USE Discrimination in housing

Housing programs, Inclusionary
- USE Inclusionary housing programs

Housing projects, Government
- USE Public housing

Howard University (Washington, D.C.)
- BT   Historically Black Colleges and Universities—District of Columbia
  Private universities and colleges
- NT   Moorland-Spingarn Research Center (Washington, D.C.)

Human population
- USE Population

Human resource development
- USE Education

Human resource management
- USE Personnel management

Huston-Tillotson College (Austin, Tex.)
- BT   Historically Black Colleges and Universities—Texas
  Private universities and colleges
  United Negro College Fund Institutions

Hybridity of races
- USE Miscegenation

Hymnals, Shape note
- USE Shape note hymnals

Hymns, American
- USE Hymns, English—United States

Hymns, English—United States
- UF   American hymns
  Hymns, American
- NT   Shape note hymnals
  Spirituals (Songs)

Hymns, Revival
- USE Revivals—Hymns

I

I.B.P.O.E.W. (Elks)
- USE Improved Benevolent Protective Order of Elks of the World

ITC
- USE Interdenominational Theological Center (Atlanta, Ga.)

Illness
- USE Diseases

Illustration of books—Awards—United States
- NT   Caldecott Medal
  Coretta Scott King Book Award

Improved Benevolent Protective Order of Elks of the World
- UF   Elks
  I.B.P.O.E.W. (Elks)
- BT   Secret societies

Improvisation (Music) *[MT68]*
- UF   Extemporization (Music)
- NT   Rap (Music)

Inclusionary housing programs *(May Subd Geog)*
> Here are entered works on programs which oblige or encourage developers of upper income housing to include a number of low or moderate income units.
>
> UF   Housing programs, Inclusionary
> RT   Poor—Housing

Independent schools
> USE Private schools

Indian-African American relations
> USE African Americans—Relations with Indians

Indian-Black relations
> USE Blacks—Relations with Indians

Indians—Relations with Blacks
> USE Blacks—Relations with Indians

Indians of North America—Mixed descent
> NT   Melungeons
>   Ramapo Mountain people
>   Wesorts

Indians of North America—Ownership, Slaves
> USE Indians of North America—Slaves, Ownership of

Indians of North America—Relations with African Americans
> USE African Americans—Relations with Indians

Indians of North America—Slaves, Ownership of
> UF   Indians of North America—Ownership, Slaves
>   Ownership, slaves by Indians
> BT   Slavery—United States

Industrial unions
> USE Trade-unions

Infant education
> USE Education, Preschool

Infants, African American
> USE African American infants

Initiations (into trades, societies, etc.)
> *[HD4889(Labor)]*
> UF   Fraternities
> RT   Secret societies

Inner cities *(May Subd Geog) [HT156]*
> Here are entered works on densely populated, usually deteriorating, central areas of large cities, inhabited predominantly by poor people, often of a specific ethnic group, and on the social and economic problems of these areas.
>
> UF   Central cities
>   Ghettos, Inner city
>   Inner city ghettos
>   Inner city problems
>   Zones of transition
> BT   Cities and towns
> RT   Urban cores

Inner city education
> USE Education, Urban

Inner city ghettos
> USE Inner cities

Inner city problems
> USE Inner cities

Inner city schools
> USE Urban schools

Institutions, Ecclesiastical
> USE Religious institutions

Institutions, Religious
> USE Religious institutions

Institutions, associations, etc.
> USE Associations, institutions, etc.

Instruction
> USE Education

Instructional materials centers—Services to minorities *(May Subd Geog)*
> BT   Minorities—Services for
> RT   Libraries and minorities

Instrumentation and orchestration (Dance orchestra) *[ML455 (History and criticism)]* *[MT86 (Instruction)]*
> BT   Dance orchestras
>   Jazz

Insurance *(May Subd Geog) [HG8011-HG9970]*
> NT   Discrimination in insurance

Insurance, Burial *(May Subd Geog)* *[HG9466-HG9479]*
> UF   Burial clubs
>   Burial insurance
>   Clubs, Burial

Insurance, Fraternal
> UF   Fraternal insurance
> BT   Friendly societies

Insurance law *(May Subd Geog)*
> NT   Discrimination in insurance—Law and legislation

Integration, Faculty
> USE Faculty integration

Integration, Racial
> USE Race relations

Integration, Social
> USE Social integration

Integration in education
> USE School integration

Integration in higher education
> USE College integration
>   Segregation in higher education

Integration in sports
> USE Discrimination in sports

Intellectuals, African American
> USE African American intellectuals

Intercultural education
> USE Multicultural education

Interdenominational Theological Center (Atlanta, Ga.)
> UF   ITC
> BT   African American theological seminaries

Historically Black Colleges and Universities—
Georgia
Private universities and colleges
United Negro College Fund Institutions
NT   Charles H. Mason Theological Seminary
(Church of God in Christ)
Gammon Theological Seminary
(United Methodist)
Johnson C. Smith Theological Seminary
(Presbyterian USA)
Morehouse School of Religion (Baptist)
Phillips School of Theology
(Christian Methodist Episcopal)
Turner Theological Seminary
(African Methodist Episcopal)

Interethnic dating *(May Subd Geog)*
UF   Cross-cultural dating
Dating, Interethnic
Interethnic relations
USE Ethnic relations

Intermarriage *(May Subd Geog) [HQ1031]*
Here are entered works which discuss collectively marriage be-
tween persons of different religions, religious denominations, races,
and ethnic groups.
UF   Marriage, Mixed *[Former Heading]*
Mixed marriage
NT   Interracial marriage
Intermarriage, Racial
USE Interracial marriage
Internal migration
USE Migration, Internal

Interracial adoption *(May Subd Geog)*
UF   Mixed race adoption
BT   Adoption
Race relations

Interracial dating *(May Subd Geog) [HQ801.8]*
UF   Bi-racial dating
Biracial dating
Dating, Bi-racial
Dating, Biracial
Dating, Interethnic
Dating, Interracial

Interracial marriage *(May Subd Geog) [HQ1031]*
UF   Intermarriage, Racial
Marriage, Interracial
BT   Intermarriage
NT   Children of interracial marriage
Interracial marriage, Children of
USE Children of interracial marriage
Intolerance
USE Toleration
Inventors, African American
USE African American inventors

Iota Phi Lambda Sorority
BT   Greek letter societies

Iron and steel workers, African American
USE African American iron and steel workers
Islam—Education
USE Islamic education

Islamic education *(May Subd Geog) [LC901-LC915]*
Here are entered works on secular education within an Islamic
framework, as well as works that discuss both secular and religious
education within that framework.
UF   Education, Islamic
Education, Muslim
Islam—Education *[Former Heading]*
Muslim education
BT   Education
NT   Islamic religious education
Islamic educators
USE Muslim educators

Islamic religious education *(May Subd Geog)*
[BP44-BP48]
Here are entered works on the study and teaching of Islam as one's
personal religion. Works on secular education within an Islamic
framework, as well as works that discuss both secular and religious
education within that framework are entered under Islamic education.
UF   Muslim religious education
Religious education, Islamic *[Former Heading]*
BT   Islamic education
Religious education

J

Jackson State University (Jackson, Miss.)
BT   Historically Black Colleges and Universities—
Mississippi
Public universities and colleges
Jackson Whites
USE Ramapo Mountain people

Japan—Race relations
NT   African Americans—Relations with Japanese
Japanese—Relations with African Americans
USE African Americans—Relations with Japanese
Japanese-African American relations
USE African Americans—Relations with Japanese

Jarvis Christian College (Hawkins, Tex.)
BT   Historically Black Colleges and Universities—
Texas
Private universities and colleges
United Negro College Fund Institutions

Jazz *(May Subd Geog) [M1366 (Music)]*
[ML3505.8-ML3509 (History and criticism)]
UF   Accordion and piano music (Jazz)
[Former Heading]
Clarinet and piano music(Jazz)
[Former Heading]
Cornet and piano music (Jazz)
[Former Heading]
Double-bass and piano music (Jazz)
[Former Heading]

Jazz—United States
Jazz duets *[Former Heading]*
Jazz ensembles *[Former Heading]*
Jazz music *[Former Heading]*
Jazz nonets *[Former Heading]*
Jazz octets *[Former Heading]*
Jazz quartets *[Former Heading]*
Jazz quintets *[Former Heading]*
Jazz septets *[Former Heading]*
Jazz sextets *[Former Heading]*
Jazz trios *[Former Heading]*
Saxophone and piano music (Jazz)
   [Former Heading]
Vibraphone and piano music (Jazz)
   [Former Heading]
Wind instrument and piano music (Jazz)
   [Former Heading]
Xylophone and piano music (Jazz)
   [Former Heading]
BT African Americans—Music
     Music
SA *headings for solo instrumental music followed by the parenthetical qualifier* (Jazz), *e.g.* Piano music (Jazz); *headings which include the words* jazz ensemble *as a statement of medium, e.g.* Concertos (Flute with jazz ensemble); Jazz ensemble with orchestra; Suites (Jazz ensemble); *and subdivisions* Methods (Jazz) *and* Studies and exercises (Jazz) *under names of instruments*
NT Big band music
     Big bands
     Boogie woogie (Music)
     Bop (Music)
     Dixieland (Music)
     Instrumentation and orchestration (Dance orchestra)
     Jazz vocals
     Ragtime music
     Swing (Music)

Jazz—To 1921

Jazz—1921-1930

Jazz—1931-1940

Jazz—1941-1950

Jazz—1951-1960

Jazz—1961-1970

Jazz—1971-1980

Jazz—1981-1990

Jazz—1991-2000

Jazz—Interpretation (Phrasing, dynamics, etc.)

Jazz—Lead sheets
UF Lead sheets for jazz

Jazz—Brazil
NT Bossa nova (Music)

Jazz—United States
USE Jazz
Jazz audiences *(May Subd Geog)* [ML3505.8-ML3509]
BT Music audiences
Jazz band music
USE Big band music
Jazz bands
USE Big bands
Jazz dance
BT Dancing
Jazz duets
USE Jazz
Jazz ensembles
USE *headings which include the words* jazz ensemble *as a medium qualifier, e.g.* Concertos (Flute with jazz ensemble); Flute with jazz ensemble; Jazz ensemble with orchestra; Suites (Jazz ensemble)
     Jazz
Jazz festivals *(May Subd Geog)*
BT Music festivals
Jazz music
USE Jazz
Jazz musicians *(May Subd Geog)*
BT Musicians
Jazz nonets
USE Jazz
Jazz octets
USE Jazz
Jazz quartets
USE Jazz
Jazz quintets
USE Jazz
Jazz septets
USE Jazz
Jazz sextets
USE Jazz
Jazz singers *(May Subd Geog)*
Jazz songs
USE Jazz vocals
Jazz trios
USE Jazz
Jazz vocals *(May Subd Geog)*
  Here are entered songs performed in jazz style by a vocalist, vocal ensemble, or chorus, generally accompanied by a solo instrument, jazz ensemble, or big band.
UF Jazz songs
     Jazz vocals—United States
     Scat singing
     Songs, Jazz
     Vocals, Jazz

BT   Big band music
       Jazz
       Popular music

Jazz vocals—Lead sheets
    UF   Lead sheets for jazz vocals

Jazz vocals—United States
    USE   Jazz vocals

Jehovah's Witnesses *(May Subd Geog)*
    [BX8525-BX8528]
    Here are entered works on members of the Watch Tower Bible and Tract Society.
    BT   African Americans—Religion

Jesse Owens Building of the United States Postal Service (Cleveland, Ohio)
    UF   Owens Building of the United States Postal Service (Cleveland, Ohio)
            Owens Finance Station (Cleveland, Ohio)
    BT   Post office buildings—Ohio

Jesus Christ—African American interpretations
    UF   Jesus Christ—Negro interpretations
            [Former Heading]
    BT   African Americans—Religion

Jesus Christ—Negro interpretations
    USE   Jesus Christ—African American interpretations

Jesus music
    USE   Contemporary Christian music

Jewelry, Black
    USE   Blacks—Jewelry

Jewish-African American relations
    USE   African Americans—Relations with Jews

Jewish-Black relations
    USE   Blacks—Relations with Jews

Jews—Relations with African Americans
    USE   African Americans—Relations with Jews

Jews—Relations with Blacks
    USE   Blacks—Relations with Jews

Jews, African American
    USE   African American Jews

Job bias
    USE   Discrimination in employment

Job discrimination
    USE   Discrimination in employment

John Brown Farm State Historic Site (North Elba, N.Y.) *(Not Subd Geog)*
    UF   Brown Farm State Historic Site (North Elba, N.Y.)
    BT   Historic sites—New York (State)

John Brown series (Gouache painting)
    USE   Lawrence, Jacob, 1917- John Brown series

John Brown's Raid, Harpers Ferry, W.Va., 1859
    USE   Harpers Ferry (W.Va.)—History—John Brown's Raid, 1859

John Henry (Legendary character)
    BT   African Americans—Folklore

John Newbery Medal books
    USE   Newbery Medal

Johnson C. Smith Theological Seminary (Presbyterian USA)
    BT   Interdenominational Theological Center (Atlanta, Ga.)

Johnson C. Smith University (Charlotte, N.C.)
    BT   Historically Black Colleges and Universities—North Carolina
            Private universities and colleges
            United Negro College Fund Institutions

Journalism, African American
    USE   African American press

Journalism, Ethnic
    USE   Ethnic press

Journalists, African American
    USE   African American journalists

Journalists, Minority
    USE   Minority journalists

Journals, Scholarly
    USE   Scholarly periodicals

Judges, African American
    USE   African American judges

Junior colleges *(May Subd Geog) [LB2328]*
    UF   Two-year colleges
    BT   Historically Black Colleges and Universities
    NT   Bishop (S.D.) State Junior College (Mobile, Ala.)
            Carver State Technical College (Mobile, Ala.)
            Clinton Junior College (Rock Hill, S.C.)
            Coahoma Junior College (Clarksdale, Miss.)
            Concordia College (Selma, Ala.)
            Denmark Technical College (Denmark, S.C.)
            Drake (J.F.) Technical College (Huntsville, Ala.)
            Hinds Junior College (Utica, Miss.)
            Lawson State Community College (Birmingham, Ala.)
            Lewis College of Business (Detroit, Mich.)
            Mary Holmes College (West Point, Miss.)
            Natchez Junior College (Natchez, Miss.)
            Prentiss Institute Junior College (Prentiss, Miss.)
            Saint Philip's College (San Antonio, Tex.)
            Shorter College (North Little Rock, Ark.)
            Trenholm State Technical College (Montgomery, Ala.)

K

Kansas-Nebraska Bill *[E433]*
    BT   Missouri compromise
            Slavery—United States

Kappa Alpha Psi Fraternity
    BT   Greek letter societies

Kentucky State University (Frankfort, Ky.)
BT   Historically Black Colleges and Universities—
            Kentucky
      Public universities and colleges
      State universities and colleges

King, Martin Luther
      USE King, Martin Luther, Jr., 1929-1968

King, Martin Luther, Jr., 1929-1968
UF   King, Martin Luther [Former Heading]
The subdivisions provided under this heading represent, for the
greater part, standard subdivisions established by LCSH useable under
any person and do not necessarily pertain to Martin Luther King, Jr., e.g.
Du Bois, William Edward Burghardt, 1868-1963—Archives.

—Abstracts

—Adaptations
      Use under individuals such as artists or composers for discus-
      sions of adaptations by others of their creative works. For discus-
      sions of an individual's adaptations of themes from others, see
      —Sources.

—Adversaries
      Use for discussions of contemporaries who opposed the person's
      point of view or work.

—Aesthetics
      Use for discussions of the individual's philosophy of art or
      beauty, whether explicitly stated or inferred from his creative
      works.

—Alcohol use
      Use for works about the person's use or abuse of alcohol. See
      also —Drug use.

—Allegory
      See —Symbolism

—Ancestry
      See —Family

—Anecdotes
      Use for collections of brief narratives of true incidents from the
      individual's life.

—Anecdotes, facetiae, satire, etc.
      See —Anecdotes
            —Humor

—Anniversaries, etc.
      Use for works dealing with the anniversary celebration itself.
      Do not use for works merely published on the occasion of an
      anniversary.

—Appreciation *(May Subd Geog)*
      Use under persons active in the fine arts, music, and performing
      arts for works on public response and reception, praise, etc. of the
      person's artistic works. For works consisting of critical analysis
      or interpretation of artistic works without biographical details, see
      —Criticism and interpretation. For works on public opinion about
      the person, see —Public opinion. For works on the person's impact
      on other persons, groups, movements, etc., see —Influence. For
      works on systems of beliefs and rituals connected with divine
      persons or saints, see —Cult.

—Archives
      Use for collections or discussions of documentary materials or
      records relating to the person's public or private activities, includ-
      ing manuscripts, diaries, correspondence, photographs, or other
items of historical interest. See also —Correspondence;
—Diaries; —Manuscripts; —Notebooks, sketchbooks, etc.

—Archives—Access control

—Archives—Catalogs

—Archives—Microform catalogs

—Art

—Art collections

—Art patronage
      Use for works about the person's support and patronage of the arts.

—Assassination

—Assassination attempt

—Assassination attempts

—Associates
      See —Friends and associates

—Attitude towards [specific topic]
      See —Views on [specific topic]

—Audiotape catalogs

—Authorship
      Use for discussions of the validity of attributing authorship of
      works to the person. For discussions of a non-literary person's
      literary ability and accomplishments see —Literary art.

—Autobiography
      USE—[name of person]

—Autographs
      Use for collections or discussions of the person's autographs or
      handwriting.

—Autographs—Facsimiles

—Autographs, Spurious
      See —Forgeries

—Awards

—Bibliography
      Use for lists of publications by or about the person. For bibliog-
      raphies of bibliographies about the person, assign the headings: 1.
      Bibliography—Bibliography—[name of person]. 2. [name of per-
      son]—Bibliography.

—Bibliography—Catalogs

—Bibliography—Exhibitions

—Bibliography—Microform catalogs

—Biography
      USE —[name of person]

—Birth
      Use for works discussing the events of an individual's birth,
      including birthdays, the date or year of the person's birth, etc. See
      also —Birthplace.

—Birthplace

—Books and reading
Use for works dealing with written material known to have been read by the person, his reading habits and interests, books borrowed from friends or libraries, etc. See also —Library.

—Burial
See —Death and burial

—Captivity, [dates]
Use for discussing periods in which the person was held captive in bondage or confinement, especially under house arrest, as a hostage, or in battle. Do not use under persons also known as literary authors. For works discussing periods in which the person was actually imprisoned in a correctional institution or prisoner of war camp, see —Imprisonment. See also —Exile; —Kidnapping, [date].

—Career in [specific field or discipline]
Use for works limited to describing events in the person's occupational life or participation in a profession or vocation. Assign an additional heading for the field. Do not use under persons also known as literary authors. For works discussing the person's actual substantive contributions or accomplishments in a specific field or topic, whether made as a result of a vocation or an avocation, see —Contributions in [specific field or topic]. See also —Resignation from office.

—Caricatures and cartoons
Use for collections or discussions of caricatures or pictorial humor about the person. See also —Comic books, strips, etc.

—Cartoons, satire, etc.
See —Caricatures and cartoons
   —Humor

—Catalogs
Use under artists and craftspersons for works listing their art works or crafts which are available or located in particular institutions or places. See also —Archives—Catalogs; —Archives—Microform catalogs; —Audiotape catalogs; —Bibliography—Catalogs —Bibliography—Exhibitions; —Bibliography—Microform catalogs; —Catalogs raisonnes; —Compact disc catalogs; —Correspondence—Catalogs; —Correspondence—Microform catalogs; —Discography; —Exhibitions; —Film catalogs; —Library—Catalogs; —Library—Microform catalogs; —Manuscripts—Catalogs; —Manuscripts—Microform catalog; —Slides—Catalogs; —Thematic catalogs; —Video catalogs.

—Catalogs raisonnes
Use for comprehensive listings of an artist's or craftsperson's works in one medium or all media, usually chronologically or systematically arranged, and accompanied by descriptive or critical notes.

—Centennial celebrations, etc.
See —Anniversaries, etc.

—Character
See —Ethics
   —Psychology
   —Religion

—Childhood and youth

—Chronology
Use for works which list by date the events in the life of a person.

—Clothing

—Coin collections

—Collectibles *(May Subd Geog)*
Use for works about items of interest to collectors which are related to the person or portray him or topics associated with him. See also —Autographs; —Museums; —Numismatics; —Portraits; —Posters.

—Comic books, strips, etc.

—Commentaries
See —Criticism and interpretation

—Compact disc catalogs

—Companions
See —Friends and associates

—Concordances
Use as a form subdivision for indexes to the principle works found in the writings of the person.

—Congresses

—Contributions in [specific field or topic]
Use for works discussing the person's actual substantive contributions or accomplishments in a specific field or topic, whether made as a result of a vocation or an avocation. Also use for discussions of the person's philosophy of system or thought on a particular topic which he propounded or imparted to others. Use this subdivision to bring out one specific field or topic for a person active in more than one field, or to bring out subtopics or aspects of a particular field to which an individual contributed. Assign an additional heading for the field or topic. Do not use this subdivision for a work discussing the person's general contributions in the discipline or field with which he is solely or primarily identified. Assign the person's name without subdivision in such cases. Do not use under persons also known as literary authors. For works limited to describing events in the person's occupational life or participation in a profession or vocation, see —Career in [specific field or discipline].

—Correspondence
Use as a form or topical subdivision for the letters from and/or to the person. Assign as additional heading for individual correspondents.

—Correspondence—Catalogs

—Correspondence—Microform catalogs

—Costume
See —Clothing

—Criticism and interpretation
Use for works consisting of critical analysis or interpretation of the person's artistic works or endeavors without biographical details. Use this subdivision only under persons active in the fine arts, music, and performing arts. For works on public response and reception, praise, etc. of the person's artistic works, see —Appreciation.

—Date of birth
See —Birth

—Death and burial
Use for works on the person's death, funeral, or burial, including the person's last illness.

—Death mask

—Diaries
Use for collections or discussions of the person's diaries. Also use for individual diaries.

—Dictionaries
See also —Encyclopedias

—Disciples
Use for works discussing persons who received instruction from the individual or accepted his doctrines or teachings and assisted in spreading or implementing them.

—Discography
Use for lists or catalogs of sound recordings by or about the person. See also —Audiotape catalogs.

—Diseases
See —Health

—Divorce

—Drama
Use as a form subdivision for plays and musical dramatic works, including operas, ballets, musical comedies, etc. about the person. For criticism or discussions of plays, etc. about an individual, assign [name of person]—In fiction, drama, poetry, etc. as a topical heading.

—Dramaturgy
Use under composers for discussions of their technique in writing operas and other dramatic works. Do not use under persons also known as literary authors.

—Drug use
Use for works about the person's use or abuse of drugs. See also —Alcohol use.

—Dwellings
See —Homes and haunts

—Early life
See —Childhood and youth

—Education
See —Knowledge and learning

—Employees
Use for works discussing persons employed by the individual, including household servants, etc.

—Encyclopedias
See also —Dictionaries

—Enemies
See —Adversaries

—Estate
Use for discussions of the aggregate of property or liabilities of all kinds that a person leaves for disposal at his death, including discussions or cases of contested estates. See also —Will.

—Ethics
Use for discussion of the individual's ethical system and values. See also —Religion.

—Ethnological collections

—Ethnomusicological collections

—Exhibitions
Use for works about exhibitions on the life or work of the person, including catalogs of single exhibitions. See also —Bibliography—Exhibitions.

—Exile *(May Subd Geog)*

—Family
Use for discussions of the person's family or relations with family members. Also use for genealogical works. Assign an additional heading for the name of the family. See also —Marriage.

—Fiction
Use as a form subdivision for works of fiction about the person. For criticism or discussions of fiction about a person, assign [name of person] in fiction, drama, poetry, etc. as a topical heading.

—Film catalogs

—Finance, Personal
Use for discussions of the person's financial affairs. See also —Estate; —Will.

—Folktales
See —Legends

—Forgeries *(May Subd Geog)*
Use for discussions of forgeries of the person's creative works or signature. In the case of individual forgeries, assign an additional heading for the name of the forger.

—Freemasonry
Use for works discussing the person's membership or participation in the Freemasons.

—Frequented places
See —Homes and haunts

—Friends and associates
Use for discussions of the person's close and immediate contacts such as companions, co-workers, etc. See also —Adversaries; —Disciples; —Employees; —Family; —Relations with [specific class of persons or ethnic group].

—Funeral
See —Death and burial

—Genealogy
See —Family

—Grave
See —Tomb

—Handwriting
See —Autographs

—Harmony
Use under composers for works discussing their uses of harmony.

—Haunts
See —Homes and haunts

—Health
Use for works about the person's state of health, including diseases suffered and accounts of specific diseases. For accounts of specific diseases assign an additional heading of the type: [disease]—Patients—[place]—Biography. See also —Alcohol use; —Drug use; —Mental health.

—Homes and haunts *(May Subd Geog)*
Use for works discussing the person's homes or dwellings, favorite places, places he or she habitually frequented, or places associated with the person in some way. See also —Birthplace; —Journeys; —Palaces.

—Homes and haunts—Guidebooks

—Humor
Use as a form subdivision for humorous works about the person as well as for works about the person's sense of humor or use of humor. For pictorial humor, see —Caricatures and cartoons.

—Iconography
See —Pictorial works

—Imitations
See —Parodies, imitations, etc.

—Impeachment

—Imprisonment
Use for works discussing periods in which the person was actually imprisoned in a correctional institution or a prisoner of war camp. For works discussing periods in which the person was held captive in bondage or confinement, especially under house arrest, as a hostage, or in battle, use —Captivity, [dates]. See also —Exile.

—In literature
Use for discussions of the person as a theme in belles lettres, including musical dramatic works and individual literary genres. For literary works about the person, or in which he or she appears as a character, assign the appropriate form subdivision, e.g. —Drama; —Fiction; —Literary collections; —Poetry.

—Indexes
See also —Concordances

—Influence
Use for works discussing the person's impact on other persons, groups, movements, etc. Assign an additional heading for the person or group influenced. For works on public response and reception, praise, etc., of the person's artistic works, see —Appreciation.

—Information services

—Interment
See —Death and burial

—Interpretation
See —Criticism and interpretation

—Interviews
Use for works consisting of transcripts of what was said during the course of interviews or conversations with the person on one or more occasions.

—Journals
See —Diaries

—Journeys *(May Subd Geog)*
Use for works about voyages and travels undertaken by the person. When the subdivision is further subdivided by place, assign as additional heading of the type [place]—Description and travel. See also —Exile.

—Journeys—Guidebooks

—Juvenile drama

—Juvenile fiction

—Juvenile films

—Juvenile humor

—Juvenile literature

—Juvenile poetry

—Juvenile sound recordings

—Kidnapping, [date]

—Knowledge—Agriculture, [America, etc.]
Use for works discussing the person's knowledge of a specific topic, whether explicitly stated or inferred from his life and work. Also use for discussions of the person's educational background in a specific topic. Assign an additional heading for the specific topic. For works on the person's opinions or attitudes on a specific topic, whether explicitly stated or inferred, see —Views on [specific topic].

—Knowledge and learning
Use for works about the person's formal or informal learning or scholarship in general. For knowledge or learning of specific topics, see —Knowledge—[topic].

—Language
See also —Literary art

—Language—Glossaries, etc.

—Last illness
See —Death and burial

—Last years
See also —Death and burial

—Leadership, Military
See —Military leadership

—Learning
See —Knowledge and learning

—Legends
Use as a form subdivision for stories about the person which have come down from the past and which are popularly taken as historical though not verifiable. See also —Romances.

—Letters
See —Correspondence

—Library
Use for works discussing the person's own library. See also —Books and reading.

—Library—Catalogs

—Library—Microform catalogs

—Library resources
Use for works describing the resources or special collections available in libraries for research or study about the person.

—Literary art
Use for discussions of a non-literary person's literary ability and accomplishments. Do not use under multi-career persons who are also recognized as literary authors.

—Literary collections
Use for literary anthologies about the person which involve two or more literary forms. For anthologies in one literary form, see the form, e.g. —Drama; —Fiction; —Poetry.

—Litigation
See —Trials, litigation, etc.

—Manuscripts
Use for works discussing writings made by hand, typewriter, etc., by or about the person. Do not use for individual works in manuscript form. See also —Archives; —Autographs; —Correspondence; —Diaries; —Notebooks, sketchbooks, etc.

—Manuscripts—Catalogs

—Manuscripts—Facsimiles

—Manuscripts—Indexes

—Manuscripts—Microform catalogs

—Map collections

—Marriage
See also —Divorce

—Medals
Use for works about medals issued to commemorate the person or his work.

—Meditations
Use as a form subdivision for works containing descriptions of thoughts or reflections on the spiritual significance of the person's life or deeds.

—Mental health
Use for works discussing the person's state of mental health, including mental illness and accounts of specific mental disorders. For accounts of specific disorders or situations, assign an additional heading of the type: [disease]—Patients—[place]—Biography; Psychotherapy patients—[place]—Biography; etc.

—Military leadership

—Miscellanea
Use for collections of curiosa relating to the person as well as for texts about the person in question and answer format.

—Monuments *(May Subd Geog)*
Use for works about monuments erected in honor of the person. See also —Museums; —Shrines; —Statues; —Tomb.

—Motives, themes
See —Themes, motives

—Museums *(May Subd Geog)*
Use for works on museums devoted to the person. See also —Archives; —Collectibles; —Death mask; —Monuments; —Relics; —Shrines; —Tomb.

—Music
See —Songs and music

—Musical instrument collections

—Musical settings
Use as a form subdivision for musical scores or sound recordings in which writings or words of the person have been set to music.

—Name
Use for discussions of the history, orthography, etymology, etc., of the person's name. See also —Titles.

—Natural history collections

—Notebooks, sketchbooks, etc.
Use for collections or discussions of the person's notebooks, sketchbooks, etc. Also use for individual works.

—Notebooks, sketchbooks, etc.—Facsimiles

—Numismatic collections
See also —Coin collections

—Numismatics
Use for works discussing the representation of the person on coins, tokens, medals, paper money, etc. See also —Medals.

—Old age
See —Last years

—Opponents
See —Adversaries

—On postage stamps
Use for works about the portrayal of the person on postage stamps.

—Oratory
Use for works discussing the person's public speaking ability.

—Outlines, syllabi, etc.

—Palaces *(May Subd Geog)*

—Pardon
Use for works about the person's legal release from the penalty of an offense.

—Parodies, imitations, etc.
Use as both a form and topical subdivision for imitations, either comic or distorted, of the person's creative works.

—Patronage of the arts
See —Art patronage

—Performances *(May Subd Geog)*
Use under performing artists or performers of all types for works about their performances. Also use under composers, choreographers, etc. for works about performances of the compositions or works.

—Periodicals

—Personal finance
See —Finance, Personal

—Personality
See —Psychology

—Philosophy
Use for discussions of the individual's personal philosophy. Do not use under names of philosophers. See also —Aesthetics; —Ethics; —Religion.

—Photograph collections

—Pictorial humor
See —Caricatures and cartoons

—Pictorial works
Use for works consisting of pictures or visual images relating to the person. See also —Art; —Caricatures and cartoons; —Comic books, strips, etc.

—Place of birth
See —Birthplace

—Places frequented
See —Homes and haunts

—Poetry
Use as a form subdivision for works of poetry about the person. For criticism or discussions of poetry about a person, assign [name of person]—In literature as a topical heading.

—Political and social views
Use for works discussing the person's political and/or social views in general. For works on specific topics, see —Views on [specific topic].

—Portraits
See also —Caricatures and cartoons; —Death mask; —Numismatics; —On postage stamps; —Posters; —Self-portraits; —Statues; —Poster collections.

—Poster collections

—Posters
Use for collections or discussions of posters depicting the person.

—Prayer-books and devotions
Use as a form subdivision, particularly under divine persons or saints, for works of devotions directed to those persons whose help or prayers are requested.

—Professional life
See —Career in [specific field or discipline]

—Psychology
Use for discussions or interpretations of the person's psychological traits, personality, character, etc. See also —Mental health.

—Public opinion
Use for works about public opinion about the person. Do not use under persons also known as literary authors. For works on public response and reception, praise, etc. of the person's artistic works, use —Appreciation.

—Public speaking
See —Oratory

—Quotations
Use for collections or discussions of quotations by or about the person.

—Reading habits
See —Books and reading

—Relations with [specific class of persons or ethnic group]
Assign an additional heading for the specific group with appropriate subdivision if necessary.

—Relations with employees
See —Employees

—Relations with family
See —Family

—Relations with friends and associates
See —Friends and associates

—Relics

—Religion
Use for discussions of the person's religious beliefs and practices. Also includes the person's knowledge or views on religion in general. See also —Ethics.

—Residences
See —Homes and haunts

—Resignation from office

—Rhetoric
See —Literary art
—Oratory

—Romances

—Satire
See —Humor

—Sayings
See —Quotations

—Scholarship
See —Knowledge and learning

—Scientific apparatus collections

—Seal
Use for works discussing the devices, such as emblems, symbols, or words used by an individual to authenticate his writings or documents.

—Self-portraits
Use for reproductions or discussions of self-portraits by the person.

—Sermons
Use as a form subdivision, particularly under divine persons or saints, for single sermons or collections of sermons about the person.

—Servants
See —Employees

—Sexual behavior

—Shrines *(May Subd Geog)*
Use for works discussing structures or places consecrated or devoted to the person and serving as places of religious veneration or pilgrimage.

—Sketchbooks
See —Notebooks, sketchbooks, etc.

—Slide collections

—Slides

—Slides—Catalogs

—Social views
See —Political and social views

—Societies, etc.
Use for works discussing organizations devoted to or specializing in the person's life or work.

—Songs and music
Use as a form subdivision for collections or single works of vocal or instrumental music about the person. For collections or single works in musical dramatic forms such as operas, ballets, musical comedies, etc., use —Drama.

—Sources
Use for discussions of the person's sources of ideas or inspiration for his endeavors or creative works. For discussions of adaptations by others of an individual's creative works, see —Adaptations.

—Spiritual life
See —Religion

—Statues *(May Subd Geog)*
Use for works discussing or containing reproductions of statues representing the person.

—Stories of operas
See —Stories, plots, etc.

—Stories, plots, etc.
Use under composers for works discussing or summarizing the stories or plots of their operas.

—Study and teaching *(May Subd Geog)*
Use for works on methods of studying and teaching about the person.

—Style, Literary
See —Literary art

—Symbolism
Use for discussions of the symbols employed by the person in his creative works.

—Table-talk
See —Quotations

—Tales
See —Legends

—Teachings
Use for works discussing in general the body of knowledge, precepts, or doctrines the person taught to others.

—Thematic catalogs
Use under composers for listings of the themes of their musical compositions. Do not use under persons also known as literary authors.

—Themes, motives

—Titles

—Tomb

—Travels
See —Journeys

—Trials, litigation, etc.
Use for proceedings or discussions of proceedings of civil or criminal actions to which the person is a party.

—Video catalogs

—Views on [specific topic]

—Views on aesthetics
See —Aesthetics

—Views on ethics
See —Ethics

—Views on politics and society
See —Political and social views

—Views on religion
See —Religion

—Views on society
See —Political and social views

—Voyages
See —Journeys

—Will
Use for discussions of the person's legal declaration regarding the disposition of his property or estate, including discussions or cases of contested wills. See also —Estate.

—Writing skill
See —Literary art

—Written works
Use under persons active in the fine arts, music and performing arts for discussions, listings, etc. of their non-literary textual works.

—Yearbooks
See —Periodicals

—Youth
See —Childhood and youth

King, Martin Luther, Jr., 1929-1968—Monuments
(May Subd Geog)

King, Martin Luther, Jr., 1929-1968—Monuments—Georgia

King Federal Building (Victoria, Tex.)
USE Martin Luther King, Jr. Federal Building (Victoria, Tex.)

King National Historic Site (Atlanta, Ga.)
USE Martin Luther King, Junior, National Historic Site (Atlanta, Ga.)

Knoxville College (Knoxville, Tenn.)
BT Historically Black Colleges and Universities—Tennessee
Private universities and colleges
United Negro College Fund Institutions

Knoxville College-Morristown Campus (Morristown, Tenn.)
BT Historically Black Colleges and Universities—Tennessee
Private universities and colleges
United Negro College Fund Institutions

Kwanza
    USE Kwanzaa
Kwanzaa *(May Subd Geog) [GT4403]*
    UF   Kwanza
    BT   Harvest festivals—United States

L

Labor, Organized
    USE Trade-unions
Labor laws and legislation *(May Subd Geog)*
    UF   Employees—Legal status, laws, etc.
         Law, Industrial
         Law, Labor
         Work—Law and legislation
         Working class—Legal status, laws, etc.
    NT   Blacks—Employment—Law and legislation
         Discrimination in employment—Law and
           legislation
         Reverse discrimination in employment—Law
           and legislation
Labor leaders, African American
    USE African American labor leaders
Labor organizations
    USE Trade-unions
Labor supply—Effect of education on
    UF   Education and employment
         Employment and education
Labor unions
    USE Trade-unions
Lane College (Jackson, Tenn.)
    BT   Historically Black Colleges and Universities—
           Tennessee
         Private universities and colleges
         United Negro College Fund Institutions
Langston University (Langston, Okla.)
    BT   Historically Black Colleges and Universities—
           Oklahoma
         Public universities and colleges
         State universities and colleges
Language and racism
    USE Racism in language
Law, Industrial
    USE Labor laws and legislation
Law, Labor
    USE Labor laws and legislation
Law enforcement *(May Subd Geog)*
    UF   Enforcement of law
    NT   Discrimination in law enforcement
Law students, African American
    USE African American law students
Lawmakers
    USE Legislators

Lawrence, Jacob, 1917- John Brown series
    UF   John Brown series (Gouache painting)
**Lawson State Community College
    (Birmingham, Ala.)**
    BT   Historically Black Colleges and Universities—
           Alabama
         Junior Colleges
         Public universities and colleges
Lawyers, African American
    USE African American lawyers
Lead sheets for jazz
    USE Jazz—Lead sheets
Lead sheets for jazz vocals
    USE Jazz vocals—Lead sheets
Leadership, African American
    USE African American leadership
Learned periodicals
    USE Scholarly periodicals
Legends *(May Subd Geog) [PZ8.1 (Juvenile)]*
    UF   Folk-tales
         Traditions
         Urban legends
Legislators *(May Subd Geog)*
    UF   Lawmakers
    NT   County council members
         Women legislators
Legislators, African American
    USE African American legislators
LeMoyne-Owen College (Memphis, Tenn.)
    BT   Historically Black Colleges and Universities—
           Tennessee
         Private universities and colleges
         United Negro College Fund Institutions
Lesbians, African American
    USE African American lesbians
Lewis College of Business (Detroit, Mich.)
    BT   Historically Black Colleges and Universities—
           Michigan
         Junior Colleges
         Private universities and colleges
Libel and slander *(May Subd Geog)*
    NT   Hate speech
Liberation movements (Civil rights)
    USE Civil rights movements
Librarians, African American
    USE African American librarians
Libraries, African American
    USE African Americans and libraries
Libraries, African American academic
    USE African American academic libraries
Libraries, Black
    USE Libraries and Blacks

Libraries and African Americans
  USE African Americans and libraries
Libraries and Blacks *(May Subd Geog)*
  UF   Black libraries
       Blacks and libraries
       Libraries, Blacks
       Libraries and Negroes *[Former Heading]*
       Library services to Blacks
  BT   Blacks
Libraries and minorities *(May Subd Geog) [Z711.8]*
  UF   Library services to minorities
       Minorities and libraries
  BT   Minorities
  RT   Instructional materials centers—Services to
         minorities
  NT   Academic libraries—Services to minorities
       African Americans and libraries
       Library orientation for minority college students
       Public libraries—Services to minorities
       School libraries—Services to minorities
Libraries and Negroes
  USE African Americans and libraries
       Libraries and Blacks
Libraries and the socially handicapped *(May Subd
  Geog) [Z711.92.S6]*
  UF   Library services to the socially handicapped
       Socially handicapped and libraries
  BT   Socially handicapped
Library orientation for minority college students
  (May Subd Geog) [Z711.2]
  BT   Libraries and minorities
       Minority college students
Library resources on Negroes
  USE African Americans—Library resources
Library services to African Americans
  USE African Americans and libraries
Library services to Blacks
  USE Libraries and Blacks
Library services to minorities
  USE Libraries and minorities
Library services to the socially handicapped
  USE Libraries and the socially handicapped
Life histories
  USE Biography
**Lincoln, Abraham, 1809-1865—Relations with
  African Americans**
Lincoln-Douglas debates, 1858 *[E457.4]*
Lincoln University (Jefferson City, Mo.)
  BT   Historically Black Colleges and Universities—
         Missouri
       Public universities and colleges
       State universities and colleges

Lincoln University (Lincoln University, Pa.)
  BT   Historically Black Colleges and Universities—
         Pennsylvania
       Public universities and colleges
  Here are listed subdivisions that have been established by LCSH
  for individual universities and colleges. For example, an alumni
  directory of Knoxville College would be constructed: Knoxville
  College (Knoxville, Tenn.)—Alumni and alumnea—Directories.

—**Accounting**
—**Accreditation**
—**Administration**
—**Admission**
—**Aerial views**
—**Alumni and alumnae**
— —**Directories**
— —**Societies, etc.**
—**Anniversaries, etc.**
—**Archives**
—**Auditing**
—**Awards**
  UF Lincoln University (Lincoln University, Pa.)—
        Prizes *[Former Heading]*
—**Bands**
—**Baseball**
—**Basketball**
—**Benefactors**
—**Bibliography**
—**Biography**
—**Buildings**
— —**Access for the physically handicapped**
—**Charters**
—**Choral organizations**
—**Coin collections**
—Course catalogs
  USE Lincoln University (Lincoln University,
         Pa.)—Curricula
—**Curricula**
  UF Lincoln University (Lincoln University, Pa.)—
        Course catalogs
      Lincoln University (Lincoln University, Pa.)—
        Curricula—Catalogs

— —**Catalogs**
 USE Lincoln University (Lincoln University, Pa.)—
  Curricula

—**Data processing**

—**Degrees**

—**Directories**

— —Telephone
 USE Lincoln University (Lincoln University, Pa.)—
  Telephone directories

—**Discipline**

—**Dissertations**

—**Employees**

— —**Political activity**

—**Endowments**

—**Entrance examination**
 Here are entered compilations of entrance examination
 questions and answers. Works on the requirements for admission to Lincoln University are entered under Lincoln University (Lincoln University, Pa.)—Entrance requirements.

—**Entrance requirements**
 Here are entered works on the requirements for admission
 to Lincoln University. Compilations of entrance examination
 questions and answers are entered under Lincoln University
 (Lincoln University, Pa.)—Entrance examinations.

— —**Biology, [Mathematics, etc.]**

— —**Mathematics**

— —**Study guides**

—**Evaluation**

—**Examinations**
 Here are entered works on examinations, as well as compilations
 of examination questions and answers. Works on examinations on
 specific topics are entered under this heading further subdivided by
 the topic, with an additional heading, if appropriate under the topic
 further subdivided by Examinations or Examination questions, etc.,
 e.g. 1. Lincoln University (Lincoln University, Pa.)—Examinations—Mathematics. 2. Mathematics—Examinations.

— —**Biology, [Mathematics, etc.]**

— —**Mathematics**

— —**Study Guides**

—**Faculty**

— —**Discipline**

— —**Pensions**
 UF Lincoln University (Lincoln University, Pa.)—
  Faculty—Salaries, pensions, etc.
  [Former Heading]

— —**Salaries, etc.**

 UF Lincoln University (Lincoln University, Pa.)—
  Faculty—Salaries, pensions, etc.
  [Former Heading]

— —Salaries, pensions, etc.
 USE Lincoln University (Lincoln University, Pa.)—
  Faculty—Pensions
   Lincoln University (Lincoln University, Pa.)—
   Faculty—Salaries, etc.

—**Finance**

—**Football**

—**Freshmen**

—**Funds and scholarships**

—**Golf** *[GV969.5H]*

—**Graduate students**

—**Graduate work**

—Guide-books
 USE Lincoln University (Lincoln University, Pa.)—
  Guidebooks

—**Guidebooks**
 UF Lincoln University (Lincoln University, Pa.)—
  Guide-books *[Former Heading]*

—**History**

— —**19th century**

— —**Civil War, 1861-1865**

— —**20th century**

— —**Chronology**

— —**Sources**

—**Language**

—**Libraries**

—**Maps**

—**Mascots**

—**Museums**

—**Open admission**

—**Orchestras**
 UF Lincoln University (Lincoln University, Pa.)—
  Orchestras and bands *[Former Heading]*

—Orchestras and bands
 USE Lincoln University—Bands
   Lincoln University—Orchestras

—Parking

—Periodicals

—Pictorial works

—Planning

—Poetry

—Portraits

—Presidents

—Prizes
　　USE Lincoln University (Lincoln University, Pa.)—
　　　　Awards

—Public opinion

—Public relations
　　UF Public relations—Lincoln University
　　　　(Lincoln University, Pa.)

—Public services

—Registers

—Regulations

—Religion

—Research grants

—Riots

—Sanitary affairs

—Societies, etc.

—Songs and music

—Sports

—Statistics

—Strike [date]

—Student housing

—Students

— —Caricatures and cartoons

— —Mental health services

— —Yearbooks

—Swimming

—Telephone directories
　　UF Lincoln University (Lincoln University, Pa.)—
　　　　Directories—Telephone
　　　　[Former Heading]

—Track-athletics

—Volleyball

—Wrestling

Linguistic minorities *(May Subd Geog)*
　　UF Minority languages

The Links, Inc. *(May Subd Geog)*
　　BT Women—Societies and clubs

Literacy tests (Election law) *(May Subd Geog)*
　　UF Voting—Literacy tests
　　BT Suffrage

Literary awards
　　USE Literary prizes

Literary movements *(May Subd Geog) [PN597]*
　　UF Movements, Literary
　　NT Negritude (Literary movement)

Literary prizes *(May Subd Geog) [PN171.P75]*
　　UF Book awards
　　　　Book prizes
　　　　Literary awards
　　　　Literature—Awards
　　　　Literature—Prizes
　　NT Coretta Scott King Book Award
　　　　Ebony's Gertrude Johnson Williams Writing
　　　　　Contest

Literature—Awards
　　USE Literary prizes

Literature—Black authors *[PN6068 (Collections)]*
　　UF Black literature
　　　　Negro literature *[Former Heading]*
　　SA *subdivision* Black authors *under headings for*
　　　　individual literature and genres; and sub-
　　　　division African American authors under
　　　　headings in the field of American litera-
　　　　ture, e.g. English poetry—Black authors;
　　　　Drama—Black authors; American litera-
　　　　ture—African American authors

Literature—Prizes
　　USE Literary prizes

**Literature, Modern—20th Century—History and
criticism**
　　NT Negritude (Literary movement)

Livingstone College (Salisbury, N.C.)
　　BT Historically Black Colleges and Universities—
　　　　North Carolina
　　　　Private universities and colleges
　　　　United Negro College Fund Institutions

Local junior colleges
　　USE Community colleges

Local officials and employees *(May Subd Geog)*
　　NT County officials and employees
　　　　Municipal officials and employees

Los Angeles (Calif.)—Riot, 1965
　　USE Watts Riot, Los Angeles, Calif., 1965

Low income housing
　　USE Poor—Housing
　　　　Public housing

Low income people
USE Poor

Lutherans, African Americans
USE African American Lutherans

Lutherans, Negro
USE African American Lutherans

Lynch law
USE Lynching

Lynching *(May Subd Geog) [HV6455-HV6471]*
Here, without further subdivision, are entered general works on lynching, lynching in the United States on a whole, and in the Southern States.
UF Lynch law
BT Criminal justice, Administration of

M

Magazine publishing
USE Periodicals, Publishing of

Magazines
USE Periodicals

Magnet centers
USE Magnet schools

Magnet schools *(May Subd Geog) [LB2818]*
Here are entered works on schools offering special courses not available in the regular school curriculum and designed, often as an aid to school desegregation, to attract students on a voluntary basis from all parts of a school district without references to the usual attendance zone rules.
UF Magnet centers
Schools, Magnet
BT Public schools
RT School integration

Malcolm X Park (Washington, D.C.)
USE Meridian Hill Park (Washington, D.C.)

Malungeons
USE Melungeons

Mammies *(May Subd Geog)*
BT Slaves—United States

Manners and customs *(Not Subd Geog) [GT]*
Here are entered general works on folkways, customs, ceremonies, festivals, popular traditions, etc., treated collectively.
UF Folkways
Traditions
BT Ethnology
SA *subdivision* Social life and customs *under names of cities, etc., and under classes of persons and ethnic groups, e.g.* African Americans—Social life and customs
NT Folklore

Manpower utilization
USE Personnel management

Manumission of slaves
USE Slaves—Emancipation

March on Washington for Jobs and Freedom, Washington, D.C., 1963
UF March on Washington for Jobs and Freedom, 1963 *[Former Heading]*
BT Civil rights demonstrations—Washington (D.C.)

March on Washington for Jobs and Freedom, 1963
USE March on Washington for Jobs and Freedom, Washington, D.C., 1963

Marginal peoples
USE Marginality, Social

Marginality, Social *(May Subd Geog) [GN367 (Ethnology)] [HM136 (Sociology)] [HN50-HN942.5 (By country)]*
UF Marginal peoples
Social marginality
BT Assimilation (Sociology)
Culture conflict
RT Socially handicapped

Maroons *(May Subd Geog)*
UF Cimarrones
RT Blacks—West Indies
BT Fugitive slaves—West Indies

Marriage, Interracial
USE Interracial marriage

Marriage, Mixed
USE Intermarriage

Marriage law *(May Subd Geog)*
NT Miscegenation—Law and legislation

Marshall Federal Judiciary Building (Washington, D.C.)
USE Thurgood Marshall Federal Judiciary Building (Washington, D.C.)

Martin Luther King, Junior, Birthplace (Atlanta, Ga.)
BT Dwellings—Georgia

Martin Luther King, Junior, Center for Non-violent Social Change (Atlanta, Ga.)
BT Civil rights organizations

Martin Luther King, Junior, National Historic Site (Atlanta, Ga.)
UF King National Historic Site (Atlanta, Ga.)
BT Historic sites—Georgia
National parks and reserves—Georgia

Martin Luther King, Jr., Day *(May Subd Geog) [E185.97.K5]*
UF Birthday of Martin Luther King, Jr.
Martin Luther King Day *[Former Heading]*
BT Holidays—United States

Martin Luther King Day
USE Martin Luther King, Jr., Day

Martin Luther King, Jr. Federal Building (Victoria, Tex.)
UF King Federal Building (Victoria, Tex.)
BT Public buildings—Texas

Mary Holmes College (West Point, Miss.)
    BT   Historically Black Colleges and Universities—
            Mississippi
            Junior Colleges
            Private universities and colleges

Mary McLeod Bethune Council House (Washington, D.C.)
    BT   Dwellings—Washington (D.C.)

Mary McLeod Bethune Council House National Historic Site (Washington, D.C.) *(Not Subd Geog)*
    BT   Historic sites—Washington (D.C.)
            National parks and reserves—Washington (D.C.)

Maryland Eastern Shore, University of (Princess Anne, Md.)
    UF   University of Maryland-Eastern Shore
            (Princess Anne, Md.)
    BT   Historically Black Colleges and Universities—
            Maryland
            Public universities and colleges
            State universities and colleges

Mass media, African American
    USE African American mass media

Mass media and African Americans
    USE African Americans and mass media

Mass media and minorities *(May Subd Geog)*
    [P96.M5]
    BT   Minorities
    NT   African Americans in the newspaper industry
            Ethnic press
            Mass media and race relations

Mass media and race problems
    USE Mass media and race relations

Mass Media and race relations *(May Subd Geog)*
    UF   Mass media and race problems
            [Former Heading]
    BT   Mass media and minorities
            Race relations

Mass political behavior
    USE Political participation

Mathematicians, African American
    USE African American mathematicians

Mayors, African American
    USE African American mayors

Medals—United States
    NT   Spingarn Medal

Medical and health care industry
    USE Medical care

Medical care *(May Subd Geog)*
    UF   Delivery of health care
            Delivery of medical care
            Health care
            Health care delivery
            Health services
            Medical and health care industry
            Medical services
            Personal health services
    SA   *subdivision* Medical care *under names of individual military services and under individual wars, classes of persons, ethnic groups, and occupational groups, e.g.*
            United States Air Force—Medical care;
            World War, 1939-1945—Medical care;
            Construction industry—Employees—Medical care; African Americans—Medical care
    NT   Discrimination in medical care
            Mental health services

Medical colleges
    UF   Medical schools
    BT   Historically Black Colleges and Universities
    NT   Charles R. Drew University of Medicine and
            Science (Los Angeles, Calif.)
            Meharry Medical College (Nashville, Tenn.)
            Morehouse School of Medicine (Atlanta, Ga.)

Medical education *(May Subd Geog)*
    Here are entered general works on education in the field of medicine.
    UF   Education, Medical
            Medical personnel—Education
    NT   Discrimination in medical education

Medical personnel—Education
    USE Medical education

Medical profession
    USE Medicine

Medical schools
    USE Medical colleges

Medical services
    USE Medical care

Medicine *(May Subd Geog)*
    UF   Medical profession
    NT   Diseases
            Minorities in medicine
    SA   *subdivision* Medicine *under ethnic groups e.g.*
            African Americans—Medicine

Mediums, African American
    USE African American mediums

Meharry Medical College (Nashville, Tenn.)
    BT   Historically Black Colleges and Universities
            Medical colleges
            Private universities and colleges

Melanin
    RT   Melanism

Melanism
    BT   Color of man
    RT   Melanin

Melungeons *(May Subd Geog)*
    UF   Malungeons
    BT   African Americans—Appalachian Region
            Indians of North America—Mixed descent
            Mulattoes

Members of Congress (United States House of
   Representatives)
   USE United States. Congress. House

Members of Congress (United States Senate)
   USE United States. Congress. Senate

Memoirs
   USE Biography

Men, African American
   USE African American men

Mennonites, African American
   USE African American Mennonites

Mental health personnel, Minority
   USE Minority mental health personnel

Mental health services *(May Subd Geog)*
   [RA790-RA790.95]
   UF   Psychiatric care
           Psychiatric services
   BT   Medical care
   SA   *subdivision* Mental health services *under
           classes of persons and ethnic groups, e.g.*
           African Americans—Mental health serv-
           ices; *and subdivision* Students—Mental
           health services *under names of individual
           educational institutions, e.g.* Lincoln Uni-
           versity (Lincoln University, Pa.)—Stu-
           dents—Mental health services
   NT   Discrimination in mental health services

Merchant seamen, African American
   USE African American merchant seamen

Meridian Hill (Washington, D.C.) *(Not Subd Geog)*
   UF   Washington (D.C.). Meridian Hill

Meridian Hill Park (Washington, D.C.)
   UF   Malcolm X Park (Washington, D.C.)

Messianism, African American *(May Subd Geog)*
   [E185.625]
   UF   African American messianism

Methodists, African American
   USE African American Methodists

Methodists, Negro
   USE African American Methodists

Middle schools
   BT   Schools

Midwives, African American
   USE African American midwives

Migration, Internal *(May Subd Geog) [HB1952]*
   Here are entered works on the movement of population from one
   section to another section of the same country.
   UF   Internal migration
           Mobility
   BT   Population
   NT   Cities and towns—Growth
           Rural-urban migration

Migration, Rural-urban
   USE Rural-urban migration

Miles College (Birmingham, Ala.)
   BT   Historically Black Colleges and Universities—
           Alabama
           Private universities and colleges
           United Negro College Fund Institutions

Militant organizations, Black
   USE Black militant organizations

Minorities *(May Subd Geog) [JC311 (Nationalism)]*
   Here are entered general works on racial, religious, ethnic or other
   minority groups. Works on the discipline of ethnology, and works on
   the origin, distribution, and characteristics of the elements of the
   population of a particular region or country are entered under Ethnology, with appropriate local subdivision. Theoretical works on the
   concept of groups of people who are bound together by common ties
   of ancestry and culture are entered under Ethnic groups. Works on
   the subjective sense of belonging to an individual ethnic group are
   entered under Ethnicity.
   UF   Ethnic minorities
           Minority groups
   BT   Ethnic groups
   RT   Assimilation (Sociology)
           Discrimination
           Ethnic relations
           Nationalism
           Race relations
           Segregation
   NT   Armed Forces—Minorities
           Children of minorities
           Church and minorities
           Church work with minorities
           English literature—Minority authors
           Ethnic art
           Ethnic attitudes
           Ethnic press
           Ethnic theater
           Libraries and minorities
           Mass media and minorities
           Minorities as artists
           Minority aged
           Minority authors
           Minority business enterprises
           Minority college graduates
           Minority farmers
           Minority lawyers
           Minority students
           Minority women
           Nationalities, Principles of
           Race discrimination
           Social work with minorities

Minorities—Crimes against *(May Subd Geog)*
   UF   Crimes against minorities
           Minority victims of crime

Minorities—Economic conditions
   UF   Minorities—Socioeconomic status *[Former
           Heading]*

Minorities—Education *(May Subd Geog)*
   [LC3701-LC3740]
   NT   Minorities—Scholarships, fellowships, etc.

Minorities—Education—Language arts, [etc.]

Minorities—Education—Law and legislation *(May Subd Geog)*
  BT   Educational law and legislation

Minorities—Education (Elementary) *(May Subd Geog) [LC3725]*

Minorities—Education (Graduate) *(May Subd Geog) [LC3727]*

Minorities—Education (Graduate)—California

Minorities—Education (Higher) *(May Subd Geog) [LC3727]*

Minorities—Education (Preschool) *(May Subd Geog)*

Minorities—Education (Primary) *(May Subd Geog)*

Minorities—Education (Secondary) *(May Subd Geog) [LC3726]*

Minorities—Employment *(May Subd Geog) [HD6305.M5]*
  UF   Minority employment
  RT   Affirmative action programs
  NT   Airlines—Minority employment
       Civil service—Minority employment
       Trade-unions—Minority membership
       Vocational guidance for minorities

Minorities—Fellowships
  USE Minorities—Scholarships, fellowships, etc.

Minorities—Health and hygiene *(May Subd Geog)*
  RT   Minorities—Medical care

Minorities—Housing *(May Subd Geog)*
  BT   Discrimination in housing
       Housing

Minorities—Humor
  USE Ethnic wit and humor

Minorities—Legal status, laws., etc. *(May Subd Geog)*
  UF   Minority rights

Minorities—Medical care *(May Subd Geog)*
  RT   Minorities—Health and hygiene

Minorities—Medical care—Law and legislation *(May Subd Geog)*

Minorities—Political activity
  UF   Ethnic politics
  BT   Political participation

Minorities—Population

Minorities—Psychological testing *(May Subd Geog)*
  UF   Psychological tests for minorities

Minorities—Psychology

Minorities—Scholarships, fellowships, etc. *(May Subd Geog)*
  UF   Minorities—Fellowships
       Minority fellowships
       Minority scholarships
  BT   Minorities—Education

Minorities—Services for *(May Subd Geog)*
  NT   Academic libraries—Services to minorities
       Instructional materials centers—Services to minorities
       Public libraries—Services to minorities
       School libraries—Services to minorities

Minorities—Social conditions
  UF   Minorities—Socioeconomic status *[Former Heading]*

Minorities—Socioeconomic status
  USE Minorities—Economic conditions
       Minorities—Social conditions

Minorities—Study and teaching *(May Subd Geog)*
  UF   Ethnic studies *[Former Heading]*

Minorities—Substance use

Minorities—Suffrage *(May Subd Geog)*

Minorities—Vocational education *(May Subd Geog)*

Minorities—Vocational guidance
  USE Vocational guidance for minorities

Minorities and libraries
  USE Libraries and minorities

Minorities and the church
  USE Church and minorities

Minorities as a theme in literature
  USE Minorities in literature

Minorities as artists *(May Subd Geog)*
  BT   Minorities

Minorities as consumers *(May Subd Geog)*
  UF   Minority consumers

Minorities in advertising *(May Subd Geog)*
  Here are entered works on the portrayal of minorities in advertising.
  BT   Advertising

Minorities in architecture *(May Subd Geog)*
  NT   Minority-owned architectural firms

Minorities in Armed Forces
  USE Armed Forces—Minorities

Minorities in art
  UF   Minorities in the arts *[Former Heading]*

Minorities in broadcasting *(May Subd Geog)*

Minorities in dentistry *(May Subd Geog)*

Minorities in engineering
  NT   Minority-owned engineering firms

Minorities in films
  USE Minorities in motion pictures

Minorities in government advertising *(May Subd Geog)*
  Here are entered works discussing the portrayal of minorities in government advertising.

Minorities in librarianship
  USE Minorities in library science

Minorities in library science *(May Subd Geog)*
UF   Minorities in librarianship
RT   Minority librarians
Minorities in literature
UF   Minorities as a theme in literature
Minorities in medicine *(May Subd Geog) [R693-R696]*
BT   Medicine
Minorities in medicine—California
Minorities in medicine—United States
Minorities in motion pictures *[PN1995.9M]*
Here are entered works discussing the portrayal of minorities in motion pictures. Works discussing all aspects of minority involvement in motion pictures are entered under Minorities in the motion picture industry.
UF   Minorities in films
SA   *specific minority groups in motion pictures, e.g.* African Americans in motion pictures
Minorities in nursing *(May Subd Geog) [RT83.3]*
Minorities in psychology *(May Subd Geog)*
Minorities in science *(May Subd Geog)*
Minorities in social work education *(May Subd Geog)*
Minorities in sports *(May Subd Geog) [GV709.5]*
BT   Sports
Minorities in technology *(May Subd Geog)*
Minorities in television *(May Subd Geog)*
Here are entered works discussing the portrayal of minorities on television. Works discussing all aspects of minority involvement in television are entered under Minorities in television broadcasting.
UF   Minorities on television
Minorities in television broadcasting *(May Subd Geog)*
Here are entered works discussing all aspects of minority involvement in television. Works discussing the portrayal of minorities on television are entered under Minorities in television.
UF   Minorities in the television industry *[Former Heading]*
Minorities in the arts
USE   Minorities in art
Minorities in the civil service
USE   Civil service—Minority employment
Minorities in the motion picture industry *(May Subd Geog)*
Here are entered works discussing all aspects of minority involvement in motion pictures. Works discussing the portrayal of minorities in motion pictures are entered under Minorities in motion pictures.
BT   Motion picture industry
Minorities in the press *(May Subd Geog)*
Here are entered works discussing the portrayal of minorities by the press.
BT   Press
Minorities in the professions *(May Subd Geog)*
NT   Minority women in the professions
Minorities in the television industry
USE   Minorities in television broadcasting

Minorities in trade-unions
USE   Trade-unions—Minority membership
Minorities on television
USE   Minorities in television
Minority aged *(May Subd Geog)*
UF   Ethnic aged
BT   Minorities
Minority artists *(May Subd Geog)*
NT   Minority women artists
Minority arts facilities *(May Subd Geog)*
Minority authors *(May Subd Geog)*
BT   Minorities
SA   *subdivision* Minority authors *under individual literatures, e.g.* English literature—Minority authors
Minority business enterprises *(May Subd Geog)*
UF   Business enterprises, Minority
      Minority-owned business enterprises
BT   Minorities
NT   Black business enterprises
      Minority-owned architectural firms
      Minority-owned engineering firms
Minority business enterprises—Federal aid
USE   Federal aid to minority business enterprises
Minority business enterprises—Finance
NT   Federal aid to minority business enterprises
Minority business enterprises—Law and legislation *(May Subd Geog)*
Minority business enterprises—United States
NT   African Americans in business
Minority children
USE   Children of minorities
Minority college administrators *(May Subd Geog)*
BT   Minority executives
Minority college graduates *(May Subd Geog)*
BT   Minorities
NT   Minority women college graduates
Minority college students *(May Subd Geog)*
UF   College students, Minority
BT   Minority students
NT   Library orientation for minority college students
Minority college students—Recruiting *(May Subd Geog)*
Minority college teachers *(May Subd Geog)*
UF   Minority higher education teachers
      Minority university teachers
      University teachers, Minority
Minority consultants *(May Subd Geog)*
Minority consumers
USE   Minorities as consumers
Minority employment
USE   Minorities—Employment

Minority executives *(May Subd Geog)*
UF   Executives, Minority
NT   African American executives
      Minority college administrators
      Minority school administrators
      Minority women executives
Minority farmers *(May Subd Geog)*
BT   Minorities
Minority fellowships
USE   Minorities—Scholarships, fellowships, etc.
Minority graduate students *(May Subd Geog)*
BT   Minority students
Minority group children
USE   Children of minorities
Minority groups
USE   Minorities
Minority handicapped *(May Subd Geog)*
UF   Ethnic handicapped
Minority higher education teachers
USE   Minority college teachers
Minority journalists *(May Subd Geog)*
UF   Journalists, Minority
Minority languages
USE   Linguistic minorities
Minority lawyers *(May Subd Geog)*
BT   Minorities
NT   African American lawyers
Minority librarians
RT   Minorities in library science
NT   Minority women librarians
Minority librarians—United States
NT   African American librarians
Minority literature (American)
USE   American literature—Minority authors
      American poetry—Minority authors
Minority mass media
USE   Ethnic mass media
Minority mental health personnel *(May Subd Geog)*
UF   Mental health personnel, Minority
Minority miners *(May Subd Geog)*
Minority municipal officials and employees *(May Subd Geog)*
UF   Municipal officials and employees, Minority
Minority-owned architectural firms *(May Subd Geog)*
BT   Minorities in architecture
      Minority business enterprises
Minority-owned business enterprises
USE   Minority business enterprises
Minority-owned engineering firms *(May Subd Geog)*
BT   Minorities in engineering
      Minority business enterprises

Minority performing arts
USE   Ethnic performing arts
Minority pharmacists *(May Subd Geog)*
Minority press
USE   Ethnic press
Minority psychologists *(May Subd Geog)*
UF   Psychologists, Minority
Minority radio broadcasting
USE   Ethnic radio broadcasting
Minority rights
USE   Minorities—Legal status, laws, etc.
Minority scholarships
USE   Minorities—Scholarships, fellowships, etc.
Minority school administrators *(May Subd Geog)*
BT   Minority executives
Minority shareholders
USE   Minority stockholders
Minority stockholders
UF   Minority shareholders
Minority students *(May Subd Geog)*
[LC3701-LC3740]
UF   Students, Minority
BT   Minorities
NT   Minority college students
      Minority graduate students
Minority teachers *(May Subd Geog)*
Minority teenagers *(May Subd Geog)*
Minority television audiences
USE   Minority television viewers
Minority television broadcasting
USE   Ethnic television broadcasting
Minority television viewers *(May Subd Geog)*
UF   Minority television audiences *[Former Heading]*
Minority theater
USE   Ethnic theater
Minority university teachers
USE   Minority college teachers
Minority victims of crime
USE   Minorities—Crimes against
Minority women *(May Subd Geog)*
UF   Women, Minority
      Women minorities
BT   Minorities
Minority women artists *(May Subd Geog)*
BT   Minority artists
Minority women college graduates *(May Subd Geog)*
BT   Minority college graduates
Minority women executives *(May Subd Geog)*
BT   Minority executives
Minority women in motion pictures
    Here are entered works discussing the portrayal of minority women in motion pictures.

Minority women in the professions *(May Subd Geog)*
    BT   Minorities in the professions
Minority women librarians *(May Subd Geog)*
    BT   Minority librarians
Minority youth *(May Subd Geog)*
Minstrel shows
    UF   African American minstrel shows
           Negro minstrel shows
    BT   African Americans in the performing arts
Miscegenation *(May Subd Geog) [E185.62*
*   (African Americans)] [GN254 (Ethnology)]*
    Here are entered works on marriage or sexual relations between persons of different races and on the resulting mixture of hybridity of races.
    UF   Hybridity of races
           Racial amalgamation
           Racial crossing
    BT   Race relations
    RT   Racially mixed people
Miscegenation—Law and legislation *(May Subd*
*   Geog)*
    BT   Marriage law
Missionaries, African American
    USE   African American missionaries
Missionaries, Negro
    USE   African American missionaries
Missions to African Americans
    USE   African Americans—Missions
Missions to Blacks
    USE   Blacks—Missions
Missions to Negroes
    USE   African Americans—Missions
           Blacks—Missions
Mississippi Valley State University (Itta Bena, Miss.)
    BT   Historically Black Colleges and Universities—Mississippi
           Public universities and colleges
Missouri compromise *[E373]*
    BT   Slavery—United States
    NT   Kansas-Nebraska Bill
Mixed marriage
    USE   Intermarriage
Mixed race adoption
    USE   Interracial adoption
Mixed race children
    USE   Children of interracial marriage
Mobility
    USE   Migration, Internal
Monologues with music *[M1625-M1626]*
    NT   Rap (Music)
Montgomery Rights March, 1965
    USE   Selma-Montgomery Rights March, 1965

Moorland-Spingarn Research Center
**   (Washington, D.C.)**
    BT   Archives—African American
           Howard University (Washington, D.C.)
Morbidity
    USE   Diseases
Morehouse College (Atlanta, Ga.)
    BT   Historically Black Colleges and Universities—Georgia
           Private universities and colleges
           United Negro College Fund Institutions
Morehouse School of Medicine (Atlanta, Ga.)
    BT   Historically Black Colleges and Universities—Georgia
           Medical colleges
           Private universities and colleges
Morehouse School of Religion (Baptist)
    BT   Interdenominational Theological Center (Atlanta, Ga.)
Morgan State University (Baltimore, Md.)
    BT   Historically Black Colleges and Universities—Maryland
           Public universities and colleges
Mormons, African American
    USE   African American Mormons
Mormons and Mormonism, Negro
    USE   African American Mormons
Morris Brown College (Atlanta, Ga.)
    BT   Historically Black Colleges and Universities—Georgia
           Private universities and colleges
           United Negro College Fund Institutions
Morris College (Sumter, S.C.)
    BT   Historically Black Colleges and Universities—South Carolina
           Private universities and colleges
           United Negro College Fund Institutions
Morrison, Toni, 1931-
    The subdivisions provided under this heading represent, for the greater part, standard subdivisions usable under any literary author heading, and do not necessarily pertain to Toni Morrison, e.g., Hansberry, Lorraine, 1930-1965—Characters—African Americans; Haskins, James, 1941—Bibliography.

    —Acting
        See —Dramatic production
        For works limited to discussions of the acting of an author's plays, assign Acting as an additional heading.

    —Adaptations
        Use for discussions of adaptations as well as for collections of adaptations of the author's works. Do not use for texts of single adaptations. For discussions of the author's adaptation of the themes of others, see —Sources.

    —Aesthetics
        Use for discussions of the author's philosophy of art or beauty, whether explicitly stated or inferred from his works. Includes the author's knowledge of the aesthetics of others.

—Allegory and symbolism
   See —Symbolism

—Allusions
   Use for contemporary (author's life span) and early brief references to the author. For works on the author's use of allusions, see —Criticism and interpretation; —Knowledge—[appropriate subdivision]; —Style; etc. See also —Quotations.

—Ancestry
   See —Family

—Anecdotes
   Use for collections of brief narratives of true incidents from the author's life. See also —Allusions.

—Anniversaries, etc.
   Use for material dealing with the celebration itself. Do not use for works merely published on the occasion of an anniversary.

—Antonyms and pseudonyms

—Appreciation *(May Subd Geog)*
   Use for works on public response and reception, group opinion (positive or negative), praise, tributes, cult, etc. For works on scholarly reception or consisting of critical analysis or interpretation, see —Criticism and interpretation, except when it is necessary to bring out the place. For works on the author's impact on other persons, groups, movements, etc., see —Influence.

—Archives
   Use for collections or discussions of documentary material or records relating to the author, including manuscripts, diaries, correspondence, photographs, bills, tax returns, or other items of historical interest. See also —Correspondence; —Diaries; —Manuscripts; —Notebooks, sketchbooks, etc.

—Archives—Catalogs

—Art

—Associates
   See —Friends and associates

—Audio adaptations
   Use for discussions of audio adaptations of the author's fiction, drama, or poetry.

—Authorship
   Use for works discussing the attribution of authorship.

—Authorship—Collaboration

—Autobiography
   See —Biography

—Autographs
   Use for collections or discussions of specimens of the author's autographs or handwriting.

—Autographs—Facsimiles

—Autographs, Spurious
   See —Forgeries

—Bibliography
   Use for lists of publications by or about the author. Use also under any topical subdivision, e.g., —Religion—Bibliography. For bibliographies of bibliographies about the author, assign the headings: 1. Bibliography—Bibliography—[author]. 2. [author]—Bibliography. Use also [author. title]—Bibliography. See also [author. title]—Bibliography.

—Bibliography—Catalogs

—Bibliography—Exhibitions

—Bibliography—First editions

—Biography
   Use also for autobiographies.

—Biography—Birth
   See —Birth

—Biography—Careers

—Biography—Chronology
   See —Chronology

—Biography—Death and burial
   See —Death and burial

—Biography—Exile
   See —Exile

—Biography—Family
   See —Family

—Biography—Health
   See —Health

—Biography—Imprisonment
   See —Imprisonment

—Biography—Last years and death
   See —Death and burial
     —Last years

—Biography—Marriage
   See —Marriage

—Biography—Old age
   See —Last years

—Biography—Psychology
   See —Psychology

—Biography—Sources

—Biography—Youth
   See —Childhood and youth

—Birth

—Birthday books
   See —Calenders. Assign —Birthday books as a
     second heading.

—Books and reading
Use for works dealing with written material known to have been seen by the author; his reading habits and interests; books borrowed from libraries or friends; etc. See also —Knowledge —[appropriate subdivision]; —Library

—Calendars
See also —Quotations

—Canon
See —Authorship
—Chronology
—Criticism, Textual

—Careers
See —Biography—Careers

—Caricatures and cartoons
Use for collections or discussions of caricatures or pictorial humor about the author.

—Censorship (May Subd Geog)

—Centennial celebrations, etc.
See —Anniversaries, etc.

—Character
See —Ethics
—Psychology
—Religion

—Characters
Use for works about the author's characters in general. For specific groups or categories of characters, see the list below and assign an additional heading, e.g. 1. Brown, William Wells, 1815-1884—Characters—Slaves. 2. Slavery and slaves in literature.

—Characters—Abandoned children

—Characters—Actors

—Characters—African Americans

—Characters—Aged

—Characters—Angels

—Characters—Artists

—Characters—Children

—Characters—Clergy

—Characters—Comic characters

—Characters—Courtesans

—Characters—Criminals

—Characters—Daughters

—Characters—Dramatists

—Characters—Eccentrics

—Characters—Fairies

—Characters—Fathers

—Characters—Fools

—Characters—Gauchos

—Characters—Gentiles

—Characters—Ghosts

—Characters—Giants

—Characters—Gypsies

—Characters—Heroes

—Characters—Heroines

—Characters—Indians

—Characters—Intellectuals

—Characters—Irish

—Characters—Jews

—Characters—Kings and rulers

—Characters—Lawyers

—Characters—Men

—Characters—Mentally ill

—Characters—Messengers

—Characters—Minnesingers

—Characters—Monsters

—Characters—Mothers

—Characters—Muslims

—Characters—Novelists

—Characters—Physicians

—Characters—Poets

—Characters—Prisoners of war

—Characters—Revolutionaries

—Characters—Rogues and vagabonds

—Characters—Saints

—Characters—Satirists

—Characters—Scientists

—Characters—Servants

—Characters—Sick

—Characters—Singers

—Characters—Single people

—Characters—Slaves

—Characters—Soldiers

—Characters—Teachers

—Characters—Valets

—Characters—Villains

—Characters—Welsh

—Characters—Women

—Characters—Youth

—Childhood and youth

—Chronology
> Use for lists with dates of the author's life and/or works, as well as for discussions thereof.

—Cipher

—Comedies
> Use for critical works only.

—Comic books, strips, etc.

—Commentaries
> See —Criticism and interpretation

—Companions
> See —Friends and associates

—Concordances
> Use as a form subdivision for indexes to the principal words found in the author's works. See also —[author. title]—Concordances.

—Congresses
> Use as appropriate under the author's name or under any topical subdivision, e.g. —Criticism and interpretation—Congresses. See also —[author. title]—Congresses.

—Contemporaries
> Use for works about persons flourishing during the author's life but not necessarily in close contact with the author. See also —Friends and associates.

—Correspondence
> Use as a form or topical subdivision for letters from and/or to the author. Assign as additional heading for individual correspondents.

—Correspondence—Facsimiles

—Correspondence—Indexes

—Costume
> See —Dramatic production
> For works only on the costuming of an author's plays, assign —Costume as an additional heading.

—Criticism, Textual
> Use for works which aim to establish authoritative texts, e.g. comparison of manuscripts and editions.

—Criticism and interpretation
> See also —Dramatic works; —Fictional works; —Poetic works; —Prose

—Criticism and interpretation—Congresses

—Criticism and interpretation—History

—Criticism and interpretation—History—19th century

—Criticism and interpretation—History—20th century

—Death and burial
> Use for works on the author's death, funeral, or burial, including the author's last illness.

—Dialects
> See —Language—Dialects

—Diaries
> Use for collections or discussions of the author's diaries. Also use for individual diaries.

—Dictionaries
> Do not use under author-title entries. See also —Encyclopedias; —Language—Glossaries, etc.

—Discography
> Use for lists or catalogs of sound recordings by or about the author.

—Diseases
> See —Health

—Drama
> Use as a form subdivision for plays and musical dramatic works, including operas, ballets, musical comedies, etc., about the author. For criticism or discussion of plays, etc., about the author, assign [name of author]—In literature as a topical heading.

—Dramatic production
> Includes aspects of stage presentation, e.g., acting, costume, stage setting and scenery, etc. For historical aspects of dramatic production, see —Stage history.

—Dramatic works
> Use for criticism only. Do not use under authors who write principally drama. See also —Comedies; —Histories; —Motion picture plays; —Radio and television plays; —Tragedies; —Tragicomedies.

—Dramaturgy
> See —Dramatic production
> > —Dramatic works
> > —Technique

—Dwellings
> See —Homes and haunts

—Editions
> See —Bibliography

—Editors

—Education
> See —Knowledge and learning

—Encyclopedias
> See also —Dictionaries

—Estate
> Use for discussions of the aggregate of property or liabilities of all kinds that the author leaves for disposal at his death. See also —Will.

—Ethics

—Exhibitions

Use for works about exhibitions as well as catalogs of single exhibitions. See also —Bibliography—Exhibitions; —Illustrations—Exhibitions; —[author. title]—Exhibitions.

—Exile *(May Subd Geog)*

—Family

Use for discussions of the author's family or relations with family members. Also use for genealogical works. Assign an additional heading for the name of the family. See also —Marriage.

—Fiction

Use as a form subdivision for works of fiction about the author. For criticism or discussion of fiction about the author, assign —[name of author]—In literature as a topical heading.

—Fictional works

Use for criticism only. Do not use under authors who write principally fiction. See also —Prose.

—Film and video adaptations

Use for discussions of motion picture or video adaptations of the author's fiction, drama, or poetry.

—Forerunners
    See —Sources
        —Criticism and interpretation

—Forgeries *(May Subd Geog)*

—Friends and associates

Use for works about the author's circle of close and immediate contacts such as patrons, co-workers, companions, etc. See also —Contemporaries; —Family.

—Genealogy
    See —Family

—Glossaries
    See —Language—Glossaries, etc.

—Grammar
    See —Language—Grammar

—Handbooks, manuals, etc.

—Handwriting
    See —Autographs

—Haunts
    See —Homes and haunts

—Health

Use for works about the author's state of health, including diseases suffered and accounts of specific diseases. For accounts of specific diseases assign an additional heading of the type [disease]—Patients—[place]—Biography.

—Homes and haunts *(May Subd Geog)*

Use for discussions of places of residence or places to which the author made repeated visits. For voyages and travels, see —Journeys.

—Homes and haunts—Guidebooks

—Histories

—Humor

Use for critical works discussing the author's humor, satire, etc., as well as for humorous works about the author. See also —Caricatures and cartoons

—Iconography
    See —Pictorial works

—Illustrations

Use for collections or discussions of pictorial representations of the author's works. Do not further subdivide by —History and criticism. See also [author. title]—Illustrations.

—Illustrations—Catalogs

—Illustrations—Exhibitions

—Illustrations, Comic
    See —Illustrations

—Imitations
    See —Parodies, imitations, etc.

—Imprisonment

—In literature

Use for discussions of the author as a theme in belles lettres, including musical dramatic works and individual literary genres. For literary works about the person, or in which he or she appears as a character, assign the appropriate form subdivision, e.g. —Drama; —Fiction; —Literary collections; —Poetry.

—Indexes

    See also —Concordances; [author. title]—Indexes

—Influence

Use for the author's impact on national literatures or literary movements. Assign an additional heading to identify the group or national literature influenced. For works on the author's impact on a specific person, group, movement, etc., assign an additional heading for the person or group influenced.

—Interviews

Use for works consisting of transcripts of what was said during the course of interviews or conversations with the author on one or more occasions.

—Itineraries
    See —Journals

—Journals
    See —Diaries

—Journeys *(May Subd Geog)*

Use for works about voyages and travels actually undertaken by the author. When —Journeys is further subdivided by place, assign an additional heading of the type [place]—Description and travel. For places of residence or places to which the author made repeated visits, see —Homes and haunts. See also —Exile.

—Journeys—Guidebooks

—Juvenile drama

Use also under other subdivisions as appropriate.

—Juvenile fiction

Use also under other subdivisions as appropriate.

—Juvenile films

Use also under other subdivisions as appropriate.

—Juvenile humor
  Use also under other subdivisions as appropriate.

—Juvenile literature
  Use also under other subdivisions as appropriate.

—Juvenile poetry
  Use also under other subdivisions as appropriate.

—Juvenile sound recordings
  Use also under other subdivisions as appropriate.

—Knowledge—Agriculture, [America, etc.]
  Use this heading, which occurs only with a subdivision, for material dealing with the author's knowledge or treatment of themes or specific subjects. Use —Knowledge and learning for works on the author's education, learning, and scholarship in general. For works that are assigned the heading [author]—Knowledge—[topic] and that discuss a specific subject as a theme in the author's works, assign as an additional subject the heading [topic] in literature.

—Knowledge—Aesthetics
    See —Aesthetics

—Knowledge—Costume
    See —Dramatic production

—Knowledge—Ethics
    See —Ethics

—Knowledge—Philosophy
    See —Philosophy

—Knowledge—Religion
    See —Religion

—Knowledge and learning
  Use for works on the author's education, learning, and scholarship in general. See also —Knowledge—[appropriate subdivision], and topics used directly under the name of the author, e.g., —Aesthetics; —Religion.

—Language
  Use for critical works dealing with the author's language in general on the linguistic rather than the artistic level. For works on language on the artistic level, see —Style.

—Language—Dialects

—Language—Glossaries, etc.

—Language—Grammar

—Language—Pronunciation

—Language—Punctuation

—Language—Style
    See —Style

—Language—Versification
    See —Versification

—Language—Word frequency

—Last years
    See also —Death and burial

—Legends
  Use as a form subdivision for stories about the author that have come down from the past and that are popularly taken as historical though not verifiable.

—Library
  Use for works about the author's personal library. See also —Books and reading.

—Library—Catalogs

—Library—Marginal notes

—Library resources
  Use for works describing the resources or special collections available in libraries for research or study about the author.

—Literary collections
  Use for literary anthologies about the author involving two or more literary forms.

—Manuscripts
    See also —Archives; —Autographs;
        —Correspondence; —Diaries;
        —Notebooks, sketchbooks, etc.

—Manuscripts—Catalogs

—Manuscripts—Facsimiles
    See also —Autographs—Facsimiles

—Marriage

—Men
    See —Relations with men

—Monuments *(May Subd Geog)*
  Use for works about monuments erected in honor of the author. See also —Museums; —Statues

—Moral ideas
    See —Ethics

—Motion picture plays
  Use for commentaries on film scripts written by the author. For discussions of motion picture adaptations of the author's fiction, drama or poetry, see —Film and video adaptations.

—Motion pictures
    See —Film and video adaptations

—Moving-picture plays
    See —Motion picture plays

—Museums *(May Subd Geog)*
  Use for works about museums devoted to the author. See also —Archives.

—Musical settings
  Use as a form subdivision for musical scores or sound recordings in which the writings or words of the author have been set to music.

—Name
  Use for discussions of the history, orthography, etymology, etc. of the author's name. See also —Antonyms and pseudonyms.

—Notebooks, sketchbooks, etc.
  Use for collections or discussions of the author's notebooks, sketchbooks, etc. Also use for individual works.

—On postage stamps
Use for works about the portrayal of the author on postage stamps.

—Outlines, syllabi, etc.

—Pageants
See —Anniversaries, etc.; —Dramatic production

—Paraphrases, tales, etc.
See —Adaptations

—Parodies, imitations, etc.
Use as both a form and critical subdivision for imitations, either comic or distorted, of the author's works. Do not use under author-title entries.

—Patriotism
See —Political and social views

—Periodicals

—Personality
See —Psychology

—Philosophy
See also —Aesthetics; —Ethics; —Political and social views; —Religion

—Pictorial works
Use for works consisting of pictures or other visual images pertaining to the author. Use under the author's name or under appropriate topical subdivisions. See also —Art; —Caricatures and cartoons; —Illustrations; —Monuments; —Portraits.

—Plots
See —Stories, plots, etc.

—Poetic works
Use for critical works only. Do not use under authors who write principally poetry.

—Poetry
Use as a form subdivision for works of poetry about the author. For criticism or discussion of poetry about the author, assign [name of author]—In literature as a topical heading.

—Political activity

—Political and social views

—Portraits
See also —Caricatures and cartoons; —On postage stamps; —Statues.

—Prohibited books
See —Censorship

—Pronunciation
See —Language—Pronunciation

—Prophecies
Use for works about prophecies made by the author.

—Prose
Use only for criticism of prose works or passages. Do not use under authors who write principally prose.

—Pseudonyms
See —Antonyms and pseudonyms

—Psychology
Use for discussions or interpretation of the author's personality or character or for psychological insight into the author's life.

—Public opinion
See —Appreciation

—Publishers

—Quotations
Use for collections or discussions of quotations by or about the author. See also —Calendars.

—Radio and television plays
Use for commentaries on scripts written by the author expressly for radio or television. For discussions of audio or video adaptations of the author's fiction, drama, or poetry, see —Audio adaptations; —Film and video adaptations.

—Reading habits
See —Books and reading

—Relations with editors
See —Editors

—Relations with family
See —Family

—Relations with friends and associates
See —Friends and associates

—Relations with men
Use for works on intimate associations. For works on relations with an individual man, assign an additional heading for the man.

—Relations with publishers
See —Publishers

—Relations with women
Use for works on intimate associations. For works on relations with an individual woman, assign an additional heading for the woman.

—Religion

—Satire
See —Humor

—Screenplays
See —Motion picture plays

—Settings

—Sexual behavior

—Sketchbooks
See —Notebooks, sketchbooks, etc.

—Social views
See —Political and social views

—Societies, etc.
Use for works discussing societies or organizations devoted to or specializing in the author.

—Songs and music
> Use as a form subdivision for collections or single works of vocal or instrumental music about the person.

—Songs and music—Discography

—Songs and music—History and criticism

—Sources
> Use for discussions of the author's sources of ideas or inspiration for his works.

—Sources—Bibliography

—Stage history

—Stage presentation
> See —Dramatic production

—Stage setting and scenery
> See —Dramatic production
> For works only on stage setting and scenery of an author's plays, assign as an additional heading —Theaters—Stage-setting and scenery; —Motion pictures—Setting and scenery; or —Television—Stage-setting and scenery.

—Statues

—Stories, plots. etc.
> Use for summaries and discussion of plot development in drama and fiction, and of action in poetic works.

—Study and teaching (May Subd Geog)
> Use for methods of studying or teaching about the author.

—Study and teaching—Audio-visual aids

—Study and teaching—Audio-visual aids—Catalogs

—Study and teaching—Outlines, syllabi, etc.
> See —Outlines, syllabi, etc.

—Style
> Use for discussions of rhetoric; figures of speech, e.g. imagery, metaphor, simile, etc.; and artistic use of language in general. —Technique is a larger concept. For works on specific linguistic topics, e.g. nouns, verbs, adjectives, syntax, pronunciation, etc. see —Language. See also —Symbolism.

—Summaries, arguments, etc.
> See —Stories, plots, etc.

—Symbolism

—Technique
> Use for discussions of structural and formal elements in drama, fiction, and narrative poetry; the art of writing, e.g., general construction, asides, soliloquies, unities, dramatic irony, scene structure, stream-of-consciousness, etc. See also —Style; —Versification.

—Textual criticism
> See —Criticism, Textual

—Themes, motives
> See —Criticism and interpretation

—Themes, motives—[specific topic]
> See —Knowledge—[specific topic]

—Theology
> See —Religion

—Tragedies
> Use for critical works only.

—Tragicomedies
> Use for critical works only.

—Translations
> Use for collections of translations.

—Versification
> Use for discussions of the author's technique of writing verse; the structural composition of poetry, including rhythm, rhyme, alliteration, etc. See also —Style.

—Video adaptations
> See —Film and video adaptations

—Voyages and travels
> See —Journeys

—Will
> Use for discussions of the author's legal declaration regarding disposition of his property or estate at his death. See also —Estate.

—Women
> See —Relations with women

—Yearbooks
> See —Periodicals

—Youth
> See —Childhood and youth

Mortality and race
> BT   Race

Mortgage lending
> USE   Mortgage loans

Mortgage loans (May Subd Geog)
> UF   Mortgage lending
> Real estate loans
> NT   Discrimination in mortgage loans

Motion picture actors and actresses, African American
> USE   African American motion picture actors and actresses

Motion picture industry (May Subd Geog)
> UF   Film industry (Motion pictures)
> Moving-picture industry [Former Heading]
> NT   Blacks in the motion picture industry
> Minorities in the motion picture industry

Motion picture producers and directors, African American
> USE   African American motion picture producers and directors

Mountain people (Ramapo Mountains)
> USE   Ramapo Mountain people

Movements, Literary
> USE   Literary movements

Movements against apartheid
USE Anti-apartheid movements

Moving-picture industry
USE Motion picture industry

Mulattoes *(May Subd Geog)* *[E185.62 (United States)]*
[GN645 (Anthropology)]
UF Octoroons
Quadroons
BT African Americans
Blacks
Racially mixed people
NT Melungeons
Ramapo Mountain people
Wesorts

Mulattoes—United States
UF Guineas (Mixed bloods, United States)
[Former Heading]
NT Black Seminoles

Multicultural education *(May Subd Geog)* *[LC1099]*
UF Intercultural education *[Former Heading]*

Multicultural education—Activity programs
UF Activity programs in multicultural education
BT Activity programs in education

Multicultural mass media
USE Ethnic mass media

Multiculturalism *(May Subd Geog)*
Here are entered works on policies or programs that foster the preservation of different cultural identities, including customs, languages, and beliefs, within a unified society such as a state or nation. Works on the condition in which numerous distinct ethnic, religious, or cultural groups coexists within one society are entered under Pluralism (Social sciences).
UF Cultural diversity policy
Cultural pluralism policy
Multiculturalism—Government policy
RT Ethnicity
Pluralism (Social sciences)

Multiculturalism—Government policy
USE Multiculturalism

Multiculturalism—Law and legislation *(May Subd Geog)*

Municipal civil service
USE Municipal officials and employees

Municipal employees
USE Municipal officials and employees

Municipal junior colleges
USE Community colleges

Municipal officers
USE Municipal officials and employees

Municipal officials and employees *(May Subd Geog)*
[JS148-JS155]
UF Civil service, Municipal
Municipal civil service
Municipal employees
Municipal officers
Town officers
BT Local officials and employees
SA *subdivision* Officials and employees *under names of cities*
NT Minority municipal officials and employees

Municipal officials and employees, Minority
USE Minority municipal officials and employees

Municipal services *(May Subd Geog)*
[HD4421-HD4730.97]
UF Municipal services within corporate limits
Public services
NT Discrimination in municipal services

Municipal services within corporate limits
USE Municipal services

Museums *(May Subd Geog)* *[AM]*
SA *subdivision* Museums *under names of individual persons, families, and corporate bodies, e.g.* Lincoln University (Lincoln University, Pa.)—Museums; *and names of individual museums, e.g.* Black American West Museum (Denver, Colo.)
RT African Americans—Museums

Music *(May Subd Geog)*
For works consisting of music of an individual ethnic group, additional subject entry is made under the heading [ethnic group]—[place]—Music, e.g. African Americans—Music.
UF Classical music
Music, Classical
Musical compositions
Musical works
SA *subdivision* Songs and music *under names of persons, corporate bodies, places, classes of persons, ethnic groups, wars, and topical headings for collections of single works of vocal or instrumental music about the topic or entity named; and subdivision* Music *under ethnic groups for music of the group*
NT Jazz
Popular music

Music, Classical
USE Music

Music, Dixieland
USE Dixieland music

Music, Gospel
USE Gospel music

Music, Popular
USE Popular music

Music, Popular (Songs, etc.)
USE Popular music

Music, Rhythm and blues
USE Rhythm and blues music

Music, Soul
USE Soul music

Music and race
UF Race and music
BT Ethnopsychology

Music audiences *(May Subd Geog)*
    NT   Jazz audiences
Music festivals *(May Subd Geog) [ML35-ML38]*
    UF   Musical festivals
    NT   Jazz festivals
Music in universities and colleges *(May Subd Geog)* *[ML63] [MT18 (Instruction)]*
    SA   *subdivision* Songs and music *under names of universities and colleges, e.g.* Lincoln University (Lincoln University, Pa.)—Songs and music
Musical compositions
    USE Music
Musical festivals
    USE Music festivals
Musical works
    USE Music
Musicians *(May Subd Geog) [ML385-ML403]*
    UF   Players, Musical instrument
    NT   Blues musicians
            Gospel musicians
            Jazz musicians
            Rap musicians
            Soul musicians
Musicians, African American
    USE African American musicians
Musicians, Black
    UF   Black musicians
            Negro musicians *[Former Heading]*
    BT   Blacks in the performing arts
Muslim education
    USE Islamic education
Muslim educators
    UF   Islamic educators
Muslim religious education
    USE Islamic religious education
Muslims—United States
    UF   Muslims in the United States
    NT   African American Muslims
            Black Muslims
Muslims, African American
    USE African American Muslims
Muslims, Black *[BP62.N4]*
    Here are entered works on persons of the Black race who are Muslims. Works on the movement known as the Nation of Islam or Black Muslims are entered under Black Muslims.
    UF   Negro Muslims *[Former Heading]*
    BT   Blacks—Religion
Muslims in the United States
    USE Muslims—United States
Mutual aid societies
    USE Friendly societies
Mutual benefit associations
    USE Friendly societies

N

NAACP
    USE National Association for the Advancement of Colored People
Nat Turner's Insurrection
    USE Southampton Insurrection, 1831
Natchez Junior College (Natchez, Miss.)
    BT   Historically Black Colleges and Universities—Mississippi
            Junior Colleges
            Private universities and colleges
Nation of Islam
    USE Black Muslims
National Alliance of Postal and Federal Employees *(May Subd Geog)*
    BT   Trade and professional associations
National Association for the Advancement of Colored People *(May Subd Geog)*
    UF   NAACP
    BT   Civil rights organizations
    Here are listed subdivisions that have been established by LCSH for use under names of individual corporate name headings. For example, a bibliography of the National Urban League would be constructed: National Urban League—Bibliography.

    —Abstracts

    —Accounting

    —Accreditation

    —Administration

    —Anecdotes

    —Anniversaries, etc.

    —Appropriations and expenditures

    —Appropriations and expenditures—Effect of inflation on

    —Archaeological collections

    —Archives

    —Art collections

    —Art patronage

    —Audiotape catalogs

    —Auditing

    —Automation

    —Awards

    —Bibliography

    —Bibliography—Catalogs

    —Bibliography—Microform catalogs

—Bibliography—Union lists

—Biography

—Biography—Dictionaries

—Biography—History and criticism

—Biography—Portraits

—Buildings

—By-laws

—Calendars

—Caricatures and cartoons

—Case studies

—Catalogs

—Centennial celebrations, etc.

—Chaplains

—Charities

—Charters

—Claims vs. ...

—Coin collections

—Collectibles (May Subd Geog)

—Comic books, strips, etc.

—Communication systems

—Compact disc catalogs

—Congresses

—Constitution

—Corrupt practices

—Databases

—Data processing

—Dictionaries

—Directories

—Discipline

—Discography

—Drama

—Elections

—Employees

—Endowments

—Equipment and supplies

—Ethnological collections

—Ethnomusicological collections

—Evaluation

—Examinations

—Exhibitions

—Fiction

—Film catalogs

—Finance

—Forms

—Genealogy

—Guidebooks

—Handbooks, manuals, etc.

—Heraldry

—Historiography

—History

—History—19th century

—History—20th century

—History—Chronology

—History—Sources

—Humor

—In literature

—Indexes

—Influence

—Information services

—Insignia

—Job descriptions

—Juvenile drama

—Juvenile fiction

—Juvenile films

—Juvenile humor

—Juvenile literature

—Juvenile poetry

—Juvenile sound recordings

—Language

—Libraries

—Library

—Library resources

—Literary collections

—Management

—Map collections

—Maps

—Maps—Bibliography

—Maps for children

—Medals

—Membership

—Microform catalogs

—Miscellanea

—Museums

—Musical instrument collections

—Name

—Natural history collections

—Numismatic collections

—Officials and employees

—Officials and employees—Charitable contributions

—Officials and employees—Discipline

—Officials and employees—Dismissal of

—Officials and employees—Furloughs

—Officials and employees—Job stress

—Officials and employees—Leave regulations

—Officials and employees—Pensions

—Officials and employees—Promotions

—Officials and employees—Rating of

—Officials and employees—Recruiting

—Officials and employees—Registers

—Officials and employees—Reinstatement

—Officials and employees—Relocation

—Officials and employees—Residence requirements

—Officials and employees—Retirement

—Officials and employees—Salaries, etc.

—Officials and employees—Salaries, etc.—Regional disparities

—Officials and employees—Selection and appointment

—Officials and employees—Supplementary employment

—Officials and employees—Titles

—Officials and employees—Transfer

—Officials and employees—Travel regulations

—Officials and employees—Turnover

—On postage stamps

—Organ

—Organs

—Party work

—Performances

—Periodicals

—Periodicals—Bibliography

—Periodicals—Bibliography—Catalogs

—Periodicals—Bibliography—Union lists

—Periodicals—Indexes

—Personnel management

—Personnel records

—Photograph collections

—Pictorial works

—Platforms

—Poetry

—Political activity

—Positions

—Poster collections

—Posters

—Presidents

—Public opinion

—Public relations

—Publishing (May Subd Geog)

—Records and correspondence

—Registers

—Religion

—Reorganization

—**Research** *(May Subd Geog)*

—**Research grants**

—**Rules and practice**

—**Sanitation**

—**Scientific apparatus collections**

—**Seal**

—**Security measures**

—**Slide collections**

—**Societies, etc.**

—**Songs and music**

—**Statistics**

—**Study and teaching** *(May Subd Geog)*

—**Study and teaching—Audio-visual aids**

—**Study and teaching (Continuing education)** *(May Subd Geog)*

—**Study and teaching (Early childhood)** *(May Subd Geog)*

—**Study and teaching (Elementary)** *(May Subd Geog)*

—**Study and teaching (Graduate)** *(May Subd Geog)*

—**Study and teaching (Higher)** *(May Subd Geog)*

—**Study and teaching (Internship)** *(May Subd Geog)*

—**Study and teaching (Preschool)** *(May Subd Geog)*

—**Study and teaching (Primary)** *(May Subd Geog)*

—**Study and teaching (Secondary)** *(May Subd Geog)*

—**Telephone directories**

—**Uniforms**

—**Video tape catalogs**

—**Vocational guidance** *(May Subd Geog)*

National Association of Black Journalists *(May Subd Geog)*
  BT   Trade and professional associations
  RT   African American journalists

National Association of Colored Women's Clubs *(May Subd Geog)*
  BT   Women—Societies and clubs

National Association of Negro Business and Professional Women's Clubs, Inc. *(May Subd Geog)*
  BT   Women—Societies and clubs

National Baptist Convention, U.S.A., Inc. *(May Subd Geog)*
  BT   Religious institutions
  SA   *names of individual churches, e.g.* Bethel Metropolitan Baptist Church (St. Petersburg, Fla.)

National Baptist Convention of America, Inc. *(May Subd Geog)*
  BT   Religious institutions
  SA   *names of individual churches, e.g.* Oakland Baptist Church (Louisville, Ky.)

National Bar Association *(May Subd Geog)*
  BT   Trade and professional associations
  RT   African American lawyers

National Coalition of 100 Black Women, Inc. *(May Subd Geog)*
  BT   Women—Societies and clubs
  RT   African American civic leaders

National Conference of Black Mayors
  BT   Trade and professional associations
  RT   African American mayors

National consciousness
  USE   Nationalism

National Council of Negro Women, Inc. *(May Subd Geog)*
  BT   Women—Societies and clubs

National Dental Association *(May Subd Geog)*
  BT   Trade and professional associations
  RT   African American dentists

National Historically Black Colleges Week *(May Subd Geog)*
  BT   Special weeks

National Medical Association *(May Subd Geog)*
  BT   Trade and professional associations
  RT   African American physicians

National monuments—Missouri
  NT   George Washington Carver National Monument (Mo.)

National parks and reserves—Alabama
  NT   Tuskegee Institute National Historic Site (Tuskegee, Ala.)

National parks and reserves—Georgia
  NT   Martin Luther King, Junior, National Historic Site (Atlanta, Ga.)

National parks and reserves—Kansas
  NT   Brown v. Board of Education National Historic Site (Topeka, Kan.)

National parks and reserves—Massachusetts
  NT   Boston African American National Historic Site (Boston, Mass.)

National parks and reserves—Washington (D.C.)
  NT   Mary McLeod Bethune Council House National Historic Site (Washington, D.C.)

National Rainbow Coalition
  UF   Rainbow Coalition
  BT   Civil rights organizations
National Urban Coalition *(May Subd Geog)*
  BT   Civil rights organizations
National Urban League *(May Subd Geog)*
  BT   Civil rights organizations
Nationalism *(May Subd Geog) [JC311-JC323*
(Political science)]
  UF   National consciousness
  RT   Minorities
Nationalism—Blacks
  USE Black nationalism
Nationalism, Black
  USE Black nationalism
Nationalism and art
  UF   Art and nationalism
Nationalities, Principles of
  UF   Nationality, Principle of
       Principle of nationalities
  BT   Minorities
  RT   Self-determination, National
Nationality, Principle of
  USE Nationalities, Principles of
Nationality (Citizenship)
  USE Citizenship
Negritude
  USE African Americans—Race identity
       Blacks—Race identity
Negritude (Literary movement) *(May Subd Geog)*
  BT   Literary movements
       Literature, Modern—20th century—History
         and criticism
Negro actors
  USE Actors, Black
       African American actors
Negro agricultural laborers
  USE African American agricultural laborers
Negro art
  USE African American art
       Art, Black
Negro artists
  USE African American artists
       Artists, Black
Negro arts
  USE African American arts
       Arts, Black
Negro athletes
  USE African American athletes
       Athletes, Black
Negro authors
  USE African American authors
       Authors, Black

Negro baseball leagues
  USE Negro leagues
Negro businessmen
  USE African Americans in business
Negro children
  USE African American children
       Children, Black
Negro children's writings
  USE African American children's writings
Negro churches
  USE African American churches
Negro clergy
  USE African American clergy
Negro college graduates
  USE African American college graduates
       College graduates, Black
Negro college teachers
  USE African American college teachers
       College teachers, Black
Negro criminals
  USE African American criminals
Negro dentists
  USE African American dentists
Negro drama
  USE American drama—African American authors
       Drama—Black authors
Negro dropouts
  USE African American dropouts
Negro elementary schools
  USE African American elementary schools
Negro engineers
  USE African American engineers
Negro-English dialects
  USE Black English
       Creole dialects, English
Negro entertainers
  USE African American entertainers
Negro executives
  USE African American executives
       Executives, Black
Negro families
  USE African American families
       Families, Black
Negro fiction
  USE American fiction—African American authors
       Fiction—Black authors
Negro firemen
  USE African American fire fighters
Negro-Indian relations
  USE African Americans—Relations with Indians
Negro inventors
  USE African American inventors

Negro-Jewish relations
    USE African Americans—Relations with Jews
            Blacks—Relations with Jews
Negro Jews
    USE African American Jews
Negro journalists
    USE African American journalists
Negro judges
    USE African American judges
Negro lawyers
    USE African American lawyers
Negro leadership
    USE African American leadership
Negro leagues *(May Subd Geog)*
    UF   Negro baseball leagues
    BT   Baseball
Negro librarians
    USE African American librarians
Negro literature
    USE American literature—African American authors
            Literature—Black authors
Negro mayors
    USE African American mayors
Negro minstrel shows
    USE Minstrel shows
Negro moving-picture actors and actresses
    USE African American motion picture actors and actresses
Negro music
    USE African Americans—Music
            African Americans—Songs and music
            Blacks—Songs and music
Negro musicians
    USE African American musicians
            Musicians, Black
Negro Muslims
    USE Muslims, Black
Negro newspapers (American)
    USE African American newspapers
Negro nurses
    USE African American nurses
Negro orators
    USE African American orators
Negro periodicals (American)
    USE African American periodicals
Negro photographers
    USE African American photographers
Negro physicians
    USE African American physicians

Negro poetry
    USE American poetry—African American authors
            Poetry—Black authors
Negro policemen
    USE African American police
            Police, Black
Negro political scientists
    USE African American political scientists
Negro press
    USE African American press
Negro quotations
    USE African Americans—Quotations
            Blacks—Quotations
Negro race
    USE Black race
Negro race in the Bible
    USE Blacks in the Bible
Negro scientists
    USE African American scientists
Negro sociologists
    USE African American sociologists
Negro soldiers
    USE African American soldiers
            Soldiers, Black
Negro songs
    USE African Americans—Music
            African Americans—Songs and music
            Blacks—Songs and music
Negro sounds
    USE African Americans—Music
Negro spirituals
    USE Spirituals (Songs)
Negro students
    USE African American students
            Students, Black
Negro teachers
    USE African American teachers
            Teachers, Black
Negro teachers, Training of
    USE African American teachers—Training of
Negro teachers and the community
    USE African American teachers and the community
Negro theological seminaries
    USE African American theological seminaries
Negro universities and colleges
    USE Historically Black Colleges and Universities
Negro veterans
    USE African American veterans
Negro wit and humor
    USE African American wit and humor
            Wit and humor—Black authors

Negro youth
USE African American youth
Youth, Black

Negrobilia
USE African Americans—Collectibles

Negroes
USE African Americans
Blacks

Negroes as businessmen
USE African Americans in business

Negroes as consumers
USE African Americans as consumers
Blacks as consumers

Negroes as cowboys
USE African American cowboys

Negroes as farmers
USE African American farmers

Negroes as seamen
USE African American seamen

Negroes as social workers
USE African American social workers

Negroes as soldiers
USE African American soldiers

Negroes in aeronautics
USE African Americans in aeronautics

Negroes in art
USE African Americans in art
Blacks in art

Negroes in dentistry
USE African Americans in dentistry

Negroes in literature
USE African Americans in literature
Blacks in literature

Negroes in medicine
USE African Americans in medicine
Blacks in medicine

Negroes in moving-pictures
USE African Americans in motion pictures
Blacks in motion pictures

Negroes in radio
USE African Americans in radio broadcasting

Negroes in the moving-picture industry
USE African Americans in the motion picture industry
Blacks in the motion picture industry

Negroes in the performing arts
USE African Americans in the performing arts
Blacks in the performing arts

Negroes in veterinary medicine
USE African Americans in veterinary medicine

Neighborhood health centers
USE Community health services

Neighborhoods, African American
USE African American neighborhoods

Networks (Associations, institutions, etc.)
USE Associations, institutions, etc.

New Negro Movement
USE Harlem Renaissance

New York (N.Y.)—History—Colonial period, ca. 1600-1775
NT New York (N.Y.)—Negro plot, 1741

New York (N.Y.)—Negro plot, 1741
BT New York (N.Y.)—History—Colonial period, ca. 1600-1775

New York (N.Y.). East Harlem
USE East Harlem (New York, N.Y.)

New York 21 Trial, New York, N.Y., 1970-1971
USE Black Panthers Trial, New York, N.Y., 1970-1971

New York City Bomb Conspiracy Trial, New York, N.Y., 1970-1971
USE Black Panthers Trial, New York, N.Y., 1970-1971

Newbery Award
USE Newbery Medal

Newbery Medal
UF John Newbery Medal books
Newbery Award
Newbery medal books *[Former Heading]*
Newbery Prize books

Newbery medal books
USE Newbery Medal

Newbery Prize books
USE Newbery Medal

Newspapers, Black
USE Black newspapers

Non-violence
USE Nonviolence

Nonviolence
UF Non-violence
NT Passive resistance

Nonviolent noncooperation
USE Passive resistance

Norfolk State University (Norfolk, Va.)
BT Historically Black Colleges and Universities—Virginia
Public universities and colleges

North Carolina Agricultural and Technical State University (Greensboro, N.C.)
BT Historically Black Colleges and Universities—North Carolina
Public universities and colleges
State universities and colleges

North Carolina Central University (Durham, N.C.)
BT Historically Black Colleges and Universities—North Carolina
Public universities and colleges

Novelists, African American
  USE African American novelists
Nurses, African American
  USE African American nurses
Nutrition—Religious aspects—Black Muslims
  NT Black Muslims—Dietary laws

O

OIC
  USE Opportunities Industrial Centers of America
Oakwood College (Huntsville, Ala.)
  BT Historically Black Colleges and Universities
      Private universities and colleges
      United Negro College Fund Institutions
Oberlin (Ohio)—History *(Not Subd Geog)*
  NT Oberlin-Wellington Rescue, 1858
Oberlin-Wellington Rescue, 1858 *[E450]*
  BT Fugitive slaves—Ohio—History
      Oberlin (Ohio)—History
      Wellington (Ohio)—History
Occupations and race
  UF Race and occupations
  BT Race
Octoroons
  USE Mulattoes
Olympic games
  USE Olympics
Olympic games (Winter)
  USE Winter Olympics
Olympics
      Here are entered comprehensive works on the Olympics. Works on
      the Olympic events of a particular year are entered under the appropriate
      name heading, e.g. Olympic Games (21st: 1976: Montreal, Quebec).
  UF Games, Olympic
      Olympic games *[Former Heading]*
      Summer Olympics
  NT Winter Olympics
Omega Psi Phi Fraternity
  BT Greek letter societies
Omnibus bill, 1850
  USE Compromise of 1850
One-parent family
  USE Single parent family
Open housing
  USE Discrimination in housing
Opportunities Industrial Centers of America
  UF OIC
  BT Civil rights organizations
Optometrists, African American
  USE African American optometrists
Oral history
      Here are entered works on the technique of recording the oral
      recollections of persons concerning their knowledge of historical
      events, as well as collections of such recollections.

  RT Oral tradition
Oral tradition *(May Subd Geog)*
  UF Tradition, Oral
  RT Folklore
      Oral history
Orators, African American
  USE African American orators
Orchestral musicians, African American
  USE African American orchestral musicians
Ordinaries *(May Subd Geog)*
  BT County officials and employees
Organizations
  USE Associations, institutions, etc.
Outlaws, African American
  USE African American outlaws
Owens Building of the United States Postal Service
      (Cleveland, Ohio)
  USE Jesse Owens Building of the United States
          Postal Service (Cleveland, Ohio)
Owens Finance Station (Cleveland, Ohio)
  USE Jesse Owens Building of the United States
          Postal Service (Cleveland, Ohio)
Owners of plantations
  USE Plantation owners
Ownership of slaves
  USE Slavery
Ownership of slaves by Indians
  USE Indians of North America—Slaves, Ownership of

P

Pageants *(May Subd Geog) [GT3980-GT4099*
      (Manners and customs)] [PN3202-PN3299]
  RT Festivals
  NT Parades
Pageants, Beauty
  USE Beauty contests
Paine College (Augusta, Ga.)
  BT Historically Black Colleges and Universities—
          Georgia
      Private universities and colleges
      United Negro College Fund Institutions
Painters, African American
  USE African American painters
Painters, Black *(May Subd Geog)*
  UF Black painters
Painting, African American
  USE African American painting
Painting, Black *(May Subd Geog)*
  UF Black painting
Pan-Africanism
  UF African relations
  RT African cooperation

Panther 21 Trial, New York, N.Y., 1970-1971
  USE Black Panthers Trial, New York, N.Y., 1970-1971

Parades *(May Subd Geog)* *[GT3980-GT4096]*
  Here are entered works on large public processions of a festive nature, usually including a marching band, and held in honor of an anniversary, person or event.
  UF Pomp
  BT Festivals
      Pageants

Parents, African American
  USE African American parents

Parents, Single
  USE Single parents

Parish schools
  USE Church schools

Parochial schools
  USE Church schools

Participation, Political
  USE Political participation

Parties, House-raising
  USE House-raising parties

Passive resistance *(May Subd Geog)*
  UF Nonviolent noncooperation
      Resistance, Passive
  BT Direct action
      Nonviolence
  NT Boycotts

Patients *(May Subd Geog)*
  RT Sick
  SA *subdivision* Patients *under individual diseases, e.g.* Cancer—Patients; *and subdivisions* Surgery—Patients *and* Transplantation—Patients *under individual organs and regions of the body, e.g.* Heart—Surgery—Patients; Heart—Transplantation—Patients

Paul Quinn College (Dallas, Tex.)
  BT Historically Black Colleges and Universities—Texas
      Private universities and colleges
      United Negro College Fund Institutions

Pedagogy
  USE Education

Pediatric pharmacology *(May Subd Geog)* *[RJ560]*
  UF Children—Drug effects

Pentecostals, African American
  USE African American Pentecostals

Peoples of mixed descent
  USE Racially mixed people

Performing arts centers
  USE Centers for the performing arts

Periodicals *(Not Subd Geog)* *[AP (General periodicals)]* *[PN4700-PN5650 (History)]*
  UF Magazines

  RT Press
  NT Periodicals, Publishing of
      Scholarly periodicals

Periodicals, African American
  USE African American periodicals

Periodicals, Learned
  USE Scholarly periodicals

Periodicals, Publishing of *(May Subd Geog)*
  UF Magazine publishing
      Publishing of periodicals
  BT Periodicals

Periodicals, Scholarly
  USE Scholarly periodicals

Personal health
  USE Health

Personal health services
  USE Medical care

Personal liberty laws *[E450]*
  Here are entered works on laws in certain Northern states protecting African Americans within their borders who had escaped from slavery in the South.
  BT Slavery—United States—Legal status of slaves in free states

Personnel administration
  USE Personnel management

Personnel management *(May Subd Geog)* *[HF5549-HF5549.5]*
  Here are entered works on that field of management which has the fundamental responsibility for recruiting, hiring, training, compensating, developing, and caring for the general welfare of employees.
  UF Corporations—Personnel management
      Employment management
      Human resource management
      Manpower utilization
      Personnel administration
  SA *subdivision* Personnel management *under names of individual corporate bodies and under types of industries and organizations, e.g.* United States. Navy—Personnel management; Construction industry—Personnel management; Hospitals—Personnel management
  NT Affirmative action programs

Petition, Right of *(May Subd Geog)* *[JC609]* *[JK1731 (United States)]*
  Here are entered works on the right of citizens to petition the government for redress of grievances.
  UF Right of petition
  BT Political rights

Pharmacists, African American
  USE African American pharmacists

Phi Beta Sigma Fraternity
  BT Greek letter societies

Phi Delta Kappa Fraternity
  BT Greek letter societies

Philander Smith College (Little Rock, Ark.)
    BT   Historically Black Colleges and Universities—
           Arkansas
           Private universities and colleges
           United Negro College Fund Institutions
Philanthropy
    USE Endowments
Phillips School of Theology
    (Christian Methodist Episcopal)
    BT   Interdenominational Theological Center
           (Atlanta, Ga.)
Philosophy, African American
    USE African American philosophy
Photographers, African American
    USE African American photographers
Physical anthropology *[GN49-GN298]*
    NT   Color of man
          Race
Physicians, African American
    USE African American physicians
Piano music (Blues) *[M20-M32]*
    BT   Blues (Music)
Piano music (Boogie woogie) *[M20-M32]*
    BT   Boogie woogie (Music)
Piano music (Jazz) *[M20-M32]*
Pigmentation
    USE Color of man
Pioneers, African American
    USE African American pioneers
Pioneers, Black *(May Subd Geog)*
    UF   Black pioneers
Plantation life *(May Subd Geog)*
Plantation owners *(May Subd Geog)*
    UF   Owners of plantations
          Planters (Persons)
    RT   Slaveholders
Planters (Persons)
    USE Plantation owners
Players, Musical instrument
    USE Musicians
Playhouses
    USE Theaters
Pluralism (Social sciences) *(May Subd Geog)*
    Here are entered works on the condition in which numerous distinct
    ethnic, religious, or cultural groups coexists within one society.
    Works on policies or programs that foster the preservation of different
    cultural identities, including customs, languages, and beliefs
    within a unified society such as a state or nation, are entered under
    Multiculturalism.
    RT   Ethnicity
          Multiculturalism
    NT   Biculturalism

Poetry—Black authors
    UF   Black poetry
          Negro poetry *[Former Heading]*
Poets, African American
    USE African American poets
Poets, Black
    UF   Black poets
Police, African American
    USE African American police
Police, Black *(May Subd Geog)*
    UF   Black police
          Negro policemen *[Former Heading]*
Polish American—African American relations
    USE African Americans—Relations with Polish
           Americans
Polish Americans—Relations with African Americans
    USE African Americans—Relations with Polish
           Americans
Political activity
    USE Political participation
Political behavior
    USE Political participation
Political consultants, African American
    USE African American political consultants
Political participation *(May Subd Geog)*
    UF   Citizen participation
          Mass political behavior
          Participation, Political
          Political activity
          Political behavior
    BT   Political rights
    SA   *subdivision* Political activity *under names of indi-*
          vidual corporate bodies and families; and
          under classes of persons, types of industries,
          and corporate bodies, military services, and
          Christian denominations, e.g. Construction
          industry—Political activity; African Methodist
          Episcopal Church—Political Activity;
          National Urban Coalition—Political activity
    NT   Minorities—Political activity
Political rights *(May Subd Geog)*
    Here are entered works on rights of citizens to participate, directly
    or indirectly, in the establishment or administration of government.
    UF   Civic rights
    BT   Civil rights
    RT   Citizenship
    NT   Petition, Right of
          Political participation
          Suffrage
Political scientists, African American
    USE African American political scientists
Political violence
    USE Riots
Politicians, African American
    USE African American politicians

Pomp
    USE Parades

Poor *(May Subd Geog)*
    [HV4023-HV4470.7 (Poor in cities)]
    UF   Low income people
          Poor—economic conditions
    RT   Poverty
    NT   Urban poor
          Welfare recipients

Poor—economic conditions
    USE Poor

Poor—Housing
    UF   Low income housing
    RT   Inclusionary housing programs

Poor People's Campaign
    BT   African Americans—Civil rights

Popular music *(May Subd Geog) [M1627-M1844*
    (Music)] [ML3469-ML3541 (History and criticism)]
    Here are entered popular vocal music and collections containing
    both popular instrumental and vocal music.
    UF   Music, Popular
          Music, Popular (songs, etc.) *[Former Heading]*
          Popular songs
          Popular vocal music
          Songs, Popular
          Vocal music, Popular
    BT   Music
    NT   Blues (Music)
          Contemporary Christian music
          Gospel music
          Jazz vocals
          Rhythm and blues music
          Soul music
          Swing (Music)

Popular music—United States *[M1630.18-M1630.2*
    (Music)] [ML3476.8-ML3481 (History and criticism)]
    NT   Rap (Music)

Popular music, Christian
    USE Contemporary Christian music

Popular songs
    USE Popular music

Popular vocal music
    USE Popular music

Population *(Not Subd Geog)*
    [HB848-HB3697 (Demography)]
    Here are entered works on the characteristics of human population,
    especially with reference to the size and density, growth, distribution,
    migration, and vital statistics, and the effect of these on social and
    economic conditions.
    UF   Human population
          Population, Human
    RT   Demography
    SA   *subdivision* Population *under names of coun-*
          tries, cities, etc. and under ethnic groups,
          e.g. African Americans—Population

    NT   Migration, Internal

Population, Human
    USE Population

Post office buildings—Ohio
    UF   Postal service—Ohio—Buildings
          [Former Heading]
    NT   Jesse Owens Building of the United States Post-
          al Service (Cleveland, Ohio)

Postage stamps *[HE6182-HE6185]*
    UF   Stamps, Postage
    NT   African Americans on postage stamps

Postal service—Ohio—Buildings
    USE Post office buildings—Ohio

Poverty *(May Subd Geog)*
    [HC79.P6 (Economic history)] [HV1-HV4630 (Relief)]
    UF   Destitution
    RT   Poor
    NT   Homelessness

Power, Black
    USE Black power

Prairie View Agricultural and Mechanical Univer-
    sity (Prairie View, Tex.)
    BT   Historically Black Colleges and Universities—
          Texas
          Public universities and colleges
          State universities and colleges

Preaching, African American
    USE African American preaching

Prejudgments
    USE Prejudices

Prejudice
    USE Prejudices

Prejudice in testing
    USE Test bias

Prejudice in textbooks
    USE Textbook bias

Prejudices *(May Subd Geog) [BF575.P9]*
    UF   Antipathies
          Bias (Psychology)
          Prejudgments
          Prejudice
          Prejudices and antipathies *[Former Heading]*
    NT   Antisemitism
          Discrimination
          Ethnocentrism
          Racism

Prejudices and antipathies
    USE Prejudices

Prejudices and antipathies (Child psychology)
    USE Prejudices in children

Prejudices in children *(May Subd Geog) [BF723.P75]*
    UF   Prejudices and antipathies (Child psychology)
          [Former Heading]
    BT   Child psychology

Prentiss Institute Junior College (Prentiss, Miss.)
- BT   Historically Black Colleges and Universities—
            Mississippi
        Junior colleges

Presbyterians, African American
- USE   African American Presbyterians

Presbyterians, Negro
- USE   African American Presbyterians

Preschool education
- USE   Education, Preschool

Presidents—United States—Racial attitudes
- UF   Presidents—United States—Views on race
            question
        Racial attitudes of American presidents
- BT   United States—Race relations

Presidents—United States—Views on race question
- USE   Presidents—United States—Racial attitudes

Presidents, College
- USE   College presidents

Press *(May Subd Geog) [PN4700-PN5650]*
- RT   Periodicals
- NT   African Americans in the press
        Blacks in the press
        Hate crimes in the press
        Minorities in the press
        Race relations and the press
        Racism in the press

Press, African American
- USE   African American press

Press and segregation
- USE   Segregation and the press

Primary education
- USE   Education, Primary

Principles of nationalities
- USE   Nationalities, Principles of

Printmakers, African American
- USE   African American printmakers

Prints, African American
- USE   African American prints

Prints, Black *(May Subd Geog)*
- UF   Black prints

Prisoners, African American
- USE   African American prisoners

Prisons and race problems
- USE   Prisons and race relations

Prisons and race relations *(May Subd Geog)*
- UF   Prisons and race problems *[Former Heading]*
        Race relations and prisons
- BT   Race relations

Private schools *(May Subd Geog) [LC47-LC57]*
- UF   Independent schools
        Schools, Private
        Secondary schools
- NT   Church schools
        Private universities and colleges

Private universities and colleges
- BT   Historically Black Colleges and Universities
        Private schools
- NT   Allen University (Columbia, S.C.)
        Arkansas Baptist College (Little Rock, Ark.)
        Barber-Scotia College (Concord, N.C.)
        Benedict College (Columbia, S.C.)
        Bennett College (Greensboro, N.C.)
        Bethune-Cookman College (Daytona Beach, Fla.)
        Charles R. Drew University of Medicine and
            Science (Los Angeles, Calif.)
        Claflin College (Orangeburg, S.C.)
        Clark Atlanta University (Atlanta, Ga.)
        Clinton Junior College (Rock Hill, S.C.)
        Concordia College (Selma, Ala.)
        Dillard University (New Orleans, La.)
        Edward Waters College (Jacksonville, Fla.)
        Fisk University (Nashville, Tenn.)
        Florida Memorial College (Miami, Fla.)
        Hampton University (Hampton, Va.)
        Howard University (Washington, D.C.)
        Huston-Tillotson College (Austin, Tex.)
        Interdenominational Theological Center
            (Atlanta, Ga.)
        Jarvis Christian College (Hawkins, Tex.)
        Johnson C. Smith University (Charlotte, N.C.)
        Knoxville College (Knoxville, Tenn.)
        Knoxville College-Morristown Campus
            (Morristown, Tenn.)
        Lane College (Jackson, Tenn.)
        LeMoyne-Owen College (Memphis, Tenn.)
        Lewis College of Business (Detroit, Mich.)
        Livingstone College (Salisbury, N.C.)
        Mary Holmes College (West Point, Miss.)
        Meharry Medical College (Nashville, Tenn.)
        Miles College (Birmingham, Ala.)
        Morehouse College (Atlanta, Ga.)
        Morehouse School of Medicine (Atlanta, Ga.)
        Morris Brown College (Atlanta, Ga.)
        Morris College (Sumter, S.C.)
        Natchez Junior College (Natchez, Miss.)
        Oakwood College (Huntsville, Ala.)
        Paine College (Augusta, Ga.)
        Paul Quinn College (Dallas, Tex.)
        Philander Smith College (Little Rock, Ark.)
        Rust College (Holly Springs, Miss.)
        Saint Augustine's College (Raleigh, N.C.)
        Saint Paul's College (Lawrenceville, Va.)
        Selma University (Selma, Ala.)
        Shaw University (Raleigh, N.C.)
        Shorter College (North Little Rock, Ark.)
        Simmons University Bible School (Louisville, Ky.)
        Southwestern Christian College (Terrell, Tex.)
        Spelman College (Atlanta, Ga.)
        Stillman College (Tuscaloosa, Ala.)
        Talladega College (Talladega, Ala.)
        Texas College (Tyler, Tex.)

Tougaloo College (Tougaloo, Miss.)
Tuskegee University (Tuskegee, Ala.)
Virginia Seminary College (Lynchburg, Va.)
Virginia Union University (Richmond, Va.)
Voorhees College (Denmark, S.C.)
Wilberforce University (Wilberforce, Ohio)
Wiley College (Marshall, Tex.)
Xavier University (New Orleans, La.)

Prizes (Rewards)
USE Awards
Professional associations
USE Trade and professional associations
Progressive National Baptist Convention *(May Subd Geog)*
BT Religious institutions
SA *names of individual churches, e.g.* Friendship Baptist Church (Atlanta, Ga.)
Protest movements (Civil rights)
USE Civil rights movements
Proverbs, African American
USE African American proverbs
Proverbs, Black
UF Black proverbs
Proverbs, Negro *[Former Heading]*
Proverbs, Negro
USE African American proverbs
Proverbs, Black
Psychiatric care
USE Mental health services
Psychiatric services
USE Mental health services
Psychics, African American
USE African American psychics
Psychological tests for minorities
USE Minorities—Psychological testing
Psychologists, African American
USE African American psychologists
Psychologists, Minority
USE Minority psychologists
Psychology, Child
USE Child psychology
Psychology, Cross-cultural studies
USE Ethnopsychology
Psychology, Ethnic
USE Ethnopsychology
Psychology, Racial
USE Ethnopsychology
Public accommodations, Discrimination in
USE Discrimination in public accommodations
Public buildings—Texas
NT Martin Luther King, Jr. Federal Building (Victoria, Tex.)

Public buildings—Washington (D.C.)
NT Thurgood Marshall Federal Judiciary Building (Washington, D.C.)
Public community colleges
USE Community colleges
Public demonstrations
USE Demonstrations
Public Health Service Study of Untreated Syphilis in the Male Negro
USE Tuskegee Syphilis Study
Public housing *(May Subd Geog)*
UF Government housing
Housing projects, Government
Low income housing
BT Housing
Public junior colleges
USE Community colleges
Public libraries—Services to minorities *[Z711.8]*
BT Libraries and minorities
Minorities—Services for
Public school closings *(May Subd Geog) [LB2832.2]*
Here are entered works which discuss the permanent closing of a public school building, due to declining enrollment, obsolescence, etc.
BT School closings
Public school closings—Law and legislation
BT Educational law and legislation
Public schools *(May Subd Geog) [L-LC]*
Here are entered works on preschool, elementary and secondary schools controlled or supported by state or local governments.
UF Grammar schools
Secondary schools
RT Schools
SA *headings beginning with the word* School
NT High schools
Magnet schools
Public services
USE Municipal services
Public two-year colleges
USE Community colleges
Public universities and colleges
BT Historically Black Colleges and Universities
NT Alabama Agricultural and Mechanical University (Normal, Ala.)
Alabama State University (Montgomery, Ala.)
Albany State College (Albany, Ga.)
Alcorn State University (Lorman, Miss.)
Arkansas at Pine Bluff, University of (Pine Bluff, Ark.)
Bishop (S.D.) State Junior College (Mobile, Ala.)
Bluefield State College (Bluefield, W.Va.)
Bowie State College (Bowie, Md.)
Carver State Technical College (Mobile, Ala.)
Central State University (Wilberforce, Ohio)
Cheyney State University (Cheyney, Pa.)
Coahoma Junior College (Clarksdale, Miss.)

Coppin State College (Baltimore, Md.)
Delaware State College (Dover, Del.)
Denmark Technical College (Denmark, S.C.)
District of Columbia, University of the
(Washington, D.C.)
Drake (J.F.) Technical College (Huntsville, Ala.)
Elizabeth City State University
(Elizabeth City, N.C.)
Fayetteville State University (Fayetteville, N.C.)
Florida Agricultural and Mechanical University
(Tallahassee, Fla.)
Fort Valley State College (Fort Valley, Ga.)
Grambling State University (Grambling, La.)
Harris-Stowe State College (St. Louis, Mo.)
Hinds Junior College (Utica, Miss.)
Jackson State University (Jackson, Miss.)
Kentucky State University (Frankfort, Ky.)
Langston University (Langston, Okla.)
Lawson State Community College
(Birmingham, Ala.)
Lincoln University (Jefferson City, Mo.)
Lincoln University (Lincoln University, Pa.)
Maryland Eastern Shore, University of
(Princess Anne, Md.)
Mississippi Valley State University
(Itta Bena, Miss.)
Morgan State University (Baltimore, Md.)
Norfolk State University (Norfolk, Va.)
North Carolina Agricultural and Technical State
University (Greensboro, N.C.)
North Carolina Central University (Durham, N.C.)
Prairie View Agricultural and Mechanical
University (Prairie View, Tex.)
Saint Philip's College (San Antonio, Tex.)
Savannah State College (Savannah, Ga.)
South Carolina State College (Orangeburg, S.C.)
Southern University (Baton Rouge, La.)
Southern University (New Orleans, La.)
Southern University (Shreveport, La.)
Tennessee State University (Nashville, Tenn.)
Texas Southern University (Houston, Tex.)
Trenholm State Technical College
(Montgomery, Ala.)
Virgin Islands, University of the (St. Thomas, V.I.)
Virginia State University (Petersburg, Va.)
West Virginia State College (Institute, W.Va.)
Winston-Salem State University
(Winston-Salem, N.C.)
Public welfare recipients
USE   Welfare recipients
Publishing of periodicals
USE   Periodicals, Publishing of
Pupils
USE   Students

Q

Quadroons
USE   Mulattoes
Quiltmakers, African American
USE   African American quiltmakers
Quilts, African American
USE   African American quilts
Quotas in employment
USE   Reverse discrimination in employment
Quotations, Black
USE   Blacks—Quotations

R

Race *[BF730-BF738 (Psychology)] [BT734 (Theology)] [CB195-CB281(Civilization)] [GN (Anthropology)] [HT1501-HT1595 (Sociology)]*
BT   Physical anthropology
NT   Black race
Ethnocentrism
Health and race
Mortality and race
Occupations and race
Race—Religious aspects *[BL65.R3]*
UF   Religion and race *[Former Heading]*
Race—Religious aspects—Christianity
UF   Race (Theology)
Race (Theology)
USE   Race—Religious aspects—Christianity
Race and art
USE   Art and race
Race and music
USE   Music and race
Race and occupations
USE   Occupations and race
Race awareness *(May Subd Geog)*
BT   Ethnopsychology
RT   Ethnic attitudes
NT   African Americans—Race identity
Blacks—Race identity
Race discrimination—Psychological aspects
Racism
Race awareness in children *(May Subd Geog)*
[BF723.R3]
BT   Child psychology
Race awareness in literature
Race discrimination *(May Subd Geog)*
Here are entered works which are limited to overt discriminatory behavior directed against racial or ethnic groups. Works on racism as an attitude as well as works on both attitude and overt discriminatory behavior directed against racial or ethnic groups are entered under Racism. Works on discrimination directed against a particular group are entered under the name of the group with subdivision Social conditions, or similar subdivision, e.g. Civil rights. When the heading Race discrimination is subdivided by place, a second subject entry is made in each case under the name of the place subdivided by Race relations.

UF   Discrimination, Racial
       Racial discrimination
BT   Discrimination
       Minorities
       Race relations
       Racism
NT   Segregation

Race discrimination—Law and legislation *(May Subd Geog)*

Race discrimination—Psychological aspects
BT   Race awareness

Race discrimination—Religious aspects

Race discrimination—United States
NT   African Americans—Civil rights

Race discrimination in consumer credit
   USE Discrimination in consumer credit

Race discrimination in credit cards
   USE Discrimination in credit cards

Race discrimination in criminal justice administration
   USE Discrimination in criminal justice administration

Race discrimination in education
   USE Discrimination in education

Race discrimination in employment
   USE Discrimination in employment

Race discrimination in higher education
   USE Discrimination in higher education

Race discrimination in housing
   USE Discrimination in housing

Race discrimination in insurance
   USE Discrimination in insurance

Race discrimination in law enforcement
   USE Discrimination in law enforcement

Race discrimination in medical care
   USE Discrimination in medical care

Race discrimination in medical education
   USE Discrimination in medical education

Race discrimination in mental health services
   USE Discrimination in mental health services

Race discrimination in mortgage loans
   USE Discrimination in mortgage loans

Race discrimination in municipal services
   USE Discrimination in municipal services

Race discrimination in public accommodations
   USE Discrimination in public accommodations

Race discrimination in sports
   USE Discrimination in sports

Race prejudice
   USE Racism

Race problems
   USE Race relations

Race problems and the press
   USE Race relations and the press

Race problems in school management
   USE Race relations in school management

Race psychology
   USE Ethnopsychology

Race question
   USE Race relations

Race relations *[GN496-GN498 (Ethnology)]* *[HT1501-HT1595 (Sociology)]*
UF   Integration, Racial
       Race problems *[Former Heading]*
       Race question
       Relations, Race
BT   Ethnology
       Social problems
RT   Ethnic relations
       Minorities
       Racism
SA   *subdivision* Race relations *under names of countries, cities, etc. and individual races and ethnic groups with pertinent topical subdivisions, e.g.* African Americans—Relations with Jews; African Americans—Civil rights
NT   Antisemitism
       Blacks—Relocation
       Culture conflict
       Interracial adoption
       Mass media and race relations
       Miscegenation
       Pluralism (Social sciences)
       Prisons and race relations
       Race discrimination
       Social service and race relations

Race relations—Folklore
UF   Race relations (in religion, folklore, etc.) *[Former Heading]*

Race relations—Religious aspects
For works limited to a place, an additional subject heading is assigned for the name of the place with the subdivision Race relations.
UF   Race relations (in religion, folklore, etc.) *[Former Heading]*

Race relations—Religious aspects—Baptists, [Catholic Church, etc.]

Race relations—Religious aspects—Christianity
UF   Church and race problems *[Former Heading]*
       Church and race relations *[Former Heading]*

Race relations (in religion, folklore, etc.)
   USE Race relations—Folklore
           Race relations—Religious aspects

Race relations and prisons
   USE Prisons and race relations

Race relations and the press *(May Subd Geog)*
UF   Race problems and the press *[Former Heading]*
BT   Press

Race relations in motion pictures

Race relations in school management *(May Subd Geog)*
> UF Race problems in school management
> *[Former Heading]*
> BT School management and organization
> NT School integration
> Segregation in education

Race relations reformers
> USE Civil rights workers

Races of man
> USE Ethnology

Racial amalgamation
> USE Miscegenation

Racial attitudes of American presidents
> USE Presidents—United States—Racial attitudes

Racial crossing
> USE Miscegenation

Racial discrimination
> USE Race discrimination

Racial identity of African Americans
> USE African Americans—Race identity

Racial identity of Blacks
> USE Blacks—Race identity

Racial integration in sports
> USE Discrimination in sports

Racially mixed people *(May Subd Geog)*
> UF Biracial minorities
> Peoples of mixed descent
> BT Ethnic groups
> RT Miscegenation
> NT Children of interracial marriage
> Creoles
> Mulattoes

Racism *(May Subd Geog)*
> Here are entered works on racism as an attitude as well as works on both attitude and overt discriminatory behavior directed against racial or ethnic groups. Works which are limited to overt discriminatory behavior directed against racial or ethnic groups are entered under Race discrimination. Works on racism directed against a particular group are entered under the name of the group with subdivision Social conditions, or similar subdivision, e.g. Civil rights. When the heading Racism is subdivided by place, a second subject entry is made in each case under the name of the place subdivided by Race relations.
> UF Race prejudice
> BT Ethnocentrism
> Prejudices
> Race awareness
> RT Race relations
> NT Antisemitism
> Race discrimination

Racism—Religious aspects

Racism—Religious aspects—[Christianity, etc.]

Racism and language
> USE Racism in language

Racism in language
> UF Language and racism
> Racism and language
> Racist language

Racism in motion pictures

Racism in textbooks *(May Subd Geog) [LB3045.64]*
> BT Discrimination in education

Racism in the press *(May Subd Geog)*
> BT Press

Racism in theological seminaries *(May Subd Geog)*
> BT Theological seminaries

Racist language
> USE Racism in language

Racist speech
> USE Hate speech

Raconteurs
> USE Storytellers

Radio broadcasting—United States
> NT African Americans in radio broadcasting

Radio stations, African American
> USE African American radio stations

Ragtime music *(May Subd Geog) [M1366 (Music)]*
[ML3505.8-ML3509 (History and criticism)]
> UF Ragtime music—United States
> BT Jazz

Ragtime music—United States
> USE Ragtime music

Rainbow Coalition
> USE National Rainbow Coalition

Ramapo Mountain people
> UF Jackson whites
> Mountain people (Ramapo Mountains)
> BT African Americans—New Jersey
> African Americans—New York (State)
> Ethnology—New Jersey
> Ethnology—New York (State)
> Indians of North America—Mixed descent
> Mulattoes

Rap (Music) *(May Subd Geog)*
> UF Rap (Music)—United States
> Rap songs
> Rappin (Music)
> Rapping (Music) *[Former Heading]*
> BT Dance music—United States
> Improvisation (Music)
> Monologues with music
> Popular music—United States

Rap (Music)—United States
> USE Rap (Music)

Rap musicians *(May Subd Geog)*
> UF Rappers
> BT Musicians

Rap songs
USE Rap (Music)
Rappers
USE Rap musicians
Rappin (Music)
USE Rap (Music)
Rapping (Music)
USE Rap (Music)
Ras Tafari movement *(May Subd Geog) [BL2532.R37]*
UF Rastafari movement
BT Black nationalism
Blacks—Religion
Cults
Rastafari movement
USE Ras Tafari movement
Real covenants *(May Subd Geog)*
UF Covenants running with land
Restrictive covenants
RT Discrimination in housing—Law and legislation
Real estate loans
USE Mortgage loans
Rebop (Music)
USE Bop (Music)
Reconstruction—African American troops
UF African American militia movement
Reconstruction—Negro troops *[Former Heading]*
BT African American soldiers
Reconstruction—Negro troops
USE Reconstruction—African American troops
Records, Slave
USE Slave records
Records of births, etc.
USE Registers of births, etc.
Recruiting of college athletes
USE College athletes—Recruiting
Red lining
USE Discrimination in credit cards
Discrimination in mortgage loans
Redlining
USE Discrimination in credit cards
Discrimination in mortgage loans
Refugees, African American
USE Freedmen
Fugitive slaves—United States
Registers of births, etc. *(May Subd Geog)*
[HA38-HA39]
UF Birth records
Births, Registers
Burial statistics
Deaths, Registers of
Records of births, etc.
Registers of deaths
Vital records

BT Genealogy
RT Vital statistics
NT Slave records
Registers of deaths
USE Registers of births, etc.
Relations, Race
USE Race relations
Relations among ethnic groups
USE Ethnic relations
Religion and race
USE Race—Religious aspects
Religious and ecclesiastical institutions
USE Religious institutions
Religious education
Here are entered works dealing with instruction in religion in schools and private life.
NT Islamic religious education
Religious education, Islamic
USE Islamic religious education
Religious institutions *(May Subd Geog)*
UF Ecclesiastical institutions
Institutions, Ecclesiastical
Institutions, Religious
Religious and ecclesiastical institutions
[Former Heading]
BT Associations, institutions, etc.
RT African Americans—Religion
NT African Methodist Episcopal Church
African Methodist Episcopal Zion Church
Black Muslims
Christian Methodist Episcopal Church
Church of God in Christ, Inc.
National Baptist Convention of America, Inc.
National Baptist Convention, U.S.A., Inc.
Progressive National Baptist Convention
Relocation of Blacks
USE Blacks—Relocation
Removal of Blacks
USE Blacks—Relocation
Renaissance, Harlem
USE Harlem Renaissance
Representatives in Congress (United States)
USE United States. Congress. House
Resettlement of Blacks
USE Blacks—Relocation
Resistance, Passive
USE Passive resistance
Restrictive covenants
USE Real covenants
Reunions, Family
USE Family reunions
Reverse discrimination *(May Subd Geog)*
BT Discrimination

Reverse discrimination—Law and legislation *(May Subd Geog)*

Reverse discrimination in employment *(May Subd Geog)*
- UF   Employment quotas
  Quotas in employment
- BT   Affirmative action programs
  Discrimination in employment

Reverse discrimination in employment— Law and legislation
- BT   Labor laws and legislation

Revival hymns
- USE   Revivals-Hymns

Revivals—Hymns *[BV460]*
- UF   Camp-meeting hymns
  Hymns, Revival
  Revival hymns
- BT   Gospel music

Rewards (Prizes, etc.)
- USE   Awards

Rhythm and blues music *(May Subd Geog) [ML3521 (History and criticism)]*
- UF   Music, Rhythm and blues
  Rhythm and blues music—United States
  Rhythm 'n' blues music
- BT   African Americans—Music
  Popular music

Rhythm and blues music—United States
- USE   Rhythm and blues music

Rhythm 'n' blues music
- USE   Rhythm and blues music

Right of petition
- USE   Petition, Right of

Right to a fair trial
- USE   Fair trial

Right to vote
- USE   Suffrage

Rights, Civil
- USE   Civil rights

Riots *(May Subd Geog) [HM281-HM283 (Psychology of)] [HV6475-HV6485]*
- UF   Civil disorders
  Political violence
- RT   Demonstrations
- SA   *subdivision* Riot, [date] *or* Riots *under names of individual educational institutions, e.g.* Jackson State University (Jackson, Miss.)—Riots

Riots—California
- NT   Watts Riot, Los Angeles, Calif., 1965

Runaway slaves
- USE   Fugitive slaves

Rural exodus
- USE   Rural-urban migration

Rural-urban migration *(May Subd Geog) [HB1955]*
Here are entered works on population shifts from a rural to an urban environment. Works on population shifts from an urban to a rural environment are entered under Urban-rural migration.
- UF   Cities and towns, Movement to
  Country-city migration
  Migration, Rural-urban
  Rural exodus
- BT   Migration, Internal
- RT   Urbanization

Rust College (Holly Springs, Miss.)
- BT   Historically Black Colleges and Universities— Mississippi
  Private universities and colleges
  United Negro College Fund Institutions

S

Sacred songs
- NT   Gospel music

Saint Augustine's College (Raleigh, N.C.)
- UF   St. Augustine's College
- BT   Historically Black Colleges and Universities— North Carolina
  Private universities and colleges
  United Negro College Fund Institutions

Saint Paul's College (Lawrenceville, Va.)
- UF   St. Paul's College
- BT   Historically Black Colleges and Universities— Virginia
  Private universities and colleges
  United Negro College Fund Institutions

Saint Philip's College (San Antonio, Tex.)
- UF   St. Philip's College (San Antonio, Tex.)
- BT   Historically Black Colleges and Universities— Texas
  Junior colleges
  Public universities and colleges

Savannah Historic District (Savannah, Ga.)

Savannah State College (Savannah, Ga.)
- BT   Historically Black Colleges and Universities— Georgia
  Public universities and colleges

Saxophone and piano music (Jazz)
- USE   Jazz

Scat singing
- USE   Jazz vocals

Scholarly journals
- USE   Scholarly periodicals

Scholarly periodicals
- UF   Journals, Scholarly
  Learned periodicals
  Periodicals, Learned
  Periodicals, Scholarly
  Scholarly journals
- BT   Periodicals

Scholars, African American
USE African American scholars
Schomberg Center for Research in Black Culture (New York, N.Y.)
BT Archives—African American
School administration
USE School management and organization
School boards—Membership, Negro
USE School boards—United States—Membership, African American
School boards—United States—Membership, African American
UF African American membership in school boards
African American school board members
School boards—Membership, Negro
[Former Heading]
BT African Americans
School busing for integration
USE Busing for school integration
School children—Transportation—Law and legislation
BT Educational law and legislation
School closings *(May Subd Geog) [LB2823.2]*
UF Closed schools
Closing of schools
Closings of schools
School closing
NT Public school closings
School closing
USE School closings
School desegregation
USE School integration
School integration *(May Subd Geog) [LC214-LC214.3]*
UF Desegregation in education
Education—Integration
Integration in education
School desegregation
BT Race relations in school management
RT Magnet schools
Segregation in education
NT Busing for school integration
College integration
De facto school segregation
Faculty integration
School integration—United States
RT African Americans—Education
School libraries—Services to minorities
BT Libraries and minorities
School life
USE Students

School management and organization *(May Subd Geog) [LB2801-LB2997 (Organization and supervision)] [LB3011-LB3095 (Management and discipline)]*
Here are entered general works on the administration and organization of schools. Works on the supervision of instruction within schools are entered under School supervision.
UF Educational administration
School administration
School organization
Schools—Management and organization
NT Race relations in school management
School organization
USE School management and organization
School principals, African American
USE African American school principals
School superintendents, African American
USE African American school superintendents
School violence *(May Subd Geog) [LB3013.3]*
UF Student violence
Violence in schools
Schools *(May Subd Geog) [L]*
RT Education
Public schools
SA *headings beginning with the word* School *and names of individual schools*
NT Elementary schools
High schools
Historically Black Colleges and Universities
Middle schools
Urban schools
Schools—Curricula
USE Education—Curricula
Schools—Management and organization
USE School management and organization
Schools, City
USE Urban schools
Schools, Denominational
USE Church schools
Schools, Magnet
USE Magnet schools
Schools, Parochial
USE Church schools
Schools, Private
USE Private schools
Schools, Urban
USE Urban schools
Scientists, African American
USE African American scientists
SCLC
USE Southern Christian Leadership Conference
Scottsboro Trial, Scottsboro, Ala., 1931
BT Trials (Rape)—Alabama
Sculpture, African American
USE African American sculpture

Sea Islands Creole dialect *(May Subd Geog)*
[PM7875.G8]
   UF   Geechee dialect
         Gullah dialect *[Former Heading]*
   BT   Black English
         Creole dialects, English—Florida
         Creole dialects, English—Georgia
         Creole dialects, English—South Carolina
Seamen, African American
   USE African American seamen
Secession *[E458-E459 (United States Civil War)]*
   BT   Slavery—United States
   RT   State rights
Secondary boycotts
   USE Boycotts
Secondary education
   USE Education, Secondary
Secondary schools
   USE Education, Secondary
         High schools
         Private schools
         Public schools
Secret societies *(May Subd Geog)*
   UF   Fraternities
   BT   Societies
   RT   Initiations (into trades, societies, etc.)
   NT   Ancient Egyptian Arabic Order Nobles Mystic Shrine, Inc.
         Improved Benevolent Protective Order of Elks of the World
Section 1983 actions (Civil rights)
   USE State action (Civil rights)
Segregation *(May Subd Geog)*
   UF   Desegregation
   BT   Discrimination
         Race discrimination
   RT   Minorities
   SA   *subdivision* Segregation *under names of ethnic groups, e.g.* African Americans—Segregation
   NT   Blacks—Relocation
         Blacks—Segregation
Segregation—Law and legislation *(May Subd Geog)*
Segregation—Religious aspects
Segregation and the press
   UF   Press and segregation
Segregation in education *(May Subd Geog)*
[LC212.5-LC212.73]
   UF   Education—Segregation
   BT   Race relations in school management
   RT   Discrimination in education
         School integration
   NT   Busing for school integration
         De facto school segregation

Segregation in education—Law and legislation *(May Subd Geog)*
   BT   Educational law and legislation
Segregation in education—United States
   BT   African Americans—Education
         African Americans—Segregation
Segregation in higher education *(May Subd Geog)*
   UF   Desegregation in higher education
         Education, Higher—Segregation
         Integration in higher education
Segregation in higher education—Law and legislation *(May Subd Geog)*
Segregation in higher education—United States
   BT   African Americans—Education
         African Americans—Segregation
Segregation in housing
   USE Discrimination in housing
Segregation in public accommodations
   USE Discrimination in public accommodations
Segregation in sports
   USE Discrimination in sports
Segregation in transportation *(May Subd Geog)*
   UF   Discrimination in transportation
   BT   Discrimination in public accommodations
Segregation in transportation—Law and legislation *(May Subd Geog)*
Segregation in transportation—United States
   BT   African Americans—Segregation
Self-determination, National
   RT   Nationalities, Principles of
Selma-Montgomery Rights March, 1965
   UF   Montgomery Rights March, 1965
   BT   African Americans—Civil rights
Selma University (Selma, Ala.)
   BT   Historically Black Colleges and Universities—Alabama
         Private universities and colleges
Seminaries, Theological
   USE Theological seminaries
Seminole Indians—Mixed bloods
   USE Seminole Indians—Mixed descent
Seminole Indians—Mixed descent
   UF   Seminole Indians—Mixed bloods *[Former Heading]*
   NT   Black Seminoles
Seminole Indians, Black
   USE Black Seminoles
Senators (United States)
   USE United States. Congress. Senate
Separatism, Black
   USE Black nationalism

Serfdom *(May Subd Geog)* *[HT751-HT815]*
UF   Servitude
RT   Slavery

Sermons, American—African American authors
UF   African American sermons (English)
      Sermons, American—Negro authors
      [Former Heading]

Sermons, American—Negro authors
USE   Sermons, American—African American
      authors

Servitude
USE   Serfdom
      Slavery

Seventh-Day Adventists, African American
USE   African American Seventh-Day Adventists

Seventh-Day Adventists, Negro
USE   African American Seventh-Day Adventists

Shape note hymnals
UF   Hymnals, Shape note
BT   Hymns, English—United States

Shaw University (Raleigh, N.C.)
BT   Historically Black Colleges and Universities—
      North Carolina
      Private universities and colleges
      United Negro College Fund Institutions

Ship captains, African American
USE   African American ship captains

Short stories, American—African American authors
UF   African American short stories (English)
      Black short stories (American)
BT   Short stories, American—Minority authors

Short stories, American—Minority authors
NT   Short stories, American—African American
      authors

Shorter College (North Little Rock, Ark.)
BT   Historically Black Colleges and Universities—
      Arkansas
      Junior colleges
      Private universities and colleges

Shows, Craft
USE   Craft festivals

Shriners
USE   Ancient Egyptian Arabic Order Nobles Mystic
      Shrine, Inc.

Sick *(May Subd Geog)* *[HV687-HV694 (Social Service)]*
RT   Diseases
      Patients
SA   *subdivision* Patients *under individual diseases,*
      e.g., Cancer—Patients

Sickness
USE   Diseases

Sigma Gamma Rho Sorority
BT   Greek letter societies

Sigma Pi Phi Fraternity
BT   Greek letter societies

Simmons University Bible School (Louisville, Ky.)
BT   African American theological seminaries
      Historically Black Colleges and Universities—
      Kentucky
      Private universities and colleges

Singers, African American
USE   African American singers

Single parent family
UF   One-parent family
RT   Single parents
      Unmarried fathers
      Unmarried mothers

Single parents
UF   Parents, Single
RT   Single parent family
NT   Children of single parents

Single people, African American
USE   African American single people

Sit-ins (Civil rights)
USE   Civil rights demonstrations

Skin
NT   Color of man

Skin, Color of
USE   Color of man

Skin pigmentation
USE   Color of man

Slave bills of sale *(May Subd Geog)*
BT   Bills of sale
      Slave records

Slave cabins
USE   Slaves—Dwellings

Slave dealers
USE   Slave traders

Slave holders
USE   Slaveholders

Slave keeping
USE   Slavery

Slave labor *(May Subd Geog)* *[HD4861-HD4865]*

Slave owners
USE   Slaveholders

Slave quarters
USE   Slaves—Dwellings

Slave records *(May Subd Geog)*
UF   Records, Slave
      Vital records
BT   Registers of births, etc.
      Vital statistics
NT   Slave bills of sale

Slave-trade *(May Subd Geog)*
[HT975-HT1445 (General)]
- BT Slavery
- NT Slave traders
  Slavery (International law)

Slave traders *(May Subd Geog)*
- UF Slave dealers
  Slavers
  Traders, Slave
- BT Slave-trade
  Slavery

Slaveholders *(May Subd Geog)*
- UF Slave holders
  Slave owners
- BT Slavery
- RT Plantation owners

Slaveholders—United States
- NT African American slaveholders

Slaveholders, African American
- USE African American slaveholders

Slavers
- USE Slave traders

Slavery *(May Subd Geog) [E441-E453*
(United States)] [HT851-HT1445 (General)]
- UF Abolition of slavery
  Antislavery
  Ownership of slaves
  Servitude
  Slave keeping
- BT Crimes against humanity
- RT Serfdom
- NT Slave-trade
  Slave traders
  Slaveholders
  Slaves

Slavery—Anti-slavery movements
- UF Antislavery movements
- RT Abolitionists

Slavery—Condition of slaves
- USE Slaves—Social conditions

Slavery—Emancipation
- USE Slaves—Emancipation

Slavery—Fugitive slaves
- USE Fugitive slaves

Slavery—Insurrections, etc.

Slavery—Justification *[E449]*

Slavery—Law and legislation

Slavery—United States *[E438 (Slavery question,*
1857-1861)] [E441-E458 (General)]
- UF Slavery in the United States *[Former Heading]*
- NT Compromise of 1850
  Indians of North America—Slaves, Ownership of
  Kansas-Nebraska Bill
  Missouri Compromise

  Secession
  Southern States—History
  Squatter sovereignty
  State rights

Slavery—United States—Colonization
- USE African Americans—Colonization

Slavery—United States—Emancipation
- USE Slaves—Emancipation—United States

Slavery—United States—Extension to the territories

Slavery—United States—Gift books
- UF Slavery—United States—Giftbooks
  [Former Heading]

Slavery—United States—Giftbooks
- USE Slavery—United States—Gift books

Slavery—United States—History

Slavery—United States—History—Colonial period,
ca. 1600-1775 *[E188] [E441-E446]*

Slavery—United States—Insurrections, etc.
- NT Southampton Insurrection, 1831

Slavery—United States—Legal status of slaves in
free states *[E450]*
- NT Personal liberty laws

Slavery (International law)
- BT Slave-trade

Slavery and slaves in literature
- UF Slaves in literature

Slavery and the church *(May Subd Geog)*
[HT910-HT921]
- UF Church and slavery

Slavery and the church—Baptists,
[Catholic Church, etc.]

Slavery in the United States
- USE Slavery—United States

Slaves *(May Subd Geog)*
- BT Slavery
- NT Freedmen
  Fugitive slaves
  Women slaves

Slaves—Biography

Slaves—Dwellings *(May Subd Geog)*
- UF Slave cabins
  Slave quarters

Slaves—Emancipation *(May Subd Geog)*
[HT1025-HT1037]
- UF Emancipation of slaves
  Manumission of slaves
  Slavery—Emancipation *[Former Heading]*
  Slaves—Manumission

Slaves—Emancipation—United States
- UF Slavery—United States—Emancipation
  [Former Heading]
  Slaves—United States—Emancipation
  [Former Heading]

Slaves—Manumission
    USE Slaves—Emancipation
Slaves—Social conditions
    UF   Slavery—Condition of slaves *[Former Heading]*
Slaves—United States
    NT   Mammies
Slaves—United States—Emancipation
    USE Slaves—Emancipation—United States
Slaves, Women
    USE Women slaves
Slaves in literature
    USE Slavery and slaves in literature
Slaves' writings, American *(May Subd Geog)*
    UF   American slaves' writings
Slum clearance
    USE Housing
           Slums
Slums *(May Subd Geog) [HV4023-HV4170]*
    UF   Slum clearance
    BT   Housing
SNCC
    USE Student Nonviolent Coordinating Committee
Social anthropology
    USE Ethnology
Social classes and language
    USE Speech and social status
Social classes and speech
    USE Speech and social status
Social integration *(May Subd Geog)*
    UF   Integration, Social
Social marginality
    USE Marginality, Social
Social problems *(May Subd Geog) [HN]*
    UF   Social welfare
    NT   Ethnic relations
           Race relations
Social service and race problems
    USE Social service and race relations
Social service and race relations *(May Subd Geog)*
    UF   Social service and race problems
           [Former Heading]
    BT   Race relations
Social status *(May Subd Geog)*
    UF   Socioeconomic status
           Status, Social
    SA   *subdivision* Social conditions *under classes of*
           persons, e.g. African Americans—Social
           conditions
    NT   Speech and social status
Social status and language
    USE Speech and social status

Social status and speech
    USE Speech and social status
Social welfare
    USE Social problems
Social work with African American children *(May Subd Geog) [HV3183-HV3185]*
    BT   African American children
Social work with African Americans *(May Subd Geog) [HV3181-HV3185]*
    UF   African Americans—Social work with
           [Former Heading]
    BT   African Americans
Social work with minorities *(May Subd Geog)*
    BT   Minorities
Social work with the socially handicapped *(May Subd Geog)*
    BT   Socially handicapped
Social workers, African American
    USE African American social workers
Socialization *[GN510 (Ethnology)] [HQ783 (Child development)] [LC192.4 (Education)]*
    Here are entered works dealing with the process by which individuals are taught to function in a group and share group values and patterns of behavior.
    UF   Enculturation
    BT   Acculturation
           Ethnology
    NT   Assimilation (Sociology)
Socially disadvantaged
    USE Socially handicapped
Socially handicapped *(May Subd Geog)*
    UF   Culturally deprived
           Culturally disadvantaged
           Culturally handicapped
           Disadvantaged, Culturally
           Disadvantaged, Socially
           Socially disadvantaged
           Underprivileged
    RT   Marginality, Social
    NT   Libraries and the socially handicapped
           Social work with the socially handicapped
Socially handicapped—Bibliography
    RT   Socially handicapped literature
Socially handicapped—Education *(May Subd Geog)*
    NT   Socially handicapped—Scholarships,
           fellowships, etc.
Socially handicapped—Education—Reading, etc.
Socially handicapped—Education (Higher) *(May Subd Geog) [LC4822]*
Socially handicapped—Employment
    USE Hard-core unemployed
Socially handicapped—Language
    BT   Speech and social status

Socially handicapped—Scholarships, fellowships, etc.
(May Subd Geog)
    BT   Socially handicapped—Education
Socially handicapped and libraries
    USE Libraries and the socially handicapped
Socially handicapped children *(May Subd Geog)*
    UF   Disadvantaged children
Socially handicapped children—Attitudes
Socially handicapped children—Education *(May Subd Geog) [LC4051-LC4100]*
    NT   Teachers of socially handicapped children
Socially handicapped children—Education—Art, [etc.]
Socially handicapped children—Education—Law and legislation *(May Subd Geog)*
    BT   Educational law and legislation
Socially handicapped children—Education (Elementary) *(May Subd Geog)*
Socially handicapped children—Education (Preschool) *(May Subd Geog)*
Socially handicapped children—Education (Preschool)—United States
    NT   Even Start programs
          Head Start programs
Socially handicapped children—Education (Primary) *(May Subd Geog)*
Socially handicapped children—Education (Secondary) *(May Subd Geog)*
Socially handicapped children, Teachers of
    USE Teachers of socially handicapped children
Socially handicapped literature *(May Subd Geog)*
    UF   Literature, Socially handicapped
    RT   Socially handicapped—Bibliography
Socially handicapped teenagers *(May Subd Geog)*
Socially handicapped women *(May Subd Geog)*
Socially handicapped youth *(May Subd Geog)*
Societies *[AS (Academics and learned societies)]* *[HS (Associations, secret societies, clubs)]*
    UF   Academics (Learned societies)
    RT   Associations, institutions, etc.
          Clubs
    SA   *subdivision* Societies, etc. *under names of individual persons, families, and topical headings; also subdivision* Societies and clubs *under age and sex groups; and names of individual societies*
    NT   Church societies
          Friendly societies
          Greek letter societies
          Secret societies
          Trade-unions
          Women—Societies and clubs
Societies, Benefit
    USE Friendly societies

Socioeconomic status
    USE *subdivisions* Economic conditions and/or Social conditions *under classes of persons, e.g.* African American students—Economic conditions; African American students—Social conditions
          Social status
Sociologists, African American
    USE African American sociologists
Sociology, Urban *(May Subd Geog) [HT101-HT395]*
    UF   Urban sociology
    RT   Cities and towns
    NT   Urbanization
Soldiers, African American
    USE African American soldiers
Soldiers, Black
    UF   Black soldiers
          Negro soldiers *[Former Heading]*
    BT   Blacks
    NT   African American soldiers
Songs, Jazz
    USE Jazz vocals
Songs, Popular
    USE Popular music
Sororities, Greek letter
    USE Greek letter societies
Sorority songs
    USE Fraternity songs
Soul food cooking
    USE African American cookery
Soul music *(May Subd Geog)* *[ML3537 (History and criticism)]*
    UF   Music, Soul
          Soul music—United States
    BT   African Americans—Music
          Popular music
Soul music—United States
    USE Soul music
Soul musicians *(May Subd Geog)*
    BT   Musicians
South Carolina State College (Orangeburg, S.C.)
    BT   Historically Black Colleges and Universities—South Carolina
          Public universities and colleges
          State universities and colleges
Southampton Insurrection, 1831 *[F232.S7]*
    UF   Nat Turner's Insurrection
          Turner's Negro Insurrection, 1831
    BT   Slavery—United States—Insurrections, etc.
Southern Christian Leadership Conference *(May Subd Geog)*
    UF   SCLC
    BT   Civil rights organizations

Southern States—History *(Not Subd Geog)*
[F206-F220]
BT   Slavery—United States
Southern University (Baton Rouge, La.)
BT   Historically Black Colleges and Universities—
Louisiana
Public universities and colleges
State universities and colleges
Southern University (New Orleans, La.)
BT   Historically Black Colleges and Universities—
Louisiana
Public universities and colleges
Southern University (Shreveport, La.)
BT   Historically Black Colleges and Universities—
Louisiana
Public universities and colleges
Southwestern Christian College (Terrell, Tex.)
BT   Historically Black Colleges and Universities—
Texas
Private universities and colleges
Special days *(May Subd Geog)*
Here are entered works on special days sponsored by individuals, organizations, or governmental bodies interested in publicizing or promoting patriotic, charitable, commercial, or other events and observances.
NT   Harriet Tubman Day
Special months *(May Subd Geog)*
Here are entered works on special months sponsored by individuals, organizations, or governmental bodies interested in publicizing or promoting patriotic, charitable, commercial, or other events and observances.
NT   Black History Month
Special weeks *(May Subd Geog)*
Here are entered works on special weeks sponsored by individuals, organizations, or governmental bodies interested in publicizing or promoting patriotic, charitable, commercial, or other events and observances.
UF   Weeks, Special
NT   Brotherhood Week
National Historically Black Colleges Week
Speech, Hate
USE Hate speech
Speech and social classes
USE Speech and social status
Speech and social status *(May Subd Geog)*
UF   Social classes and language
Social classes and speech
Social status and language
Social status and speech
Speech and social classes
BT   Social status
NT   Socially handicapped—Language
Spelman College (Atlanta, Ga.)
BT   Historically Black Colleges and Universities—
Georgia
Private universities and colleges
United Negro College Fund Institutions
Women's colleges

Spingarn Medal
BT   Medals—United States
Spiritual churches, African American
USE African American Spiritual churches
Spiritual churches, Black
USE African American Spiritual churches
Spiritualist churches, African American
USE African American Spiritual churches
Spiritualist churches, Black
USE African American Spiritual churches
Spiritualist movement, African American
USE African American Spiritual churches
Spiritualist movement, Black
USE African American Spiritual churches
Spirituals (Songs) *(May Subd Geog) [M1670-M1671 (Music)] [ML3556 (History and criticism)]*
UF   African American spirituals
Negro spirituals *[Former Heading]*
BT   African Americans—Music
Folk songs, English—United States
Hymns, English—United States
Sports
NT   Discrimination in sports
Minorities in sports
Squatter sovereignty *[E415.7 (American politics)] [JK318 (Constitution history: United States)]*
BT   Slavery—United States
St. Augustine's College (Raleigh, N.C.)
USE Saint Augustine's College (Raleigh, N.C.)
St. Paul's College (Lawrenceville, Va.)
USE Saint Paul's College (Lawrenceville, Va.)
St. Philip's College (San Antonio, Tex.)
USE Saint Philip's College (San Antonio, Tex.)
Stage
USE Theater
Stamps, Postage
USE Postage stamps
State action (Civil rights) *(May Subd Geog)*
Here are entered works on claims under the 14th amendment to the United States Constitution and under the Civil Rights Act of 1871, wherein a private citizen seeks damages or redress because of improper governmental intrusion into his life.
UF   Action, State (Civil rights)
Section 1983 actions (Civil rights)
BT   Civil rights—United States
State rights *[JK310-JK325]*
UF   States' rights
BT   Slavery—United States
RT   Secession
State universities and colleges
UF   1890 Land-grant and Tuskegee University
BT   Historically Black Colleges and Universities
NT   Alabama Agricultural and Mechanical University (Normal, Ala.)

Alcorn State University (Lorman, Miss.)
Arkansas at Pine Bluff, University of
(Pine Bluff, Ark.)
Delaware State College (Dover, Del.)
Florida Agricultural and Mechanical University
(Tallahassee, Fla.)
Fort Valley State College (Fort Valley, Ga.)
Kentucky State University (Frankfort, Ky.)
Langston University (Langston, Okla.)
Lincoln University (Jefferson City, Mo.)
Maryland Eastern Shore, University of
(Princess Anne, Md.)
North Carolina Agricultural and Technical State
University (Greensboro, N.C.)
Prairie View Agricultural and Mechanical
University (Prairie View, Tex.)
South Carolina State College (Orangeburg, S.C.)
Southern University (Baton Rouge, La.)
Tennessee State University (Nashville, Tenn.)
Tuskegee University (Tuskegee, Ala.)
Virginia State University (Petersburg, Va.)

States' rights
USE   State rights

Status, Social
USE   Social status

Stillman College (Tuscaloosa, Ala.)
BT   Historically Black Colleges and Universities—
Alabama
Private universities and colleges
United Negro College Fund Institutions

Storytellers *(May Subd Geog)*
UF   Raconteurs
Tellers of stories
RT   Storytelling

Story-telling
USE   Storytelling

Storytelling *(May Subd Geog) [GR72.3 (Folklore)]*
[LB1042 (Education)] [Z718.3 (In libraries)]
UF   Story-telling *[Former Heading]*
Telling of stories
RT   Folklore
Storytellers

Student busing for school integration
USE   Busing for school integration

Student life and customs
USE   Students

Student movements, African American
USE   African American student movements

Student Nonviolent Coordinating Committee *(May
Subd Geog)*
UF   SNCC
BT   Civil rights organizations

Student violence
USE   School violence

Students *(May Subd Geog) [LB3602-LB3618 (Student
life)]*
UF   Pupils
School life
Student life and customs
RT   Education
SA   *subdivision* Students *under names of individual
educational institutions, e.g.* Lincoln Univer-
sity (Lincoln University, Pa.)—Students
NT   African American students

Students, Black *(May Subd Geog)*
UF   Black students
Negro students *[Former Heading]*
BT   Blacks—Education
NT   College students, Black

Students, Minority
USE   Minority students

Students' songs—United States
UF   Students' songs, American *[Former Heading]*
NT   Fraternity songs

Students' songs, American
USE   Students' songs—United States

Study, Courses of
USE   *subdivisions* Curricula *under specific types of
educations or schools and under names of
individual schools, e.g.* Technical education—Curricula; High schools—Curricula;
Library schools—Curricula; Lincoln University (Lincoln University, Pa.)—Curricula; Education *under names of individual
denominations, sects or orders;* Instruction and study *under headings in the field
of music; or* Study and teaching *under subjects* Education—Curricula

Study of Untreated Syphilis in the Male Negro
USE   Tuskegee Syphilis Study

Suffrage *(May Subd Geog)*
[JK1846-JK1936 (United States)]
UF   Franchise Right to vote
Voting rights
BT   Political rights
NT   Literacy tests (Election law)

Suffrage—United States
NT   African Americans—Suffrage

Summer Olympics
USE   Olympics

Sunday schools, African American
USE   African American Sunday schools

Surgeons, African American
USE   African American surgeons

Swing (Music) *(May Subd Geog)*
UF   Swing (Music)—United States
BT   Jazz
Popular music

Swing (Music)—United States
USE Swing (Music)

Syphilis—Research—Alabama
NT Tuskegee Syphilis Study

Syphilis—Research—United States
NT Tuskegee Syphilis Study

T

Tales *(May Subd Geog) [GR74-GR76 (Folklore)]*
Here are entered collections of stories in prose, especially traditional, popular tales of uncertain origin such as legends, fables, etc.
UF Folk tales
Folktales

Talladega College (Talladega, Ala.)
BT Historically Black Colleges and Universities—Alabama
Private universities and colleges
United Negro College Fund Institutions

Teachers—Integration
USE Faculty integration

Teachers, African American
USE African American teachers

Teachers, Black
UF Black teachers
Negro teachers *[Former Heading]*
NT College teachers, Black

Teachers of socially handicapped children *(May Subd Geog)*
UF Socially handicapped children, Teachers of
BT Socially handicapped children—Education

Technical education—Curricula *[T65]*

Teenage boys, African American
USE African American teenage boys

Teenage girls, African American
USE African American teenage girls

Teenage mothers, African American
USE African American teenage mothers

Teenagers, African American
USE African American teenagers

Television producers and directors, African American
USE African American television producers and directors

Tellers of stories
USE Storytellers

Telling of stories
USE Storytelling

Tenement-houses *(May Subd Geog)* -
[HD7286-HD7390 (Economics)]
BT Cities and towns
Housing

Tennessee State University (Nashville, Tenn.)
BT Historically Black Colleges and Universities—Tennessee

Public universities and colleges
State universities and colleges

Test bias *(May Subd Geog) [LB3060.62]*
UF Bias in tests
Prejudice in testing
BT Discrimination in education

Texas College (Tyler, Tex.)
BT Historically Black Colleges and Universities—Texas
Private universities and colleges
United Negro College Fund Institutions

Texas Southern University (Houston, Tex.)
BT Historically Black Colleges and Universities—Texas
Public universities and colleges

Text-book bias
USE Textbook bias

Textbook bias *(May Subd Geog) [LB3045.6]*
UF Bias in textbooks
Prejudice in textbooks
Text-book bias *[Former Heading]*
BT Discrimination in education

Theater *(May Subd Geog) [PN2000-PN3299]*
Here are entered works on drama as acted on the stage. Works on facilities used to stage drama are entered under Theaters.
UF Stage
Theatre
NT African American theater
Black theater

Theater festivals
USE Drama festivals

Theaters *(May Subd Geog)*
Here are entered works on facilities used to stage drama. Works on drama as acted on the stage are entered under Theater.
UF Playhouses

Theaters—New York (State)
NT Apollo Theatre (New York, N.Y.)

Theatre
USE Theater

Theologians, African American
USE African American theologians

Theological seminaries *(May Subd Geog)*
[BV4019-BV4160]
UF Clergy—Education
Divinity schools
Seminaries, Theological
NT Racism in theological seminaries

Theological seminaries, African American
USE African American theological seminaries

Theology, African American
USE Black Theology

Theology, Black
USE Black Theology

Thurgood Marshall Federal Judiciary Building (Washington, D.C.)
UF   Marshall Federal Judiciary Building (Washington, D.C.)
BT   Public buildings—Washington (D.C.)

Toasts (African American folk poetry) *[PS477.5.T6 (Collections)]*
Here are entered those narrative poems from African American oral tradition which are usually rhymed, rhythmic, epical representations of extended conflicts between protagonists, expressed in nonstandard Black English, created for and during male recitative performances.
UF   Toasts (Negro folk poetry) *[Former Heading]*
BT   American poetry—African American authors

Toasts (Negro folk poetry)
USE   Toasts (African American folk poetry)

Token integration
USE   De facto school segregation

Tolerance
USE   Toleration

Toleration
UF   Bigotry
      Intolerance
      Tolerance
RT   Discrimination

Topical songs (Negro)
USE   African Americans—Songs and music
      Blacks—Songs and music

Topical songs (Negroes)
USE   African Americans—Songs and music
      Blacks—Songs and music

Tougaloo College (Tougaloo, Miss.)
BT   Historically Black Colleges and Universities—Mississippi
      Private universities and colleges
      United Negro College Fund Institutions

Town officers
USE   County officials and employees
      Municipal officials and employees

Trade and professional associations *(May Subd Geog) [HD2421-HD2429 (Trade associations)] [HD6350-HD6940 (Trade-unions)] [HD6496.5-HD6497 (Professional associations)]*
Here are entered works on associations devoted to the interests of particular trades or professions, without special regard to the relations of employers and employees.
UF   Professional associations
BT   Associations, institutions, etc.
NT   National Alliance of Postal and Federal Employees
      National Association of Black Journalists
      National Bar Association
      National Conference of Black Mayors
      National Dental Association
      National Medical Association

Trade-unions *(May Subd Geog) [HD6350-HD6940.7]*
UF   Industrial unions
      Labor, Organized
      Labor organizations
      Labor unions
      Unions, Labor
      Unions, Trade
      Working-men's associations
BT   Societies
SA   *subject headings beginning with the words* Trade-union; *and names of individual trade unions*
NT   Coalition of Black Trade Unionists

Trade-unions—African American membership *(May Subd Geog)*
UF   African American trade unionists
      African American union members
      Trade-unions—Negro membership *[Former Heading]*
      Trade-unions—United States—Afro-American membership *[Former Heading]*
RT   Coalition of Black Trade Unionists

Trade-unions—Minority membership
UF   Minorities in trade-unions
BT   Minorities—Employment
RT   Discrimination in employment
      Trade-unions, Black

Trade-unions—Negro membership
USE   Trade-unions—African American membership

Trade-unions—United States—African American membership
USE   Trade-unions—African American membership

Trade-unions, Black
UF   Black trade-unions
RT   Trade-unions—Minority membership

Traders, Slave
USE   Slave traders

Tradition, Oral
USE   Oral tradition

Traditions
USE   Folklore
      Legends
      Manners and customs

TransAfrica Forum
BT   Civil rights organizations

Trappers, African American
USE   African American trappers

Trenholm State Technical College (Montgomery, Ala.)
BT   Historically Black Colleges and Universities—Alabama
      Junior colleges
      Public universities and colleges

Trial, Fair
USE   Fair trial

Trials (Conspiracy)—New York (State)
NT   Black Panthers Trial, New York, N.Y., 1970-1971

Trials (Rape)—Alabama
NT   Scottsboro Trial, Scottsboro, Ala., 1931

Turner Theological Seminary (African Methodist Episcopal)
BT   Interdenominational Theological Center (Atlanta, Ga.)

Turner's Negro Insurrection, 1831
USE   Southampton Insurrection, 1831

Tuskegee Institute National Historic Site (Tuskegee, Ala.)
BT   Historic sites—Alabama
        National parks and reserves—Alabama

Tuskegee Study
USE   Tuskegee Syphilis Study

Tuskegee Syphilis Study
UF   Public Health Service Study of Untreated Syphilis in the Male Negro
        Study of Untreated Syphilis in the Male Negro
        Tuskegee Study
        Untreated Syphilis in the Male Negro Study
BT   Syphilis—Research—Alabama
        Syphilis—Research—United States

Tuskegee University (Tuskegee, Ala.)
BT   Historically Black Colleges and Universities—Alabama
        Private universities and colleges
        State universities and colleges
        United Negro College Fund Institutions

Two-year colleges
USE   Junior colleges

Tyler, Texas, Black Film Collection
UF   Black Film Collection, Tyler, Texas

U

UNCF
USE   United Negro College Fund, Inc.

Underground railroad *[E450] Subdivided by state*
RT   Fugitive slaves—United States

Underprivileged
USE   Socially handicapped

Unemployed
NT   Hard-core unemployed

Unions, Labor
USE   Trade-unions

Unions, Trade
USE   Trade-unions

Unitarian Universalists, African American
USE   African American Unitarian Universalists

United Negro College Fund, Inc.
UF   UNCF
RT   United Negro College Fund Institutions

United Negro College Fund Institutions
BT   Historically Black Colleges and Universities

RT   United Negro College Fund, Inc.
NT   Barber-Scotia College (Concord, N.C.)
        Benedict College (Columbia, S.C.)
        Bennett College (Greensboro, N.C.)
        Bethune-Cookman College (Daytona Beach, Fla.)
        Claflin College (Orangeburg, S.C.)
        Clark Atlanta University (Atlanta, Ga.)
        Dillard University (New Orleans, La.)
        Edward Waters College (Jacksonville, Fla.)
        Fisk University (Nashville, Tenn.)
        Florida Memorial College (Miami, Fla.)
        Huston-Tillotson College (Austin, Tex.)
        Interdenominational Theological Center (Atlanta, Ga.)
        Jarvis Christian College (Hawkins, Tex.)
        Johnson C. Smith University (Charlotte, N.C.)
        Knoxville College (Knoxville, Tenn.)
        Knoxville College-Morristown Campus (Morristown, Tenn.)
        Lane College (Jackson, Tenn.)
        LeMoyne-Owen College (Memphis, Tenn.)
        Livingstone College (Salisbury, N.C.)
        Miles College (Birmingham, Ala.)
        Morehouse College (Atlanta, Ga.)
        Morris Brown College (Atlanta, Ga.)
        Morris College (Sumter, S.C.)
        Oakwood College (Huntsville, Ala.)
        Paine College (Augusta, Ga.)
        Paul Quinn College (Dallas, Tex.)
        Philander Smith College (Little Rock, Ark.)
        Rust College (Holly Springs, Miss.)
        Saint Augustine's College (Raleigh, N.C.)
        Saint Paul's College (Lawrenceville, Va.)
        Shaw University (Raleigh, N.C.)
        Spelman College (Atlanta, Ga.)
        Stillman College (Tuscaloosa, Ala.)
        Talladega College (Talladega, Ala.)
        Texas College (Tyler, Tex.)
        Tougaloo College (Tougaloo, Miss.)
        Tuskegee University (Tuskegee, Ala.)
        Virginia Union University (Richmond, Va.)
        Voorhees College (Denmark, S.C.)
        Wilberforce University (Wilberforce, Ohio)
        Wiley College (Marshall, Tex.)
        Xavier University (New Orleans, La.)

United States—Armed Forces—African Americans
UF   African American military personnel
        African Americans in military service
        African Americans in the Armed Forces
        United States—Armed Forces—Negroes
        [Former Heading]
NT   African American seamen
        African American soldiers
        African American veterans
        United States. Air Force—African Americans
        United States. Army—African American troops
        United States. Marine Corps—African American troops

United States. Marine Corps—African Americans
United States. Navy—African Americans

United States—Armed Forces—Negroes
  USE United States—Armed Forces—African Americans

United States—Civilization—African influences
  BT   Africa—Civilization

United States—Civilization—African American influences
  UF   United States—Civilization—Negro influences *[Former Heading]*
  BT   African Americans

United States—Civilization—Negro influences
  USE United States—Civilization—African American influences

United States—History—Civil War, 1861-1865—African Americans *[E540.N3]*
  UF   United States—History—Civil War, 1861-1865—Negroes

United States—History—Civil War, 1861-1865—Negroes
  USE United States—History—Civil War, 1861-1865—African Americans

United States—Ethnic relations *[E184.A1]*
  NT   African Americans—Relations with German Americans
        African Americans—Relations with Polish Americans

United States—Race question
  USE United States—Race relations

United States—Race relations *(Not Subd Geog)* *[E184-185.98]*
  UF   African Americans—Relations with whites
        United States—Race question *[Former Heading]*
  SA   *names of individual racial and ethnic groups, e.g.* African Americans
  NT   African Americans—Relations with German Americans
        African Americans—Relations with Indians
        African Americans—Relations with Japanese
        African Americans—Relations with Polish Americans
        Presidents—United States—Racial attitudes

United States. Air Force—African Americans
  UF   African American Air Force personnel
        Air Force personnel, African American
  BT   United States—Armed Forces—African Americans
  NT   African American air pilots

United States. Army—African American troops
  Here are entered works on the organization, administration, and history of African American units within the United States Army. Works on African American personnel in the United States Army are entered under African American soldiers.
  UF   United States. Army—Negro troops *[Former Heading]*

  BT   African American soldiers
        United States—Armed Forces—African Americans

United States. Army—Negro troops
  USE United States. Army—African American troops

United States. Congress—Black Caucus
  UF   Black Congressional Caucus

United States. Congress. House
  UF   Members of Congress (United States House of Representatives)
        Representatives in Congress (United States)

United States. Congress. Senate
  UF   Members of Congress (United States Senate)
        Senators (United States)

United States. Marine Corps—African American troops
  BT   African American soldiers
        United States—Armed Forces—African Americans

United States. Marine Corps—African Americans *[E185.63]*
  BT   African American soldiers
        United States—Armed Forces—African Americans

United States. Navy—African Americans
  Here are entered works on the organization, administration, and history of African American units within the United States Navy. Works on African American naval personnel and merchant seamen collectively are entered under African American seamen.
  UF   United States. Navy—Negroes *[Former Heading]*
  BT   African American seamen
        United States—Armed Forces—African Americans

United States. Navy—Minorities *(Not Subd Geog)* *[VB323-VB324]*

United States. Navy—Negroes
  USE United States. Navy—African Americans

Universities and colleges, African American
  USE Historically Black Colleges and Universities

Universities and colleges, Black
  USE Historically Black Colleges and Universities

University of Arkansas at Pine Bluff (Pine Bluff, Ark.)
  USE Arkansas at Pine Bluff, University of (Pine Bluff, Ark.)

University of Maryland-Eastern Shore (Princess Anne, Md.)
  USE Maryland Eastern Shore, University of (Princess Anne, Md.)

University of the District of Columbia (Washington, D.C.)
  USE District of Columbia, University of the (Washington, D.C.)

University of the Virgin Islands (St. Thomas, V.I.)
  USE Virgin Islands, University of the (St. Thomas, V.I.)

University presidents
  USE College presidents

University teachers, Black
    USE College teachers, Black

University teachers, Minority
    USE Minority college teachers

Unmarried fathers
    RT   Single parent family

Unmarried mothers
    RT   Single parent family

Untreated Syphilis in the Male Negro Study
    USE Tuskegee Syphilis Study

Urban areas
    USE Cities and towns

Urban cores *(May Subd Geog)*
    RT   Inner cities

Urban development
    USE Urbanization

Urban dialects *(May Subd Geog) [P40.5U73]*
    UF   Dialects, Urban
            Urbanisms (Linguistics)
    BT   Cities and towns

Urban education
    USE Education, Urban

Urban folklore *(May Subd Geog)*
    Here are entered works on folklore which is found in urban areas.
    UF   Urban legends
            Urban lore
    BT   Folklore

Urban housing
    USE Housing

Urban legends
    USE Legends
             Urban folklore

Urban lore
    USE Urban folklore

Urban policy *(May Subd Geog)*
    Here are entered works discussing governmental policy directed at solving urban problems including housing, education, health, employment, transportation, criminal justice, poverty, race relations, etc.
    UF   Cities and state
            Urban problems
    NT   Education, Urban

Urban poor *(May Subd Geog) [HV4023-HV4470.7]*
    Here are entered general works on the urban poor and, with local subdivision, works limited to the urban poor of regions, countries, states, etc. Works on the poor of individual cities, city regions, or metropolitan areas are entered under the heading Poor with local subdivision.
    BT   Poor

Urban problems
    USE Urban policy

Urban-rural migration
    UF   City-country migration

Urban schools *(May Subd Geog) [LC5101-LC5143]*
    UF   City schools
            Inner city schools
            Schools, City
            Schools, Urban
    BT   Schools

Urban sociology
    USE Sociology, Urban

Urbanisms
    USE Cities and towns

Urbanisms (Linguistics)
    USE Urban dialects

Urbanization *(May Subd Geog)*
    UF   Cities and towns, Movement to
            Urban development
    BT   Cities and towns
            Sociology, Urban
    RT   Rural-urban migration

Utilization of drugs
    USE Drug utilization

V

Veterans, African American
    USE African American veterans

Vibraphone and piano music (Jazz)
    USE Jazz

Violence in schools
    USE School violence

Virgin Islands, University of the (St. Thomas, V.I.)
    UF   University of the Virgin Islands
            (St. Thomas, V.I.)
    BT   Historically Black Colleges and Universities—
            Virgin Islands
            Public universities and colleges

Virginia Seminary College (Lynchburg, Va.)
    BT   African American theological seminaries
            Historically Black Colleges and Universities—
            Virginia
            Private universities and colleges

Virginia State University (Petersburg, Va.)
    BT   Historically Black Colleges and Universities—
            Virginia
            Public universities and colleges
            State universities and colleges

Virginia Union University (Richmond, Va.)
    BT   Historically Black Colleges and Universities—
            Virginia
            Private universities and colleges
            United Negro College Fund Institutions

Vital event statistics
    USE Vital statistics

Vital rates
    USE Vital statistics

Vital records
    USE Registers of births, etc.
         Slave records
Vital statistics *(Not Subd Geog) [HA154-HA4737]*
    UF   Vital event statistics
         Vital rates
    RT   Demography
         Registers of births, etc.
    SA   *subdivision* Casualties (Statistics, etc.) *under
         individual wars, e.g.* World War, 1939-
         1945—Casualties (Statistics, etc.); *and
         subdivision* Statistics, Vital *under names
         of countries, cities, etc. and under ethnic
         groups for compilations of birth, mar-
         riage, and death statistics*
    NT   African Americans—Statistics, Vital
         Slave records
Vocal music, Popular
    USE Popular music
Vocals, Jazz
    USE Jazz vocals
Vocational guidance for minorities *(May Subd Geog)*
    UF   Minorities—Vocational guidance
    BT   Minorities—Employment
Voluntarism *(May Subd Geog) [HN49.V64]*
    UF   Voluntary action
         Volunteer work
         Volunteering
         Volunteerism
    RT   Associations, institutions, etc.
    SA   *headings beginning with* Volunteer
Voluntary action
    USE Voluntarism
Voluntary associations
    USE Associations, institutions, etc.
Voluntary organizations
    USE Associations, institutions, etc.
Volunteer work
    USE Voluntarism
Volunteering
    USE Voluntarism
Volunteerism
    USE Voluntarism
Voorhees College (Denmark, S.C.)
    BT   Historically Black Colleges and Universities—
         South Carolina
         Private universities and colleges
         United Negro College Fund Institutions
Voting—Literacy tests
    USE Literacy tests (Election law)
Voting rights
    USE Suffrage

W

Washington (D.C.). Meridian Hill
    USE Meridian Hill (Washington, D.C.)
Watts Riot, Los Angeles, Calif., 1965
    UF   Los Angeles (Calif.)—Riot, 1965
         [Former Heading]
    BT   Riots—California
Weeks, Special
    USE Special weeks
Welfare recipients *(May Subd Geog)*
    UF   Public welfare recipients
    BT   Poor
Welfare recipients—Housing
    BT   Housing
Wellington (Ohio)—History *(Not Subd Geog)*
    NT   Oberlin-Wellington Rescue, 1858
Wellness
    USE Health
Wesorts *(May Subd Geog) [E184.W5]*
    BT   African Americans—Maryland
         Ethnology—Maryland
         Indians of North America—Mixed descent
         Mulattoes
West Indians—Relations with African Americans
    USE African Americans—Relations with West Indians
West Virginia State College (Institute, W.Va.)
    BT   Historically Black Colleges and Universities—
         West Virginia
         Public universities and colleges
Whalers, African American
    USE African American whalers
Wilberforce University (Wilberforce, Ohio)
    BT   Historically Black Colleges and Universities—
         Ohio
         Private universities and colleges
         United Negro College Fund Institutions
Wiley College (Marshall, Tex.)
    BT   Historically Black Colleges and Universities—
         Texas
         Private universities and colleges
         United Negro College Fund Institutions
Wind instrument and piano music (Jazz)
    USE Jazz
**Winston-Salem State University (Winston-Salem,
N.C.)**
    BT   Historically Black Colleges and Universities—
         North Carolina
         Public universities and colleges
Winter Olympic Games
    USE Winter Olympics

Winter Olympics *(Not Subd Geog) [GV841.5-GV842]*
> UF   Olympic Games (Winter) *[Former Heading]*
>   Winter Olympic Games *[Former Heading]*
> BT   Olympics

Wit and humor—Black authors
> UF   Black humor (Black authors)
>   Negro wit and humor *[Former Heading]*

Wit and humor, African American
> USE   African American wit and humor

Women—Clubs
> USE   Women—Societies and clubs

Women—Societies and clubs *[HQ1871-HQ2030.7]*
> UF   Women—Clubs
>   Women's clubs
>   Women's organizations
> BT   Associations, institutions, etc.
>   Clubs
>   Societies
> SA   *names of individual societies, clubs, etc., e.g.*
>   *The Chums, Inc. (Norfolk, Va.)*
> NT   The Links, Inc.
>   National Association of Colored Women's Clubs
>   National Association of Negro Business and
>   Professional Women's Clubs, Inc.
>   National Coalition of 100 Black Women, Inc.
>   National Council of Negro Women, Inc.

Women, African American
> USE   African American women

Women, Black
> UF   Black women
>   Women, Negro *[Former Heading]*

Women, Minority
> USE   Minority women

Women, Negro
> USE   African American women
>   Women, Black

Women artists, African American
> USE   African American women artists

Women artists, Black *(May Subd Geog)*
> UF   Black women artists

Women athletes, African American
> USE   African American women athletes

Women authors, African American
> USE   African American women authors

Women authors, Black *(May Subd Geog)*
> UF   Black women authors

Women chemists, African American
> USE   African American women chemists

Women city council members *(May Subd Geog)*
> UF   City councilwomen
>   Councilwomen, City
> BT   City council members

Women civil rights workers *(May Subd Geog)*
> BT   Civil rights workers

Women civil rights workers—United States
> NT   African American women civil rights workers

Women civil rights workers, African American
> USE   African American women civil rights workers

Women clergy, African American
> USE   African American women clergy

Women college presidents
> BT   College presidents

Women composers, African American
> USE   African American women composers

Women composers, Black *(May Subd Geog)*
> UF   Black women composers

Women cooks, African American
> USE   African American women cooks

Women county council members *(May Subd Geog)*
> UF   Councilwomen, county
>   County councilwomen
> BT   County council members

Women diplomats, African American
> USE   African American women diplomats

Women executives, African American
> USE   African American women executives

Women legislators
> BT   Legislators

Women mathematicians, African American
> USE   African American women mathematicians

Women minorities
> USE   Minority women

Women musicians, African American
> USE   African American women musicians

Women poets, African American
> USE   African American women poets

Women slaves *(May Subd Geog)*
> UF   Slaves, Women
> BT   Slaves

Women's colleges
> UF   Colleges for women
> BT   Historically Black Colleges and Universities
> NT   Bennett College (Greensboro, N.C.)
>   Spelman College (Atlanta, Ga.)

Women's clubs
> USE   Women—Societies and clubs

Women's organizations
> USE   Women—Societies and clubs

Wood-carving, African American
> USE   African American wood-carving

Work—Law and legislation
> USE   Labor laws and legislation

Working class—Legal status, laws, etc.
> USE   Labor laws and legislation

Working men's associations
> USE   Trade-unions

World Community of al-Islam in the West
　　USE　Black Muslims
World War, 1939-1945—African Americans
　　[D810.N4]
　　UF　World War, 1939-1945—Negroes
　　　　[Former Heading]
World War, 1939-1945—Negroes
　　USE　World War, 1939-1945—African Americans

X

Xavier University (New Orleans, La.)
　　BT　Historically Black Colleges and Universities—
　　　　Louisiana
　　　　Private universities and colleges
　　　　United Negro College Fund Institutions
Xylophone and piano music (Jazz)
　　USE　Jazz

Y

Youth—Education
　　USE　Education
Youth, African American
　　USE　African American youth
Youth, Black
　　UF　Black youth
　　　　Negro youth *[Former Heading]*

Z

Zeta Phi Beta Sorority
　　BT　Greek letter societies
Zones of transitions
　　USE　Inner cities
Zoning, Exclusionary *(May Subd Geog)*
　　[HT169.9.E82]
　　UF　Exclusionary zoning
　　BT　Discrimination in housing

CPSIA information can be obtained
at www.ICGtesting.com
Printed in the USA
BVHW011954251119
564550BV00016B/36/P